TOM CARTWRIGHT

THE FLAME STILL BURNS

TOM CARTWRIGHT
THE FLAME STILL BURNS

Stephen Chalke

FAIRFIELD BOOKS

Fairfield Books
17 George's Road, Fairfield Park, Bath BA1 6EY
Tel 01225-335813

Copyright © Stephen Chalke

First published 2007
ISBN 978-0-9544886-6-6

Page and jacket design by Niall Allsop
Printed and bound in Great Britain by Bath Press Ltd, Bath

CONTENTS

CHAPTER 1

"TOM WAS DIFFERENT"

Maybe Tom Cartwright was not one of the true greats of cricket; he did not reach the heights of a Bradman or a Laker. Nor perhaps was he one of the game's great entertainers; he did not capture the imagination of the crowd in the manner of a Milburn or a Miller.

Yet, within the game, among those who have known him, he shines out as a very special cricketer, a man who has lived his life with a flame of integrity that he has never compromised.

He started out with Warwickshire as a fresh-faced seventeen-year-old, catching the headlines with his classical batting. But by the time he was in his late twenties he was principally a medium-paced bowler, a tormentor of county batsmen up and down the land. Then in his thirties he began a long life of coaching. First he was at Taunton where he guided a raw Ian Botham to bowling success. Then he moved to his wife's native Wales where, for almost thirty years, he has travelled about the hills and valleys, passing on his craft to generations of aspiring youngsters. Through it all he has remained true to himself and to his love of cricket.

"There is something completely honest about him," Mike Brearley, the former England captain, says. "That's what I liked about him straightaway. And I liked his thoughtfulness, his championing of the underdog, his humour. He had a sharp edge to him. He was sharp at showing up hypocrisy, and you don't always like that. But he did it in a warm way that most people could take. I can still see him speaking ... chuckling."

A child of Coventry, Tom grew up in the days when the city was the heart of British engineering, and in his early cricketing years he spent several winters working alongside craftsmen building the intricate Humber cars, the Pullman and the Snipe. His family were Labour folk, who believed in discipline, hard work and honesty, and Tom took their values into his cricket.

"Tom was the ultimate professional," says Jim Stewart, his Warwickshire team-mate and another from Coventry. "He was like the old professionals of twenty years earlier. A professional professional, if you like. He lived cricket."

Always immaculately turned out, always putting his all into his performance, Tom can look back proudly on a 26-year playing career with many high points. He is the only Warwickshire professional ever to complete the double of 1,000 runs and 100 wickets in a summer. He is the only Somerset bowler ever to be the leading wicket-taker in the country. And – with Sir Richard Hadlee – he is one of only two post-war cricketers to have hit a double century and to have achieved the feat of taking 15 wickets in a match.

Yet what made his career were not just the high points. It was the hard work and dedication that brought him such success across many long summers.

"He was so reliable," his Warwickshire and England captain Mike Smith says. "Day in, day out, you knew that he'd do you a good job."

"He was quite exceptional," says Alan Smith, another Warwickshire captain. "He didn't have bad days. It was almost unthinkable for him to bowl badly or be out of sorts. And of course he was capable of bowling a lot of overs."

What overs he bowled! In the twelve English summers between 1962 and 1973, he sent down 10,719 of them in first-class cricket – and another 915 in one-day games. They were all delivered with wholehearted effort, as if it were an offence against his craft to take it easy, a compromising of his standards just to go through the motions. In one extraordinary spell in August 1967, in seven consecutive three-day matches, he bowled 383 overs and took 61 wickets. It was the summer that an experimental law prevented any polishing of the ball, and he finished it with 147 wickets, the leading wicket-taker in England.

"Bowling is bloody hard work," he told one interviewer of the time, "but medium-pacers should thrive on hard work."

"When I started playing county cricket," Somerset's Peter Roebuck recalls, "there was a type of complaining old professional. When the rain came along, they thought it was terrific. They were getting paid the same, and they didn't have to work. But Tom was different. He didn't think like that. He was a working man, a proud working man, and he wanted to do his work. He wasn't lazy; he wanted to bowl his overs."

"Work was always evident with Tom," Mike Brearley says. "Effort and work. What you put in, you get out. He would fully fit any puritan's dream."

What success he had in those twelve English summers! No bowler took more wickets than he did, and only one – the great Brian Statham – took his wickets at a lower average. Day after day, week after week, year after year in county cricket he tested the best of batsmen.

"I hated batting against him," Tom Graveney admits. "I could never see how I was going to score a run."

"He was the man you could never hit off the square," Mike Brearley says. "He became a sort of myth in county cricket. He and Derek Shackleton."

"He was a joy to watch as a bowler," says Brian Close, his captain at Somerset. "He was a supreme artist, a master of accuracy, of variation and total concentration. He did a great deal to teach our bowlers a new set of values."

"He was such an accurate bowler," Somerset's Peter Robinson says. "He bowled close to the wicket, with a high action. He really was a master craftsman with the ball."

In time the master craftsman became a coach. He had come to cricket through the enthusiasm of a dedicated schoolteacher, Eddie Branson, and at Edgbaston he had fallen under the spell of Tiger Smith, the gruff no-nonsense coach who had kept wicket for the county back in the Edwardian age. Now it was his turn to maintain and extend that magical chain that passed knowledge from one generation to the next; it was immediately clear that as a coach he had a special gift.

"He wasn't the archetypal old pro," Vic Marks, one of his first protégés at Taunton, says. "He wasn't severe, down on you; he didn't treat you in a patronising way. He was excited by all us young guys. Not only did he know our names – which a lot of coaches wouldn't have done – he had ideas that were designed for each of us individually. In that era of bog-standard truisms, he was very different."

"Tom understood the mechanics of the game," Peter Roebuck says. "And not many do, even now – although a lot think they do. In those days it was unusual to get that level of assistance, particularly as a young player."

It was a golden time at Taunton as Tom nurtured a new generation, among them Peter Roebuck, Ian Botham, Vic Marks and Viv Richards. "We still think of ourselves a bit, even now, thirty years on, as his boys," Vic Marks says.

The compliments flow.

Mike Brearley: "What a fine man he was and what a terrific bowler! He represented the best of county cricket."

Brian Close: "Tom was a wonderful bowler. Under English conditions there wasn't a finer one at that time. A great bowler. The difference between a good bowler and a great bowler is that the great bowler can keep up the pressure for much longer periods. Make no mistake about it, Tom was a great bowler."

Ian Botham: "He always had time, always had faith in me. I couldn't have had a better man to teach me the art of bowling."

Vic Marks: "Tom's one of my two favourite people in cricket. Him and Arthur Milton."

Tom Cartwright is a man of integrity, a steadfast man who has given his life to cricket. But at times, despite his soft voice and patient manner, others have encountered that integrity, that steadfastness, as curmudgeonliness, as obstinacy. Occasionally at Edgbaston there were contractual disputes – about differential rates of pay or the right to bring families to away matches – and Tom was never one to bite his tongue if he thought he was right.

"He reminds me of some of the characters in George Eliot," Mike Brearley says – and, of course, George Eliot grew up not far from Tom's childhood home in North Coventry. "Caleb Garth in *Middlemarch*, a man of total integrity. He would never do anything that had a smattering of dishonesty according to his standards. But Tom didn't get on a high moral ground; he wasn't moralistic. He'd say his piece, and you knew where he stood. He'd be humorous about human failure, and that's the chuckle."

At the end of 1969, when Tom was still at his peak as a bowler, he found himself in dispute with his native county, parting company with them to sign for Somerset. Warwickshire tried to prevent him from playing the next summer, but he challenged their ruling and in a ground-breaking hearing at Lord's won the argument.

Warwickshire was an affluent county club, with aspirations to win the championship, while Somerset was at rock bottom, run on a shoestring and firmly rooted to the foot of the table. "We had no bowling," Peter Robinson says. "It was like trying to fight a war with rifles when the others have got cannons. But then Tom came." The following year Brian Close arrived. Then the youngsters emerged, and the club found itself enjoying the best period in its history.

But, after seven wonderful years in the West Country, Tom got locked in another dispute. The committee wanted him to play when he, the proud professional, did not believe that he was fit enough to do so properly, and again he walked away. He left the generation of youngsters just as they were coming into full bloom, and he set up home in Wales.

"Tom has never changed," says Jim Stewart. "He's always stuck to his beliefs."

County cricket was not a world peopled by radicals, and Tom stood out in a quiet, yet insistent way. He was a proud worker, a man of the highest standards, but at times – when there were disputes – the committee men would see him as 'a shop steward', 'a barrack room lawyer', even 'a car worker'.

To his wife Joan, daughter of a Welsh tin plate worker, Tom's opinions were mild compared with those she had imbibed in her childhood – "He thinks he's very left-wing, but he isn't really at all" – but, according to Vic Marks, "As far as cricket was concerned, Tom was a rabid left-winger, very obstinate. But he had a good impish sense of humour as well."

Tom played only five Tests for England. He was unlucky with injuries, and the theory of the time deemed him not fast enough as a bowler to be successful in Australia. But he did tour South Africa in 1964/5, and he was picked to tour that country again four years later, a surprise selection in a party that did not include Basil D'Oliveira.

As the row erupted over D'Oliveira's omission, Tom was struggling with a shoulder injury. Could he get fit? Could he be persuaded to declare himself fit?

It was a turbulent time and he finally withdrew his name, setting in motion the chain of events that led to an end to all Test cricket between the two countries for the next 25 years.

"Why didn't he go to South Africa?" Vic Marks asks. "That's what we all want to know."

*

This book is the story of a fine cricketer, a very English cricketer, who learnt his game in the days of uncovered pitches and three-day county cricket, those long-lost days before television and commercial sponsors held sway, when cricket was – in Tom's words – 'the people's summer game'.

As a young car worker in Coventry, Tom loved listening to the political talk in the tea breaks when they all sat round and put the world to rights.

As a young player he loved to listen to his seniors talking cricket in the evening. "He was a shy lad when he started," his team-mate Alan Townsend says. "You could take him out for a drink, and he'd sit there quietly, listening all night."

Gradually he became a senior player himself, and it was his turn to do the talking. "Tom was the last to leave," Brian Langford, his first captain at Somerset, recalls, "but he wouldn't drink. He'd talk cricket all evening. His pint lasted all night. And the young ones all listened to him. He knew so much about cricket, more than anyone I've met. You spend day in, day out with people, and after a bit you get fed up with hearing the same things. But Tom wasn't always saying the same things. With him there was always something different."

Now Tom has turned seventy, and for the writing of this book he has happily driven from Neath to Cardiff for regular lunch-time meetings in *Y Mochyn Du*, the pub on the corner outside Glamorgan's Sophia Gardens ground. Never a freeloader, he insists on paying the bill. Then in a quiet corner he eats his shepherd's pie and enjoys the chance to reminisce.

But a session never ends without his putting the world of cricket to rights. There are so many themes: the destruction of county cricket, the dominance of the 'men in suits', the steady stream of top-down, paperwork initiatives, the failure to maintain standards of fair play and discipline.

"Not many people want to take up issues, you know. They don't. They really don't." He breaks off to take another mouthful of pie. "Sometimes I wish I could walk away, but I can't."

CHAPTER 2
A CHILD OF COVENTRY
1935 – 1950

22 July 1935. In a rented miner's cottage in Alderman's Green, North Coventry, Lily Cartwright gave birth to her fourth and last child. It was a boy, her only boy, a brother for Joan, Sheila and little Lily, and he was given the same two Christian names as his father, William Thomas. To avoid confusion he soon became Thomas William but, like his father, he was known as Tom.

Sixteen years earlier, as a pair of 14-year-olds, Lily Whitmore and Tom Cartwright had met at Christian Endeavour classes at the local Methodist chapel, and each Sunday they walked from the chapel to Wyken Slough, a large expanse of water that had formed when the local mine subsided. There they courted for eight years, always under the same oak tree.

Wyken Slough is not such a quiet spot now, with the lorries on the nearby M6 thundering by all day, but the oak tree stands as solid as ever, just as the marriage of Tom and Lily remained steadfast and strong – with barely a night apart – from 1927 till death finally separated them in 1996.

It was not a marriage blessed by the Cartwrights. They were prosperous greengrocers, with four horses and carts for deliveries, and they had hoped for better for their boy Tom than a miner's daughter such as Lily. None of the family's money would come to them and there was little social contact, but Tom was a man of principle. "He idolised Mum," their first-born Joan says, and he settled to a modest life, working in the car industry. Baby Tom's arrival meant that there were six of them living in the cottage with its two bedrooms, living room and kitchen – and the lean-to their father had built out the back.

Joan recalls that occasionally in the 1930s her father's mother would appear on a Saturday night, taking her into the centre of Coventry in a horse-drawn landau carriage. "She'd pop into a bar for a quick snifter and, if I'd been a good girl, she'd take me to the faggot-and-pie shop, a half-tiled place with a high counter. She'd buy me a faggot, a portion of chips and some mushy peas, on a little white dish, and she'd stand over me while I sat and ate them."

The city of Coventry had an ancient centre, with timber-framed Tudor houses and narrow, twisting streets with little shops, but, beyond that, there were scores of modern factories, producing motor cars, bicycles, aircraft and machine tools. There was unemployment in the 1920s when the bicycle industry went into decline but by the 1930s, when the Depression took its grip, men from all over the British Isles were arriving for work in the city. In 1937 alone nearly 10,000 newcomers arrived.

It was an exciting city. Frank Whittle had invented the jet engine not many miles to the north, Armstrong Siddeley were manufacturing aeroplanes on the south side, and most of the great names of the British car industry had factories: Daimler, Rover, Humber, Standard Triumph, Jaguar, Singer, Morris, Alvis and many more. Coventry felt like the very hub of British engineering.

Tom's father settled to a staff job at Riley. He drove the silver works van, with the big diamond emblem on the side, and he worked as a mechanic for Percy McClure, who raced the Riley cars at Donnington. "My father used to go with him," Tom says. "Once, when I was very small, I went too. It's one of my earliest memories. Percy McClure's car was blue, and he took me on his lap in it."

War changed their lives. Tom was only four, too small to understand, but Joan was eleven and she still recalls the scene in their house when the four children returned from Sunday School on the third of September 1939. Around the table sat their father and mother, together with their next-door neighbour Miss Sharratt, an elderly seamstress who took in worn-out children's coats, turned them inside out and made them once more respectable. They were listening intently to the radio, and they hushed the incoming children. "Shh .. shh … be quiet, please." The sombre tones of Neville Chamberlain announced that Britain was now at war. "We all thought that aeroplanes were going to come over and bomb us there and then, but Dad sat us down and explained to us that it wouldn't be like that."

The bombs did come, however. With the city's main power station across the field at the back of their house, the first raid saw a bomb landing in a nearby road. "We got on our bikes the next day," Joan recalls, "and we raced up to look at the crater. Little did we think that we would have hundreds and hundreds more."

Their father built an Anderson shelter, with a sandbagged entrance, bunk beds and a hurricane lamp, and through the summer and autumn of 1940 – as more and more of the population took to leaving the city at night – they slept in the shelter, together with their neighbours, and they learnt to distinguish the different roars of the British and German planes. When they heard with terror an explosion that was particularly close, their father reassured them: "Don't worry," he said. "You don't hear the one that hits you."

The power station miraculously survived, but twice the canal was broken and water flooded into the brook and across Alderman's Green Road, leaving hundreds of fish lying everywhere.

Then came the night of Thursday 14 November 1940, the night that changed the city of Coventry for ever. "It was seven o'clock," says Sheila, the second oldest. "We were having our tea, and Dad had just got home from work on his bicycle when the siren sounded. We knocked on the wall to Miss Sharratt, and we all went down the shelter."

In one long, clear night, code-named Moonlight Sonata, wave after wave of the Luftwaffe flew over, retaliating for the raid that week on Munich and determined to knock out all the factories that had been turned over to the war effort. Altogether that night 500 aeroplanes dropped 1,500 high explosive bombs and 30,000 incendiaries, and not one plane was brought down by anti-aircraft fire.

The Alvis and Standard factories were soon in flames, the Owen and Owen department store was reduced to rubble and, though the cathedral clock hauntingly chimed the hours all night, the cathedral itself was a blazing torch beyond saving by midnight. The water mains were shattered, there was no supply of gas or electricity, and the tram wires were all down. By the time the All Clear sounded at six in the morning, there was death and destruction everywhere: 80% of buildings damaged or destroyed, 568 people killed and 863 seriously injured.

"When we came up from the shelter," Sheila says, "Mum looked towards Coventry, and she said, 'Look at the dawn breaking.' And Dad said, 'That's not the dawn. It's Coventry on fire.'"

"There were no slates on the roof," Joan says, "and no glass in the windows. And on the other side of the power station, there were eleven people killed in one road. One family – the name was Roberts – they put the children under the stairs and, because there was no more room, they sat themselves on either side of the kitchen table. When the children came out in the morning, they were still sat there, and the children thought they were OK. But they were dead from the blast."

On a gloomy, wet morning thousands of people made their way out of the city, getting lifts in cars and lorries, and the Cartwright family was among them, heading for Marsh Gibbon, a village near Bicester, where their father had family. For four weeks, while their father went back to Coventry and cleared up the mess, they stayed in the countryside.

Then, with Christmas approaching, they returned. "Dad took us through the centre of Coventry," Sheila remembers, "and it still sticks in my mind that you could see into all the cellars beneath the houses, and there were small piles of wood everywhere, all still smouldering. 'This is what you've come home to,' Dad said. He'd got the house all cleaned up and a beautiful tea laid. And, when we were all sitting round the table, the sirens went. Mum said, 'I want to go back.' And Dad said, 'Not bloody likely. You're home to stop.'"

It would turn out to be the longest separation of their 69-year marriage, and now they had to grow used to living amid the ruins. "Every day I'd walk with my grandma, Mum's mother, to Bell Green," Joan says. "We'd catch a bus and join the queues at the shops. We went to the butcher's near Pool Meadow. We knew what time their sausages came. Then we'd cut through by the cathedral, which was all in ruins, and go down the Arcade to the biscuit shop to buy broken biscuits."

"I was too young to understand," Tom says. "In a way, for a small boy, it was all very exciting. One night, when we were in the shelter and one of the bombs dropped very close, there was a great whoosh, the hurricane lamp was taken right off its hook, out into the garden, and in came all this dust and earth. And of course we were completely in the dark. We got to know all the guns, like Big Bertha and the pom pom guns. They all had names. The bombs in the fields behind us left massive holes that filled up with water, and it was a playground. We used to go round collecting the shrapnel in buckets."

"They put barbed wire round the fields," Sheila says, "but for us it was somewhere to play. You didn't see it for what it was."

"Because we were so close to the power station," Tom says, "there were ack-ack guns all round us, and the soldiers were in and out of our house all the time. At Christmas they took us across to the barracks for a big party."

A second major attack occurred on two successive nights in April of the following year, but their lives went on. Joan left school: "I never officially left. All of a sudden Mum said, 'You can go to work now,' and I got a job at Riley, making carburettors for aeroplanes. From 7.30 in the morning to seven at night, when I'd cycle home for dinner. All day Saturdays, too, and sometimes Sunday mornings. And, because Dad was driving the van and I was on piece work, I was earning as much as him."

Two years later she was joined by her next sister: "I was on Inspections," Sheila says. "Joan was in the Machine Shop. We had an uncle in the stores, and Mum's father was on the gate."

They were a close family. "We weren't rich but we weren't poor," Sheila says. "We had a complete rig-out for Sunday school. We always had winter clothes and summer clothes, two changes for school, and we weren't ever short of food." They were proud working folk, strong believers in the Labour Party, and their pride came with a strict discipline. "You were brought up to call people Mr and Mrs, to say please and thank you. I was 25 when I got married and, right up till then, I was still having to get home by nine o'clock."

Sheila's husband John confirms this. "We'd be sitting in the cinema and, halfway through the film, Sheila would say, 'We've got to go.' We're only now seeing the ends of them all on television."

"I used to worry like mad," Sheila says. "Dad was very strict, but you loved him and you could have fun with him."

"Black was black, and white was white," John says. "He was straight down the middle. You knew where you were with him. Tom is just the same."

"He taught us to know the difference between right and wrong," Tom says. "Between truth and lies. And to treat other people in the way you'd like other people to treat you."

The worst of the war seemed to have passed the city by 1944, but one day a telegram arrived. "The telegram boy would often go past on his bike," Tom recalls. "People used to dread him. They waited and held their breath till he'd gone past. But that day he stopped, and we found out that my Uncle Les was missing in Italy. Missing, presumed dead."

Several weeks passed before the boy stopped once more. "I can still see clearly that second telegram, sitting on the table with nobody wanting to open it. But it was good news. He'd turned up. Somehow in the action he'd got separated from the rest of them." Les was his mother's brother, the only cricketer in the family, and he came to play an important part in Tom's life. "When he came back from the war, he played for the Riley team, and on Saturday afternoons he and his wife took me along to watch the games. Then, when I was 14, they roped me in."

The end of the war brought immediate change to the factories. "We were doing aircraft work," Sheila remembers, "and it went straight back to car work. And one Friday afternoon they came in and they said to us women, 'You're all finished. The men want their jobs back. It'll be an all-male factory from Monday.' I got a job in another factory, making chains. I was there about a year, but I remember coming home and saying to Mum, 'It's full of old maids.' There were all these women whose husbands and boy friends had gone out to the Far East, and nobody knew where they were. I said, 'I shall never get married if I stay here.' So I went off to Courtaulds, where Lily was working, and that's where I met John."

Meanwhile Tom was still a pupil at Foxford School, an elementary school where the sporting facilities were rudimentary. But there he encountered a man whose value was far greater than any number of beautiful pitches and well-equipped sports halls: Eddie Branson, a schoolmaster with a passion for cricket.

Mr Branson taught music, and Tom's sisters remember him taking them for singing. "He was such a gentleman," Lily says. "He had this favourite phrase. If he got angry, it was always 'You blithering idiot'. And he had this tuning fork. 'Ping,' it would go, and we'd sing songs like *Greensleeves* and *Frère Jacques*."

The Cartwrights were like most of the children he taught, with little music in the family. "Dad used to sing *Show me the way to go home* and *Chick,*

chick, chick, chick, chicken," Sheila recalls. Nevertheless Mr Branson left his mark. "He used to talk about Handel," Tom says, "and it went way above most of our heads. I was one of the growlers at the back of the class, but now I listen to *Classic FM* all the time. I often think of him when I'm listening."

"His first love was cricket," Lily says, and Tom recalls how he helped to prepare for the matches. "He used to get us out of Metalwork on Thursday afternoon and Woodwork on Friday morning, to do the pitch. There was no square. It was just an undulating field; some weeks we played in the hollow, some on the hump. We'd put a lot of water on it and push a big roller up and down. And we'd get out all the weeds with a pen knife. He would mow the pitch and do the markings, and we would weed and roll, weed and roll. We also had to wash and polish the balls."

In the summer of 1947 Tom was eleven years old, but he was good enough not only to play for the school but to be picked for the Coventry Boys' representative side. "Eddie Branson asked me to come and help out on the day of the trials, and he said, 'Bring your things. You never know, somebody may want to go early.' On the day, I was doing the scorebook and he said, 'Get changed and put some pads on.' And I did well. All the other kids were older than me, and I batted and batted. When we all gathered round and they read out the team, I was in it. And it all went on from there."

At this stage there was little interest in cricket at home, and Tom remembers his mother's response when he arrived back. "We were playing at Jackers Road, and on the way back I ran through the hole in the hedge and snagged my shirt. When I got in, she was ironing. 'Mum, I've been picked to play for Coventry Schools.' I blurted it out. She stopped her ironing. 'That's nice,' she said. She hadn't a clue. I was full of excitement, and it was like somebody sticking a pin into me. Then she looked at me. 'What *have* you done to your shirt?'"

Back at school, Eddie Branson improvised some practice facilities. "There was an area of allotments beside some temporary buildings, to encourage people to learn about gardening. He had a strip of concrete laid, got a net from Morris Motors and in lunchtime and breaks we practised. And, because he bowled leg breaks and googlies and he wanted us to face some fast bowling, he got these Irish builders to throw the ball at us."

These were the years of post-war reconstruction. The city of Coventry had a town architect whose ambition was to implement the principles of the Garden City movement, with out-of-town estates, a pedestrianised centre and a new cathedral that would symbolise the city's resurgent spirit. On Saturday 22 May 1948 great crowds gathered for the opening of the new Broadgate, with Princess Elizabeth – pregnant with her first child – going on to lay the foundation stone of a new shopping district. Her speech was full of the ideals of the time:

> If we can summon to our aid in peace those high qualities with which we met the evil challenge of war, and if the spirit which the citizens of Coventry showed on the night of November 14, 1940, can be reborn in the hearts of our people today, then we shall indeed see the fruits of peace.

It was a time of hard work, where people of vision were trying to create a better world, and, in his own small role as Secretary of the Coventry Schools Cricket Association, Eddie Branson was playing his part. In *Nutshell*, the newsletter of the Coventry branch of the National Union of Teachers, he outlined the progress being made:

> In no other game has there been a sterner challenge to enthusiasm than in schools' cricket. So often in the past the only facilities for coaching have been pot-holed playgrounds surrounded by menaced and menacing windows. The hope of playing a match under fair conditions was vain fancy, and the reality, the rough bare earth or untended grass patch.

> For sheer malevolence little can equal the Bad Wicket of cricket. Its whole purpose is to destroy a boy's faith in himself, his teacher, and the game.

> Fortunately, during the coming season, the evil will be well-nigh exorcised from school cricket. The magnificent response of local clubs for the loan of their grounds, the new fields of the Education Committee, the matting and practice wickets provided for several schools, all promise to ensure the conditions under which the game may flourish as never before.

Eddie Branson arranged for the Coventry Schools side to spend a day at Edgbaston at the start of each summer. "I was also in the Coventry Schools soccer side," Tom recalls, "and it was at that point that I decided that I was going to play for Warwickshire and England at cricket and Coventry and England at soccer."

He played in the Coventry Boys' football team for three winters, captaining them in his last year at school, and, when he went to work at Rootes, he played as an amateur at Aston Villa, mostly on its fourth team. He wore the number seven shirt, and he still recalls his first game in the third team. "We were playing Shrewsbury second team. I was on the right wing, and Peter McParland was on the left. He'd not long come over from Ireland." In six years' time McParland would be the hero of the Midland side, scoring both goals in a famous Cup Final victory over the great Busby Babes of

Manchester United. But Tom recalls more clearly that McParland's first goal in the claret-and-blue of the Villa was headed in from his cross.

Mention of the Busby Babes brings back another memory. "Coventry Schools played Dudley Schools, and I'm sure Duncan Edwards played for them against us. I think they beat us six-nil."

Coventry Boys football team 1948/49
Winners of the Birmingham Schools Shield
Tom, front left. George Cole, standing behind him, was Coventry's scrum half
for many years; Terry Barnes, standing third from right,
was on the staff at Edgbaston for a while.

"We all thought he was going to be a footballer," his sister Joan says. "It used to be the hoity-toities who played cricket and the roughs who played football. Then we were told that Warwickshire were interested in him. I remember saying, 'I thought he was going to play for the City. In the number seven shirt.'"

"The first time we went over to Edgbaston," Tom says, "Eddie Branson said to me, 'Do you think you'd like to be a county cricketer?' And I said, 'Yes, I would.' He said, 'It's up to you, how hard you work.' And I did work hard. I've got a lad in my Under-14 team here in Glamorgan, and I say to him sometimes, 'For goodness sake, James, smile a bit; it's got to be fun as well.' I don't know, but I think I may have been a bit like that."

In 1949 Tom was captain of the Foxford School side, and his cricketing prowess was starting to affect the family. "Dad had played a little cricket with the chapel in the Bible Class League," he says, "but he didn't really follow the game. But I remember that my mum took me over to Edgbaston to see the New Zealanders in 1949."

Wickets for Pritchard and Hollies, fifties by Dollery, Ord, Townsend and Coventry's own Fred Gardner, this was a heady first taste of Warwickshire cricket, and there was also a first sight of the future captain of Pakistan, A.H. Kardar: "a glamorous character, tall and serene."

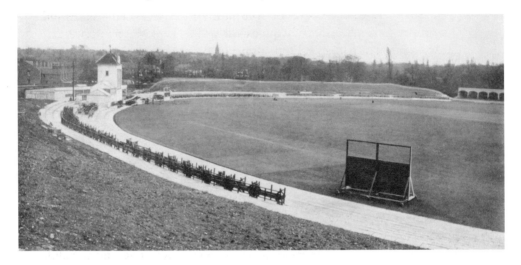

"Edgbaston was nothing like it is now. There was a wooden double decker stand, a shale bank to the left side of the pavilion, and lots of planks on stumps of wood. It was a great trek to get there: bus into Coventry, train to Birmingham New Street, then tram to the ground. I'd been to some of the soccer grounds in the Midlands, and that was exciting. But cricket has something more. There's an elegance, a beauty about a cricket ground, with everybody properly dressed."

Perhaps in our more easy-going times, we make the mistake of associating such decorum with élitism and social repression, but for Tom, a lad from a proud working-class family in a great industrial city, it is the very thing that gives cricket its extra magic: "If I go onto a ground in the morning, an hour before a game, it's the loveliest of times. Especially at a club ground, in a nice place. There may be a mower still ticking and the groundsman marking the ends, but there's a silence as well. You can stand and think and listen. You've got the birds singing, the craftsman working, the mower ticking, the smell of everything. That's something that makes cricket different from all other games. I used to love to go out to open the batting at the start of a match and to see the white lines and the 22 yards of beautiful strip. No ball marks, no foot marks. All the preparation. It's something very special."

With the leaving age raised to fifteen, Tom spent one more year at school, captaining both Foxford and Coventry Boys at both soccer and cricket. He was the first boy to play for three years in the Coventry soccer side, the first to play for four years in the cricket side, and his performances on the cricket field in 1950 are recorded in ink in the front of a book presented to him when he left school. In 24 matches he scored 937 runs at an average of 58.5 and took 112 wickets at 4.4.

In one match against Binley School he hit 139 not out. "I got nine sixes and 13 fours, I can still remember that quite clearly, and I kept wicket afterwards." It was a performance that led Eddie Branson to write about him to the *News Chronicle*, and as a result he was presented with a harrow-sized cricket bat.

They were figures that could have made him big-headed, but Eddie Branson did his best to make sure that that did not happen. "That last winter we had a school match one evening and a Coventry Schools match the next day, and I didn't play in the school game. And I didn't go and watch. The next morning after assembly he took me aside, and for about a minute he tore me apart. Said I was too big for my boots. 'Who did I think I was?' And it certainly put me straight, because I'd never seen him like that before."

Tom listens quietly as I tell him a story I have heard about a young cricketer playing away from home in a club match some years ago. He threw his bat through the pavilion window when he was given out, and the club tried to lodge a complaint. But they were told that he was already on a last warning and would face a lengthy ban. "He's a future England cricketer. Do you want to set him back like this?" They withdrew their complaint, and he progressed in due course into the England side where he handled himself badly and never fulfilled his potential. Tom replies immediately: "They wouldn't have been setting him back. It was letting him off that cost him a long international career. There's no question of that."

Tom left school in the month of his 15th birthday, and he still treasures the book *The Young Cricketer* that Eddie Branson presented to him, still recalls how he soaked up all its articles from Trevor Bailey on fast bowling and Brian Close on 'How I Came To Play for England' right through to John Arlott's loving description of the Hambledon Club playing on Broadhalfpenny Down in the 1770s. Eddie Branson was not a top cricketer, but he had done his job. He had lit in Tom a flame that would burn and burn.

Tom returns in 1956 to present a briefcase to Eddie Branson on the occasion of his leaving Foxford School. "I was working at Rootes all day, petrified about having to make the presentation in the evening."

When Tom left Warwickshire in 1969, Eddie Branson wrote to Leslie Deakins the secretary: 'I consider myself fortunate to have had the opportunity to have been of some help to him in the very beginning of his cricket life, and nothing I value more highly than the gratitude and respect he has shown at all times. Not his "to scorn the base degrees by which he did ascend."'

"He was the first person who treated me as a young adult. Towards the end he started to ask me my opinion about people who were in the team, and nobody had ever treated me like that before."

Tom compares that world of his growing up, when the city of Coventry set about rebuilding itself, when dedicated schoolteachers gave their time after hours, to the world in which he now works, a world in which teachers – burdened with paperwork – no longer have time for such activities, a world in which children, if they are to play cricket, have to be taken to clubs where often their parents pay for expert coaching.

"You cannot replicate in club cricket what schoolteachers can do. You haven't got the time. You haven't got the bodies there. You rely on the kids coming to the club.

"The only people we ever saw at games were a few mums, occasionally grandads if they lived long enough after retirement. Dads were all working; they didn't do flexible hours like they do now. Now they're there at all the matches, and there's this demand, this expectancy all the time. They're paying out money for it all, and they expect results. And I'm not sure the kids are allowed just to enjoy it.

"An awful lot of the link between the kids and the teachers has been lost in schools. Out on the field there was no us and them, none of that gulf. Eddie became a different person to us, and we probably didn't seem as bad to him when we were back in the classroom. These days, when I meet teachers, not many of them seem to look forward to going to school. Everybody I talk to wants to finish."

But Tom doesn't want to finish, and in July 2005 he was with his Wales Under-16 team, playing Cornwall at the Callington club ground. There after many years he met up with Lorna and Liz, the two daughters of his inspirational schoolmaster.

"Dad always stayed after school every night," Liz remembers. "We had tea at half past five, and he was always home at twenty past. He stayed to do coaching. And Saturday mornings, he was never around. Every day he seemed to be organising cricket, always off to the phone box up the road with all his penny coins."

"He went to Trent Bridge the day you made your debut," Lorna says. "It was one of the most special days in his life."

"In the late '50s," Liz says, "we used to get the *Coventry Evening Telegraph* every night and look at the back page. 'What did Tom do?' And you seemed to be scoring 20, 25, 30, no spectacular scores, and that went on for several years. Then you switched over to bowling, and your career suddenly took off. The whole family lived and died on your efforts. And Dad used to complain about the selectors. We didn't really know if he was being partial, but we all suffered the injustices."

Tom is clear. "If you put an Eddie Branson in every school in this country, you'd transform cricket. People like him provided opportunity, and that's the key. People giving up their time, giving their enthusiasm. He wasn't an expert, he was an enthusiast. And I'd rather have an enthusiast working with kids any day. The expert can crush enthusiasm. He can turn people off wanting to play."

The sun shines, his team goes back out after tea, and Tom lingers in the pavilion with Lorna and Liz.

"It's a good life, cricket," he says. "You have so many friends, so much fun. It goes on and on, and it never stops. And I wouldn't have had it, wouldn't be here with you today, if it hadn't have been for your father. My whole destiny has come from what he did."

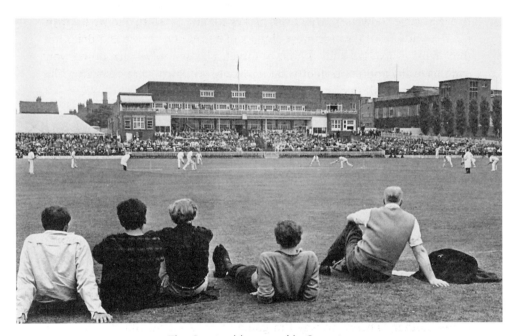

The Courtaulds ground in Coventry
"This is where I sat as a boy. You could see everything about the fielders; they almost trod on you. In the intervals we'd play cricket with a bottle and a tennis ball. And at 5.30 people from all the car factories would come down the path between the works and the pavilion and stand seven or eight deep, watching."

CHAPTER 3

THE BOY IN THE BLUE CAP
1950 – 1952

Tom was fifteen in July 1950, and it was time to leave school. He dreamed of being an all-the-year-round sportsman, with Warwickshire and Aston Villa, but in the meantime he had to find more routine employment. As part of preparing the pupils for work, Foxford School arranged a series of day-long outings to the main employers in the area.

"We went to all sorts of places: Dunlops, Courtaulds, car factories, sweet factories. We even spent a day at Keresley Pit. It was quite a deep pit. We were on a train for a long time, then we had to crawl through water and, when we reached the face, the blokes were all working by hand, wearing helmets with lights on them. And they were all wearing football shorts or their wives' long drawers, with big beer bellies hanging over. They couldn't stand up, and there were no cutters. It was all done with picks, with the miners hacking away at a low angle. They let us have a go. Then we went up to the pithead showers with all these blokes coming off shift, and we sat with them in the canteen, eating great chunks of bread and cheese and drinking thick cups of tea. It's a day I'll never forget. Unless you've been down, you can't have any appreciation of what it's like to go down there every day like that. They were all so cheerful."

This was not for Tom. He had grown up with the story of how his mother's father had been a miner at Exhall Colliery and had been part of the rescue party that went in after a disaster. "The first body he came across was his next door neighbour, and I don't think he ever went down again. He spent the rest of his working life as a gateman at Riley."

One job offer came from the personnel manager at Courtaulds, who was the captain of their works cricket team, and Tom went there for interview with his mother. "He wanted me to be an apprentice pipe-fitter. I remember sitting there, thinking what a boring thing that was, connecting pipes. The apprenticeship would have lasted till I was 21, and that would have stopped me becoming a cricketer. But he kept saying that I was never going to be a cricketer; he more or less put me down for the job. When I got outside, I said to my mother, 'There's no way I'm going there.' And she didn't argue. She was dead keen for me to play cricket, anyway."

By this time his father was at Armstrongs aircraft works, but Tom opted for the car industry. More than a quarter of the UK's cars were being produced in Coventry, you could earn a good wage without an apprenticeship and – with the factories all having teams in the strong Coventry Works League –

his cricketing prowess soon brought him employment. At Rootes the works manager was the cricket chairman.

Life in the car factory
A painting by Tom done in art class at school

The standard of car production at Rootes varied greatly. At one extreme were the Hillman Minxes, where the track ran round at a pre-determined speed and the workers stood at different points, performing repetitive tasks. Jim Stewart, later to be a team-mate of Tom's at Edgbaston, spent some winters doing night shifts on the Minxes, and he recalls the tedium of fixing on back axles hour after hour. "If you cross-threaded one, you didn't have time to put it right. You just put a cross, and somebody rectified it at the end. You were paid by how many there were at the end of the shift, and some nights it was in excess of 200. It was the best money I'd ever earned, but there were some dud cars made. You were unlucky if you bought one that had come off the track near the end of a night or on a Friday afternoon."

At the other extreme were the Humber Pullmans, where highly skilled coach-builders completed only four or five a week. "It was brilliant to see them," Tom says. "I used to go and watch them. It was like they were putting a Meccano set together. Even the silencer, they had the asbestos in a big tank and they built it. They didn't just take one off a shelf. They were meticulous. They weren't going to see the car again, but they had this great pride in making the thing as perfect as they could. They'd bolt on the chassis, and it was nothing to take it off and put it on again."

Tom himself worked on the Humber Super Snipe. He fitted the junction boxes in the wiring of the engines and, with everybody needing to be ready before the track was manually pushed forward and only five produced a day, his experience was closer to that of the Pullman coach-builders than to Jim Stewart's on the Minx.

"If you worked on a production line like the Minx," Tom says, "you could end up almost like a zombie. There were hordes of people on the line, and they were being used like animals. And they weren't being given any responsibility for their work so the sense of achievement wasn't the same. In time some bad people got into positions in the unions, people who were blinkered in their attitudes. Then you got years of confrontation. If people are looking after the interests of others, they do need to have a wider vision."

Jim Stewart, working on the Minxes in the mid-to-late '50s, remembers constant stoppages. But Tom's memories are more of the teamwork he learned – "You were in a gang where everybody depended on everybody else to be doing their job well, not to be making mistakes, not to be creating hold-ups" – though he does recall the morning in November 1951 when the union convenor suddenly called out, "Meeting at half past eleven."

"The track stopped, and we had this big meeting at the top of the line. 'We've been to see the management,' the convenor said. He was standing on a soap box. 'We can't get anywhere so we're calling a strike.' We all downed tools and walked out. Then we all went down to Pool Meadow and caught the Midland Red bus to Villa Park where England were playing Northern Ireland."

There on a sunny Tuesday afternoon they became part of a crowd of 57,889 and saw Nat Lofthouse score both goals in a 2-0 England victory. "We were back in Pool Meadow by a quarter to six, at much the time we would have been coming home from work. 'What do you mean, you've been to a football match?' my father said. 'No, no, there's been a walkout. We're on strike.' I think we went in as normal the next day."

Tom has never forgotten those formative years in the factory, growing into a man alongside men who, in the days before television, had all sorts of interests. Some tended allotments, some were pigeon pokers, some played in brass bands, some – like his father – had little aviaries, and always there was lively debate and discussion. "There was plenty of banter. People didn't sit isolated. There were some bright people there, and they'd talk about all sorts of things. But the really serious talk was always about sport.

"I liked it at Rootes. I really did. You could get pretty mucky, but I can honestly say, I really enjoyed my time there."

Tom's cricket took him in the summer of 1951 to the prestigious Coventry and North Warwickshire Club, where he played in the second eleven under the captaincy of Eddie Liggins, later to become Sir Edmund, President of the Law Society. Cricket was taking him into a new social world, and his father was slow to realise the progress he was making.

"I know the local coal merchant went to see my father when I was still at school. 'You don't go and watch Tom,' he said. 'One day he'll play for England.' And my father shrugged it off. It was only later he got interested. But my mother would come on her bike, everywhere we played virtually, and she got quite knowledgeable – well, about my performances, anyway."

One day Derief Taylor arrived at the Coventry and North Warwickshire Club. A West Indian by birth, he had come to Warwickshire through Tom Dollery who had met him in North Africa in the war and, as a batsman and slow left-arm bowler, he had played a few games for the county in the previous three summers: "I remember seeing him one year at the Courtaulds ground," Tom says. "He was wearing white batting gloves, and he got given out lbw. The ball had hit his glove, down by the pad, and all the way back to the pavilion he kept turning round and waving his glove."

Now he was the county's juniors coach, a great enthusiast who devoted long hours to Warwickshire: "He lived at the club almost; when he wasn't there, he was out on the road". He was on the lookout for promising youngsters – or, as he called them in his Jamaican accent, 'youts'.

"He'd come to see the chairman's son, who was at Warwick School, and, while he was at the ground, he spent a lot of time with me. 'Who's this?' he asked. And they said, 'No, no, we've brought you over to see John.'"

Derief Taylor reported back to the head coach Tiger Smith, who had already registered Tom's potential from the pre-season visits to Edgbaston that Tom had made as a Coventry Schoolboy with Eddie Branson.

"He took us there each year for a day during the Easter holidays. We'd have a little tour of the pavilion, then we'd change in the visiting dressing room. I can remember seeing that Ray Lindwall had signed his name over one peg, and I put my gear on that one. We used to go over to the hard-surface nets and spend the morning being coached by the first-team players, people like Alan Townsend, Fred Gardner, Bert Wolton. Then in the afternoon, while they practised, we'd watch and send the balls back to them. And we'd catch the train home. The first time I went there, that was the first time I became aware of first-class cricket. And I thought, 'What an incredible life! What an amazing thing to be doing this every day!'"

On 15 August 1951 Tom played at Edgbaston for the Warwickshire Youths against the Essex Amateurs, scoring 57 in an opening partnership of 103, his first appearance in the county scorebooks that are preserved at the ground. When the Essex side batted, they faced the bowling of O.S. Wheatley and

D.W. White, two youngsters of Tom's age, and were all out for 59. "Butch White," Tom remembers, "bowled in-swingers, very wide of the crease, at about Monty Panesar's pace. Then he went off to National Service, and the next thing we heard he'd signed for Hampshire as an opening bowler. We were all amazed but, when we played against him, he was whistling the ball around everybody's ears. His father had played club cricket with Dennis Amiss's father, and Dennis always seemed to get more round his ears than anybody."

Three weeks later, accompanied by his father, Tom travelled by train to Edgbaston for a trial, and after the net session he remembers Tiger Smith sitting down with his father. "Tiger asked him, 'Would you be happy for him to come on the staff?' And on the train going home, Dad said to me, 'There's a chance they'll take you.'"

The letter from Warwickshire duly arrived, offering Tom a contract for the summer only, worth five pounds a week – "less than I was earning at Rootes" – and without hesitation he accepted a place on the staff, to start in April 1952.

That summer of 1951 Warwickshire had won the championship title for only the second time in their history, for the first time since 1911. But the players were distant figures to Tom. Twice a summer they came out from leafy Edgbaston to the Courtaulds works ground in industrial Coventry, and in August 1951 it was on that ground, thanks to a patient century by Coventry's own Fred Gardner, that they secured their 16th victory and thus became champions.

"Fred was a local hero, a bit of an idol, and he also played for Coventry City. He was somebody you could almost touch because he was from where you were from. But the others – Eric Hollies, Tom Pritchard, Tom Dollery – as boys we'd sit around the boundary at Courtaulds; they were almost standing on us, and we'd look at everything about them, their cotton Oxford boots, their trousers, their shirts – but they were so distant from us. They were magic figures. County cricketers were superstars in those days. There was no television. All you did was read about them in the *Coventry Evening Telegraph*."

After a winter at Rootes, Tom set out for Edgbaston. "I was going into a different world. Even getting on the train in those days, going up to the city of Birmingham, I'd see people with briefcases and rolled umbrellas, and we didn't have anybody like that where we were living."

Two summers earlier he had been at school, breaking records with both bat and ball, now he was earning his living as a cricketer – though only as a batsman. "There were nine seam bowlers on the staff, and I couldn't get a bowl. So I tried to bowl off-spin, but I still didn't bowl in the games. Only when I went home on Saturdays and played for Rootes in the Coventry Works League, and then I'd bowl seam."

The record books list Tom as having played cricket for three counties but, as he will proudly tell you, he was twice loaned out to the opposition in his first month at Edgbaston and he is actually T.W. Cartwright of Warwickshire, Somerset, Glamorgan, Devon and Merionethshire.

"I hadn't a clue who Merioneth were. They could have come from China. But they turned up for a pre-season friendly one short; I was a bit of a dogsbody at that stage, a run-around player, and I was given to them."

Jack Bannister, a 21-year-old quick bowler, was playing for Warwickshire, and he recalls the two-day game. "Tiger Smith said to them, 'You can have this lad Cartwright.' Tom came in at the end of the first day at ten or eleven, and he was still not out the next morning when they were all out and had to follow on. And their captain said to him, 'You've got your pads on. You can open.' And he kept us out there for three or four hours."

There were so many players on the staff that his performance for Merionethshire was not sufficient to get Tom selected for the first second-team game in early May at Northampton. But he played a fortnight later against Lancashire at Edgbaston and made a fifty before being caught and bowled by the England cricketer Bob Berry. At Stafford in the next match he made 65; then he found himself coming on as twelfth man in a first-eleven fixture at Edgbaston when Freddie Brown, captain of England the previous summer, was batting. "There was a big crowd in, and I was running around on the midwicket boundary. I was sixteen years old, and I was on the field with Freddie Brown."

On another occasion Tom's world expanded further as, during a rain break at Edgbaston, he found himself in the dressing room with the American comedy duo Bud Abbott and Lou Costello. He watched amid laughter as they played the table-top horse-racing game Escalado. "They bet in dollars and, when Lou Costello lost, he paid his dues by getting out this wad of five-pound notes, the big white ones, and tearing a corner off one of them. Then he borrowed my pads and went out for a net."

Tom made two more fifties in the second eleven, with a highest score of 76 against Nottinghamshire at Edgbaston, a game that ended in a draw when the veteran Notts openers Wally Keeton and Harry Winrow made easy runs in the second innings. Keeton at 47 was a few months older than Tom's father, a contemporary of the legendary Harold Larwood, while Winrow at 36 was also on the way down, on the verge of emigrating to South Africa where years later he and Tom would cross paths a second time.

"He had a shoe shop in East London and, when we were on tour in 64/5, he was umpiring our match against Border. I hadn't seen him since that second eleven game in 1952, and there he was, out on Jan Smuts Ground at East London. I was batting and I got to 98. Then Ackerman bowled me a leg break. I got right forward, missed it and there was a big appeal for a stumping. And Harry at square leg said, 'Not out'. When he came in afterwards, he gave me a nice big wink. I wasn't sure what it meant. I got a hundred, but I was never really sure."

The summer of 1952 brought Warwickshire no repeat of the triumph of their championship year. Their victories fell from 16 to eight, and they dropped to tenth in the table. So, with an eye to the future, as August drew to a close, they promoted Tom to the first team for the county's final fixture, at Trent Bridge. He was 17 years and 39 days old, and only Fred Santall in 1920 and Roly Thompson in 1949 had ever made a younger championship debut for Warwickshire.

Tom was to replace John Thompson, the schoolmaster amateur whose holiday cricket was over for another year, and, with the team making their way up from Lord's at the end of play on Friday, Tom had to make the journey to Nottingham on his own, had to find the Flying Horse hotel and to sit there, a shy young man waiting for his team-mates to arrive.

The world of hotels was still a new one to him, and the Flying Horse was not like anywhere he had stayed with the second eleven. "An olde worlde hotel. They had Maid Marian's Room, Robin Hood's Room, Friar Tuck's Room. And in the morning a maid would bring a cup of tea into your room. I remember lying there at 7.30, thinking that the chaps on the day shift at Rootes had already started."

Then there was the head porter, a passionate supporter of Nottinghamshire cricket. "He had beautiful, copperplate handwriting. We had newspapers delivered to our rooms, and every morning he'd written on them all, things like 'BUTLER GOES THROUGH WARWICKSHIRE' or 'HARDSTAFF: ANOTHER BRILLIANT HUNDRED'. There'd be a comment on every paper."

Nottinghamshire liked to start their Saturday games as late at twelve o'clock, in the hope that this would attract office workers making their way home from the city centre, and by ten past one, when the second Warwickshire wicket fell, a crowd of more than two thousand was sitting in gentle sunshine. The scoreboard read 84 for two, and they applauded politely as out from under an elegant canopy in front of the pavilion stepped Cartwright, the 17-year-old newcomer. Among the crowd was Eddie Branson, clapping with extra vigour, but Tom was in too much of a haze to notice him.

"I was only just seventeen, and I was walking out to bat for Warwickshire. For the first time. It was an amazing experience. When I looked around the field, I could see men like Joe Hardstaff, Harold Butler, Reg Simpson, all these faces that I recognised from cigarette cards. And I was walking out into the middle, surrounded by them all."

The summer of 1952. Hope in the air. A new queen on the throne and talk of a second Elizabethan Age. No more wartime identity cards, and rations for meat and tea increasing. *High Noon* in the cinema, with Gary Cooper and the new star Grace Kelly. And the beginning of the jet age, with the first passenger flights of the Comet.

These were 'the broad sunlit uplands' that Churchill had so famously promised in the war – though further afield there were darker clouds: fierce fighting in Korea, refugees streaming out of East Berlin and in the Transvaal that day a speech by the South African Prime Minister renewing his commitment to a system of racial segregation.

But Trent Bridge and the Transvaal were worlds apart as Tom walked out to the middle. He had no county cap, not even a second eleven one, just a little blue thing that his mother had insisted on buying him in Nuneaton, and he was still using the harrow bat that he had been given by the *News Chronicle*.

"Tiger Smith always said that it was better to have a bat slightly too small than one too big," he recalls, aware now of technicalities that he knew nothing of when he went out to bat that day at Trent Bridge. "To play properly, you've got to extend your arms fully. And, if the bat is too big, the brain tells the top arm to bend a little and that allows the bottom hand to take over. On every coaching course I run, I take them through that."

He took guard and prepared for his first ball from the leg-spinner Peter Harvey. "A googly. I remember that I was a bit sheepish, but I think I picked it. And, after I'd played it, I smiled down the wicket."

'He played forward,' wrote Bill Hall, veteran reporter on the *Birmingham Post*, 'and, taking it full toss, stroked it to mid-off, showing that indefinable quality of style.'

30 August, 1952. It was the last Saturday in county cricket's summer schedule, the last game that Warwickshire would play as reigning champions before passing the pennant to Surrey, who were in action twenty miles away at Leicester where Peter May was on his way to a chanceless century. May was foremost among the emerging post-war generation – Cowdrey and Sheppard, Statham and Trueman – who were bringing fresh hope to English cricket.

"I used to go across to Edgbaston on the train from Coventry. There was a group of us, all on the staff, and in the train they would be asking, 'Do you think I'll make the grade?' And I would never take part in that. I just didn't enter into it. As far as I was concerned, the idea of playing cricket every day was just pure excitement. It never occurred to me that I wouldn't. I never wanted even to contemplate it."

When he came in for lunch, Tom had only seven runs to show for fifty minutes' batting, but his style had already impressed Bill Hall:

> Cartwright is tall and long-limbed. He is chiefly a forward player, using his reach rather than his feet to command spin bowling. His swing of the bat is a full one but is controlled to the point of leisureliness. Temperamentally, too, he is well equipped. His forward play, which in a nervous player is apt to degenerate into an apprehensive shove, was confident from the start. Altogether it was a most promising beginning.

"Tom Dollery was captain," Tom says. "Before I went out, he said, 'Just go and play. If we need to score quickly, we'll do it.'"

He picked up no sense that the older professionals were jealously guarding their places against the threat of the youngster, nor did the encouragement come only from his own team. "The man who really impressed me was Joe Hardstaff. He looked after me the whole time I was batting. He was fielding in the covers, and he would stop for a word between overs. 'Well done, stick it out a bit more,' that sort of thing."

Hardstaff was the greatest of the cigarette cards around the young Tom, featuring in his little boyhood book of *Famous Cricketers*. An England regular before the war, Hardstaff had hit 169 not out against Australia at The Oval in 1938. Then, in England's first post-war Test, he had punished the Indians with an exhilarating 205 not out. Now he was 41 years old and still good enough to be in the top ten in the national averages.

JOSEPH HARDSTAFF

One of our most stylish bats, this Notts and England player has given many polished and hard-hitting performances. Starting his Test career in 1935 when he played against South Africa, he has since played for England in nearly all the International series. 1937 was his first big year when after having a very successful tour in Australia he came home to run up an aggregate of 2,540 runs for an average of 57.72. Also during that season he won the Lawrence trophy for the quickest hundred, made in 51 minutes, and got his highest score of 266 against Leicester. He featured sixth on last season's batting list with an average of 64.75, and proved yet again that his fielding is invariably safe. Toured the West Indies during the 1947/48 winter.

"He was such a good-looking man. He was tall, and he had this copper hair that was probably streaked a bit by then. He was a great figure in the game, but he didn't make me feel in awe of him. In a funny kind of way he came down to my level, made me feel as if I was part of it all."

After lunch Tom swept the leg-spinner Harvey for his first boundary, and this brought further comment from Bill Hall:

> Cartwright reached forward to Harvey's leg-spin and deliberately pulled it across his stumps. It is a stroke much out of favour nowadays – although W.G. Grace was not ashamed to be photographed playing it – but its presence at Trent Bridge on Saturday showed that here was a young batsman who had not been too tightly pressed into the conventional mould and who was being allowed to find his own way.

"I used to sweep a lot in those days. It's a good shot if it's played properly; it keeps the board ticking, and it destroys the rhythm of the slow bowlers. Several people swept at Warwickshire, though you didn't see it so much with the other counties. And I remember, early on, Joe Hardstaff said to me, 'If you don't sweep any more in this innings, I'll buy you as much pop as you can drink. And every time you sweep, you buy me a pint. Okay?' That was the deal. 'Don't do it,' he'd say. 'Don't try to hit across the ball.' And I kept saying, 'Yes, sir. Thank you, sir.' I think I did obey him to a pretty large extent."

Without the sweep his innings grew even slower but, as his captain had promised, his partners were happy to force the pace. Dick Spooner fell for 87, caught in the covers. Then came Alan Townsend, opening up with a four and a six before being bowled for 23. Tom Dollery, 'batting superbly' and bringing up his 2,000 runs for the summer, hit 72 at nearly a run a minute, then the dashing Don Taylor added 54 in just three-quarters of an hour.

What company the young Tom was keeping! The previous summer Dollery had been the hero of all Warwickshire, the first professional cricketer to lead a county to the championship title, and three winters earlier Don Taylor had written himself into *Wisden* back in his native New Zealand, when he and the great Bert Sutcliffe had become the only openers in cricket history to put on more than 200 in each innings of a game. Waiting to bat after them were the senior professional Charlie Grove, in his fortieth year and still sharp enough to be fourth in the national bowling averages, and the leg-spinner Eric Hollies, forever famous as the man who bowled Bradman second ball in the Don's farewell Test innings.

This was the magic with which Tom had grown up: the cigarette cards that were swapped in the playground, the autographs he collected when Warwickshire came to Courtaulds, the voice of John Arlott on the radio:

Bradman pushes the ball gently in the direction of the Houses of Parliament which are out beyond mid-off. It doesn't go that far, it merely goes to Watkins at silly mid-off. No run, still 117 for one. Two slips, a silly mid-off, and a forward short leg close to him, as Hollies pitches the ball up slowly. ...He's bowled! ... *(The applause and cheers last for nearly a minute)* ... Bradman, bowled Hollies, nought. ... Bowled ... Hollies ... Nought.

Now I wonder if you see a ball very clearly on your last Test in England, on a ground where you've played some of the biggest cricket of your life, and when the opposing team have just stood round and given you three cheers, and the crowd has clapped you all the way to the wicket ... I wonder if you really see the ball at all.

"John Arlott was one of the key people who inspired me to play cricket. His voice was fascinating, and he painted pictures that made it inevitable that I wanted to play."

Now it was Tom's name that was being mentioned on the Light Programme as listeners received regular updates from Trent Bridge. And at lunch and tea he was sitting with Eric Hollies. "I remember him asking me what year I was born. '1935? I played for England before you were born.' It was an amazing experience to be in the same team as them all."

Did Eric ever tell Tom about the ball that bowled Bradman? "I never heard him mention it. But he did talk about Wally Hammond. He thought he was the best batsman he'd played against – though he said he was a difficult man, especially when they went to the West Indies together in 1934. There was a day in the nets when he was annoyed with Eric and he was hitting every ball like a rocket straight back at him."

Tom was approaching his fifty when the new ball was taken. 'Twice he was badly beaten by Butler and after tea, when he was 70, he gave a chance in the slips off that bowler.' Some of the crowd started to leave, making their way across the river in time for the six o'clock football match – Notts County against the Forest in Division Two – and the message came out to Tom that the declaration was imminent. "So I had a bit of a slog." He chanced his arm against leg-spinner Peter Harvey and was 'caught off' a mis-hit swipe'.

CARTWRIGHT, CAUGHT ROWE, BOWLED HARVEY, 82.

Tom was 17 years 39 days old. Only once since the county championship had been formally established in 1890 had a batsman younger than Tom made a fifty: the Hastings schoolboy John Nason, hitting 53 at the age of 17 years 21 days, in 1906. And Tom had gone on to 82. Even 54 years later, it remains the highest championship score ever made by a batsman under the age of 17½.

"I'd liked to have gone on and seen if I could get 100, but I'd had time and I hadn't done it. And everybody in the team was really good. Nobody had a moan about my being slow. They all said, 'Well played', though nobody made a huge fuss. People didn't in those days. The unwritten law at Warwickshire was that you knew your place. You changed in the uncapped players' dressing room. You knocked on the door before you went into the capped players. It wasn't overbearing or unpleasant. It was beneficial; you knew who you were playing with."

Back at the Flying Horse he sat quietly in the corner. "By then I was spaced out. I was only a kid, and it had been quite a bewildering day. Going out to bat in that company, I should have felt out of my depth, but somehow I didn't. I was fairly confident. And Joe Hardstaff had an enormous influence on how I felt afterwards. Each nod and wink and smile. I thought about him a lot. To have a man like that be so generous, it had a profound effect."

He had made the headlines – and not just those penned by the head porter at the Flying Horse. 'Cartwright was Slow but Good,' ran the one in Monday's *Nottingham Guardian*. 'He gave a remarkable exhibition for one so young.'

But on Monday his efforts were put into perspective by the Notts captain Reg Simpson. In the same time of four hours which it took Tom took to reach his 82, Simpson hit a glorious double century, the tenth of his career. A fearless player of quick bowling, he had the reporter from the *Nottingham Guardian* in raptures:

> There were times when he was almost contemptuous of the strong visiting attack, and towards the end of his innings he was walking down the pitch to the fast bowlers before they had delivered the ball, conclusive proof of his mastery.

"He was just a name to me, somebody I'd no idea about, but he played with such grace. He had this great ability to leave the bouncer without ducking or diving. Just a little flick of the head, and he'd watch it go past. He was an amazing man to watch."

Tom fielded all day in the covers, where he took a good catch to dismiss Joe Hardstaff for one. Then Nottinghamshire declared with a first innings lead of five and on Tuesday, when Warwickshire were looking for quick runs for a declaration of their own, Tom went in at number seven and scored an unbeaten 22, adding 88 with Dick Spooner: 'Cartwright usually managed to take a single quickly so that Spooner was able to take most of the bowling.'

Notts were left 257 to win and, with Freddie Stocks blazing his way to 99 and Simpson and Hardstaff also providing quick runs, 'so merrily did the Notts batsmen accomplish their task that they had a quarter of an hour of extra time to spare at the end.' With 1,245 runs in three days, *Wisden* reckoned it 'some of the best cricket played at Trent Bridge during the summer', and the headline in the *Nottingham Guardian* read 'WHAT A GRAND FAREWELL!'

It only remained for Bill Hall in the *Birmingham Post* to reflect on his first sight of the 17-year-old from Coventry: 'His appearance in county cricket next season will be watched with great interest.'

"There was no chance for me to get carried away," Tom says. "I had no more games, nowhere to go on from what I'd done. I was back working at Rootes the next week."

CARTWRIGHT, CAUGHT ROWE, BOWLED HARVEY, 82, AND NOT OUT, 22.

Fifty-four years have passed, and the framed scorecard hangs in the hallway of Tom's house. A golden three days at the start of a lifetime in cricket.

The next spring found the same group of youngsters travelling in the train from Coventry to Birmingham, and they were still wondering if they were going to make the grade. But not Tom, whose shy exterior concealed a solid inner core.

"Perhaps I was arrogant, but I just thought they were being negative. Cricket was such a positive thing in my life. I couldn't wait to get up in the morning. It was one of the joys of going to bed to get it over with, to get up again and go in the next day. I can remember that trip through the Broadgate in Coventry, where you get off the bus to go down to the station, and I was almost skipping my way down. It was a wonderful time. An incredible time. So full of joy."

Pre-season training, the 1950s way
(left to right) Derief Taylor, Eric Hollies, Bert Wolton, Tom Dollery, Dick Spooner,
Charlie Grove, Alan Townsend, Ian King, Keith Dollery, unidentified head,
Ray Weeks, Tom Cartwright, Norman Horner, Brian Lobb, Jimmy Ord, Tom Pritchard

NOTTINGHAMSHIRE v WARWICKSHIRE

Trent Bridge. 30 August, 1 & 2 September 1952

NOTTINGHAMSHIRE WON BY 4 WICKETS

WARWICKSHIRE

F.C. Gardner	lbw b Butler	13	b Stocks		44
R.T. Spooner +	c Birtle b Harvey	87	(6) c sub b Matthews		67
J.S. Ord	st Rowe b Harvey	20	(2) st Rowe b Harvey		22
T.W. Cartwright	c Rowe b Harvey	82	(7) *not out*		22
A. Townsend	b Matthews	23	(3) c Giles b Stocks		35
H.E. Dollery *	c Clay b Birtle	72	(5) c Giles b Birtle		63
D. Taylor	*not out*	54	(4) b Butler		0
C.W. Grove	c & b Harvey	0			
W.E. Hollies					
J.D. Bannister					
R. Weeks					
Extras	*b 5, lb 5*	10	*b 6, lb 2*		8
	(for 7 wkts, dec) **361**		(for 6 wkts, dec) **261**		

1-42, 2-84, 3-155, 4-188, 5-296, 6-354, 7-361
1-59, 2-83, 3-84, 4-147, 5-173, 6-261

Butler	22	2	54	1	26	4	76	1
Matthews	22	4	83	1	21.2	3	68	1
Harvey	31.1	8	104	4	6	1	10	1
Birtle	16	1	49	1	9	1	28	1
Stocks	21	3	61	0	23	3	71	2

NOTTINGHAMSHIRE

R.T. Simpson *	c Bannister b Weeks	200	b Bannister		48
R.J. Giles	b Townsend	42	(5) b Bannister		20
F.W. Stocks	c & b Hollies	32	c Spooner b Hollies		99
J. Hardstaff	c Cartwright b Weeks	1	(2) c Hollies b Weeks		39
C.J. Poole	b Hollies	54	(4) c Weeks b Bannister		11
J.D. Clay	b Hollies	14	c Spooner b Hollies		12
P.F. Harvey	b Hollies	4	(8) *not out*		1
H.J. Butler	*not out*	5	(7) *not out*		23
C.S. Matthews	*not out*	5			
E. Rowe +					
T.W. Birtle					
Extras	*b 7, lb 2*	9	*b 2, lb 2*		4
	(for 7 wkts, dec) **366**		(for 6 wkts) **257**		

1-114, 2-194, 3-201, 4-318, 5-349, 6-350, 7-359
1-69, 2-137, 3-155, 4-215, 5-230, 6-249

Grove	16	0	64	0	5	0	25	0
Bannister	14	0	54	0	8.4	1	46	3
Townsend	18	2	52	1	8	0	40	0
Hollies	26	1	82	4	18	1	96	2
Weeks	34.5	11	105	2	8	1	46	1

Umpires: T.W. Spencer and C.H. Welch

The young Tom at Edgbaston

CHAPTER 4

LEARNING THE GAME

1953

Tom returned to Edgbaston in April 1953. He was the county's brightest prospect, as Alan Townsend remembers: "The first time I saw him, I thought he's going to be good. He was so easy. And he was a very quick learner. He was my double as a younger lad. Very shy, quiet. But from the beginning, we all thought he was going to be an England batter."

Tom was keen to learn, a quality Warwickshire quickly recognised. He started the season in the first team and before each match, when Tom Dollery and Eric Hollies walked out to the middle, they asked Tom to join them. "I just walked up and down with them as they were talking about the pitch, and at seventeen that was like being in Santa's Grotto."

They were father figures, and each in his own way was to leave a strong imprint on the shy youngster: Dollery as a dynamic and uncompromising captain, Hollies as a patient and genial master of the craft of bowling.

"Tom Dollery was a bright bloke," Tom says. "He could have gone to university. To speak to him in the field, I never felt he was there at that moment. He'd already planned that and was thinking way ahead. He was a real leader of men; the team would have gone anywhere with him. He stood at slip, and he had that ability to attract people's attention all over the field. I can't speak for the older players, but he was never out of my vision. If you weren't looking he'd give a little clap, but he had this presence all the time. It was a natural thing."

In 1949, in his first full season as Warwickshire captain, Dollery had been the only professional cricketer in charge of a county side. In the words of Eric Hollies, 'He knew that he was on trial and that on his shoulders rested the responsibility not only of Warwickshire but also of raising professional cricket to a new high standard. And he thrived on the added responsibility.' Always an attacking batsman Dollery scored 2,000 runs for the first time, he led the county to fourth place in the table – their highest since the first world war – and he still found time to run a successful benefit year. Then two years later he became the first professional captain to lead a county to the championship title.

Wisden called him 'the most skilful of all the county captains'. His team played purposeful cricket, his declarations always seemed to come off and – with the England selectors calling none of them away – the title was won in mid-August with only 13 players having been used.

The son of a master engraver, Dollery had passed the entrance exam to Reading School, an independent grammar school, and it was perhaps surprising that his leadership qualities had not surfaced during the war.

"He'd been in the desert in North Africa," Tom says, "directing fire from artillery observation posts. He was in the number one position, the closest to the enemy, and people doing jobs like that, their survival rate wasn't that good.

"During my national service, when I was playing for the Royal Artillery, there was a man called Major-General Pratt who used to umpire the odd game. He was white-haired and a typical major-general. The first time I saw him, I was fielding next to him at square leg. 'How's your Tom Dollery?' he said. Tom had been in his regiment, and he'd been a bit of a harum-scarum. He always did live life to the full, and I think he'd gone from gunner to sergeant and back more than once. 'Best Number One I ever had, you know,' this chap said to me."

The war was now over, but it was never far away in Dollery's captaincy. "We'd talk about having drinks on the field, and he'd say, 'Drinks? What do you want drinks for? In the desert we had two pints of water a day – and that was for you *and* your vehicle.' ... I wasn't there but I remember some of the boys coming back from a second team match in Chester, when he was their captain. Somebody had messed around with the newspapers, and he'd had these comics pushed under his door in the morning. He lined them up outside the hotel. He sent the coach off, got them in twos and marched them to the ground. ... If he saw somebody preening himself in front of a mirror, he'd come up: 'How do you think you'd have coped on the cobbled streets of Belgium?' ... Later in life he had a pub in Hatton, and he wouldn't serve men with long hair. He couldn't come to terms with that. What he'd be like now with ear-rings and things, I don't know."

Tom Dollery was an adventurer both in life and on the cricket field, but Eric Hollies was an altogether different character. He was a contented home-lover, married to his childhood sweetheart Cissie, and was always happiest when he could get back to her and their daughter Jackie. He was not one who was tempted by the distractions that arose during weeks away from home or, as he once put it to Jeanne Dollery, "Me, I'm a one-dog, one-bone man."

"Eric was happy with his lot," Tom says. "I remember him saying to me, 'It's all right to admire the flowers in someone else's garden, but you don't pick them.'"

Hollies was from Old Hill in the Black Country, son of the master plumber Billy Hollies whose underarm leg-spin bowling was legendary in the Birmingham League. Billy's party piece was to put a beer barrel in front of the wicket and spin the ball around it to hit the stumps, and his son inherited his sense of fun.

"Eric was a bit of a joker," Tom says. "The Black Country was only at the other end of Warwickshire, but it was a place all of its own. He used to read out these letters he got from people there, and it was like they were written in a foreign language. And every so often he'd tell one of his stories about Enoch and Eli. There was no way you could understand it all.

"There were certain batsmen he could get out for a pastime. George Cox of Sussex was one. It was like he had an Indian sign on him. George used to come out laughing, almost offering Eric his wicket. Eric was always having fun on the field, but he never let it disturb his concentration."

Hollies was not a big spinner of his leg-break, not like, say, Roly Jenkins at Worcester, who liked to sit in the bar in the evening and describe balls he had bowled that had pitched on middle-and-leg and spun into the hands of second slip. The two were great friends, but Hollies was never one to be over-impressed by such talk. "My best ball, Roly," he would say in his soft Black Country voice, "pitches on middle stump and hits middle stump."

"Tom Dollery used to call Eric the toothache bowler," Tom says. "I've never seen a leg-spinner as accurate as him. He often used him as a tight bowler, to slow the run rate down."

Through his career Roly Jenkins conceded 3.12 runs an over. Kent's Doug Wright 3.18, Somerset's Johnny Lawrence 3.04 and Middlesex's Jim Sims 3.07. The leg-spinner was expected to be more expensive. But Eric Hollies, through a career that stretched from 1932 to 1957, conceded his runs at only 2.21 an over. Even the impressively accurate Shane Warne comes in at 2.73.

"Eric ran in off ten or twelve paces, and he had so much control. In a way he was a two-part bowler. In the first innings on pitches that weren't so helpful, he'd bowl quicker and give the ball less spin. Then in the second innings, if the pitch was worn and his margin of error had become greater, he would spin it more. He would have been good in one-day cricket because he had so much control.

"He had an inbuilt, natural ability. He hardly ever went to nets to practise. That summer of 1953 he slipped a disc, and he missed some weeks. He had to lie flat on his back. Then he turned up at the nets before a match at Edgbaston, and he bowled no more than half a dozen balls. The first one went straight on the spot, and they all followed. And he just turned to Tom Dollery and said, 'I'm OK, skipper' and walked off."

Wisden completes the story.

SATURDAY 25 JULY 1953, WARWICKSHIRE VERSUS ESSEX AT EDGBASTON.

HOLLIES, BACK AFTER A THREE-WEEK ABSENCE, 28.5 OVERS, THREE WICKETS FOR 27.

"I learned so much from being around when he was there. When I first started, he said to me, 'When you can come off the field, whether you've got wickets or not, and you can put your hand on your heart and say truthfully, I bowled well again today, that's when you become a bowler, when that happens every day. And the only way you can achieve that is by being in control at your end.' He taught me to be honest with myself. If you bowled a bad ball or something went wrong, not to look for other reasons than you. He talked about conquering yourself."

They were words that in time would play a vital part in Tom's breakthrough as a bowler, but not in 1953 and not for several more years. For now Tom was a batsman, and in the third game of that summer he returned to Trent Bridge and, opening the innings, he bettered by one run his score there in 1952.

CARTWRIGHT, CAUGHT STOCKS BOWLED GOONESENA, 83.

To this day, in the whole history of the county championship, Tom remains the only batsman twice to reach a score of 80 before his 18th birthday.

His 83 was the highest score of a rain-affected match, but Tom's main memory is of fielding in the covers and admiring the Notts batsmen. "Joe Hardstaff made a fifty. I remember his back-foot strokes. He seemed to be defending, and the ball was flying through the covers; once it had gone past you, you had no hope of catching it. It was pure timing. Reg Simpson was very much the same; I think he'd probably modelled himself on Joe. Their arms seemed to flow, not at a fast speed but with long arms. Tiger used to talk about fully extending the arms; he always said that good players seemed to have longer ones than anybody else. That was a feature of Jim Parks, his arms always seemed to be longer than they should be for a man of his size. And it was the thing I noticed about Ian Botham the first time I saw him, how he had beautiful arms. They worked so perfectly together."

Rain ruined the final day at Trent Bridge, and the Warwickshire team made their way by coach to London where they were due to play Surrey, the champion county against their predecessors. There was a celebratory dinner arranged for the two teams at the House of Commons on Monday evening, and the Warwickshire players booked into the Portland Arms in Maida Vale where, after dinner, they moved into the lounge, sat down with their various drinks and talked cricket.

Tom was seventeen years old, and there was so much experience all round him: men who had seen action in the war, men who had travelled from Australia and New Zealand to play this county cricket, men like Eric Hollies and Charlie Grove who had already turned forty.

"Charlie was the senior professional. Very meticulous. Didn't smoke, didn't drink. He'd been a sergeant-major in the war. You jumped to attention when he looked at you. I would sit in the corner. And at about twenty past ten Charlie would look across at me, and he'd tap his watch. I'd plead for ten minutes, but I knew not to push it. I loved sitting there, listening to them talking, but I never said anything."

May 1953. An FA Cup winners' medal at last for Stanley Matthews. A British expeditionary team, under Edmund Hillary, setting out on their assault on Mount Everest. Frankie Laine singing *I Believe*. And a nation preparing for the coronation of their young Queen.

It was a time of hope. There was full employment, little inflation, a new National Health Service and a wide-scale programme of house building. The war had been won, rationing was nearing its end and people were mostly happy to have returned to lives of routine.

"There was much more of a rhythm of life then. A rhythm of going to work and coming home at the same time each day, a rhythm of learning a trade and progressing with it, a rhythm even in people's leisure pursuits, and it gave people good manners and a consideration for others. People had settled lives. They did things which were within their reach – going out into the country, doing the garden, spending a day at cricket. Now people are striving for things they can't attain, the structures break down and the natural rhythm is lost."

The post-war surge in attendance at county cricket matches was dying away, but the game retained its familiar patterns and Tom could grow and develop within a structure that had a reassuring feeling of permanence.

County cricket. A four-month round of two three-day matches a week. A championship that captured the public imagination. The averages every week in the papers. And the cream at the top rising to the England team, an England team that would go more than seven years without losing a Test series.

"There was a rhythm of introducing young cricketers into the game, a rhythm that was constant. You joined a county club, you went about learning your job and in time, when somebody was injured or went off to play for England, you got your chance. By playing six days a week you got into form and, if you did well, there was an inevitability that your performances would be noted by writers and selectors. The fixture list wasn't disjointed, the counties didn't look for an overseas player whenever there was a vacancy, the selectors didn't make their minds up in April who was going to be in the England squad and who wasn't. The whole thing had a rhythm, an unbroken rhythm, and it provided a depth of quality, an intensity of competition between bat and ball in the county game."

Deep in the heart of Wales Tom works hard to help the young cricketers of today to progress in the game: to learn its manners, to develop its skills, to experience its pleasures. But he is not sure that the structures around him make that progress as easy as it was for him in the 1950s. "I'm a great believer in rhythm. When things are good, you get a good rhythm."

Tom had made the most impressive of starts to his first-class career. In an era in which only the very best batsmen sustained career averages above forty, his first four matches had yielded him 262 runs at an average of 42. There was already talk that he would be England's answer to Ian Craig, the 17-year-old Australian who in January had hit a double century for New South Wales against the South Africans and who was now touring England with Lindsay Hassett's Australians.

But Tom was just beginning, and the gentle-paced Trent Bridge pitch on which he had scored 83 on Thursday was a world away from the spiteful, rain-affected strip that awaited him in Kennington on Saturday.

The Oval was not an easy pitch for batsmen in those years, and in the hotel lounge the previous night there had been talk of their last visit to the ground, when the turf had been so loose and dusty that all 40 wickets had fallen by five o'clock on the second day. So, when Eric Hollies – ever the joker – arrived at the ground on Saturday morning, he presented the groundsman Bert Lock with a trowel and a small bag of cement.

The Australians were at Lord's, playing MCC, but, when the 'No Play Today' signs went up there, some of the spectators made their way across London to swell the large Surrey crowd that were waiting eagerly as the ground staff mopped up the water and brought out the sawdust.

Just after mid-day Tom was walking to the middle with his boyhood idol from Coventry, Fred Gardner. Warwickshire had lost the toss, and Tom stood at the non-striker's end as big Alec Bedser prepared to bowl the first ball.

They ran a two and a one during the over. Fred Gardner played out a maiden from Stuart Surridge. Then came a sharp shower to liven the pitch still further and, when they returned, Tom found himself on strike, facing Alec Bedser. Over came the big arm, down the pitch came the ball and it thudded against his front pad. Within moments Tom was looking at a raised finger and returning all the way to the pavilion. He had made his first duck in first-class cricket. "I'm absolutely certain it was missing leg stump," he says, managing a chuckle 53 years later. "Laurie Gray was the umpire. He had a hip problem, and he got down in a funny position, a bit wide of the stumps to give the bowler room. From where he was, it probably looked smack in front."

By the end of the over his misery was being shared by the New Zealander Don Taylor, caught in the crowded arc of predatory fielders in the Surrey leg trap.

Surrey's captain Stuart Surridge had revolutionised their fielding. He had put his best fielders close to the bat, even if they were the bowlers, and that had allowed him to move the leg trap much closer to the batsman. "Stuart was a noisy, demonstrative man, very much a physical presence close to the wicket. Just handling the attack, moving the field, you were aware of him. It was very daunting, but it wasn't sledging. It was just a positive assertion that they were going to get you out, and this was how they were going to do it."

Alec Bedser was in his element on the drying pitch. His stock ball was an in-swinger aimed towards the leg stump, where close fielders crouched, waiting for the edge. Then, with his massive hands, he would send down his legendary leg-cutter, and the ball would pitch and turn back towards the off. By lunch he had taken five wickets, and the Warwickshire innings was in ruins at 38 for six.

"You could see the pitch steaming as you looked across it. It was that kind of day. A quick drying sun, and it did become crusty."

Twenty minutes after lunch the innings was over. Warwickshire were all out for 45, and Alec Bedser – with figures of eight for 18 – was leading his team off the field. Within a month he would be leading off the England team at Trent Bridge, having taken 14 Australian wickets in the match. Despite the damp this was to be the most golden of his many golden summers, with 162 wickets in 1,253 overs. He was a master craftsman who – like Tom in years to come – never shirked from hard work.

Replying to Warwickshire, the Surrey batsmen slumped to 81 for seven, but Laker, Surridge and Lock all took to swinging the bat adventurously and the innings only closed at 146 when Lock's attempt to hook Charlie Grove resulted in his sustaining a cut over the left eye and being driven to hospital. It was a game packed with incident.

At half past five Tom was making his way to the middle once more. Still wearing the little blue cap his mother had bought him in Nuneaton but having graduated that summer to a full-size bat, he took guard on a pair and for a long time wondered if he could ever score a run.

"It was very difficult to put a bat on Alec Bedser. I remember Arthur Mac standing up behind me, right up to the wicket, and leaping up to take the ball. The ball was pitching and going over my shoulder, and Eric at first slip was berating Alec for not bowling straight enough. And Laker at the other end was just as difficult. It was the first time I'd played against Surrey. I'd never seen any of them before. Going down to London, staying in the hotel, playing at The Oval, a big Saturday crowd, there was so much to take in. It was all a bit overpowering.

"Eventually, after what seemed a very long time, I decided to chance it. I swept Laker, top-edged it and it flew over Arthur Mac's head for three runs."

With Fred Gardner he took the score to 20. It was a higher partnership than any in the Warwickshire first innings, and alas it would prove a higher one than any that was about to follow.

Jim Laker trapped him lbw for nine. Then, by the time the total had reached 32, seven wickets were down, three of them – Spooner, Dollery, Hitchcock – in a hat-trick to Laker. At 20 for no wicket and the close of play approaching, Alan Townsend had been running himself a hot bath in the pavilion – and in the turmoil he had broken away to pad up, forgetting to turn off the taps. Yet so quickly was he going out to bat and so quickly coming back – run out for a duck – that on his return the water had still not filled the tub.

"People were running around in the dressing room," Tom remembers. "There wasn't a moment when people weren't putting pads on. Tom Dollery was saying to people, 'Get padded up. You're in.' And they'd say, 'No, I've been in, skipper.' It was that kind of comedy."

Bedser and Laker bowled unchanged. "They were imposing their will – and not just on the batter at the other end. They were imposing their will on the people still to come in. They'd created all that kerfuffle in the dressing room."

By twenty to seven the scoreboard read 52 for nine and Eric Hollies – on a pair – was taking guard to Alec Bedser. Hollies was the supreme non-batsman; in 471 first-class innings he had never once reached 25, and he appealed to the bowler's good nature. "Give me one to get off the mark, Alec; I won't hit it far." Bedser agreed, sending a gentle delivery down the leg side and, according to Eric, "I hit it all right – straight to the fielder at short leg." It was the sixth duck of the innings, making ten in the match for the visitors.

"I'll never forget that game," Tom says. "County cricket on uncovered pitches was a great learning environment. I learned more in my time at the wicket in that game than I learned in any period of any other game."

The Oval, Saturday 16 May 1953.
Cartwright, lbw Bedser, 0, lbw Laker, 9.

The game was over, though not the trip to London. The teams were due at the House of Commons on Monday night. "Tom Dollery rang back to the club," Alan Townsend says, "to find out if we could come home. And the club said, 'Oh no, you've got to stay.'"

So, while the streets of central London on Sunday saw a rehearsal of the Coronation procession, Tom wandered about Regent's Park with Keith Dollery, his Australian team-mate, stopping to watch the cricket matches that clustered together in the field beside the zoo. The next day they watched the Australians at Lord's, then went to dinner at Westminster.

"It was very formal. I sat between two ladies with tiaras and flowing gowns. I'd never seen so many glasses, so many pieces of cutlery in my life. I was terrified. All I could do was watch and copy."

"I was sat next to Anthony Eden," Alan Townsend recalls, "and he was sloshed. We were trying to eat properly, and he was prodding his peas all over the table."

After the meal they were ushered past a long queue into the Strangers' Gallery of the Commons, where a Town and Country Planning Bill was being debated. "Winston Churchill came in," Alan says. "He had a dicky bow on, and he'd obviously been out to dinner somewhere. He started chattering to Emanuel Shinwell across the table, and this poor MP was trying to talk about river pollution. We couldn't get over it. And what was going on downstairs, underneath in the Crypt, with all the couples cuddling away, was nobody's business. We were all absolutely staggered."

They returned to Edgbaston on Tuesday to find that a well-wisher had sent each of the duck-makers a set of sherry glasses – with the catch-phrase from Wilfred Pickles' radio show, 'Give 'em the glass, Barney.'

"My mother thought they were marvellous," Tom says. "She didn't see the other side."

The glasses still sit in his side cabinet, a reminder of a match in which he learnt so much. It is a match that could not happen today, with pitches that are covered against rainfall and inspectors travelling the country to ensure that groundsmen prepare surfaces that will last for four days.

Games like that one at The Oval would be a nightmare for the sponsors and marketing men of the modern game, but Tom is without doubt that they provided a learning experience that raised the skills of the game faster than they are raised today.

"Uncovered pitches put pressure on players. They were like a market force, making sure the most skilful reach the top. As a batsman you had to have a level of skill sufficient to compete and to stay in. But it's also much tougher to bowl on a helpful pitch, when the pressure is on you to deliver. On a covered one, you can play percentage cricket."

Undoubtedly the game in England has evolved into one that is more friendly to the batsmen. But many argue that this is good for the bowlers, forcing them to raise the level of their skills.

"That's the biggest load of rubbish. You only achieve high levels of technical skill in the bowling by having pitches that are slightly conducive to the bowlers so they can see something happen with the ball and want to repeat it. If you provide pitches where that doesn't happen, you're never going to raise the potential or the achievement of the bowlers. Their control will be used in a negative way. And if you reduce the skill of the bowlers, you reduce the skill of the batsmen. I find it amazing that people can't see that."

SURREY v WARWICKSHIRE

The Oval. 16 May 1953

SURREY WON BY AN INNINGS AND 49 RUNS

WARWICKSHIRE

F.C. Gardner	c Laker b A. Bedser	7	c Laker b A. Bedser	7
T.W. Cartwright	lbw A. Bedser	0	lbw Laker	9
D. Taylor	c Fletcher b A. Bedser	0	lbw b A. Bedser	20
R.T. Spooner +	c Whittaker b A. Bedser	16	c and b Laker	0
H.E. Dollery *	c Lock b A. Bedser	8	c Surridge b Laker	0
R.E. Hitchcock	c Whittaker b Lock	3	c A. Bedser b Laker	0
A. Townsend	c McIntyre b Lock	7	run out	0
R. Weeks	*not out*	0	c Surridge b A. Bedser	0
C.W. Grove	c Fletcher b A. Bedser	3	c Constable b Laker	10
K.R. Dollery	c Brazier b A. Bedser	0	*not out*	0
W.E. Hollies	c Laker b A. Bedser	0	c sub b A. Bedser	0
Extras	*lb 1*	1	*b2, lb 3, nb 1*	6
		45		**52**

1-3, 2-3, 3-8, 4-27, 5-30, 6-36, 7-42, 8-45, 9-45, 10-45
1-20, 2-22, 3-26, 4-26, 5-26, 6-32, 7-32, 8-49, 9-52, 10-52

A. Bedser	13.5	4	18	8	13.4	7	17	4
Surridge	6	1	17	0				
Lock	7	3	9	2				
Laker					13	6	29	5

SURREY

E.A. Bedser	b K. Dollery	5
D.G.W. Fletcher	c Townsend b Weeks	13
B. Constable	c Grove b K. Dollery	37
T.H. Clark	c K. Dollery b Hollies	2
A.F. Brazier	c Townsend b Hollies	6
G.J. Whittaker	b K. Dollery	0
A.J. McIntyre +	c & b K. Dollery	9
J.C. Laker	c H. Dollery b Hollies	18
W.S. Surridge *	b Grove	19
A.V. Bedser	*not out*	5
G.A.R. Lock	*retired hurt*	27
Extras	*lb 4, nb 1*	5
		146

1-5, 2-27, 3-50, 4-61, 5-65, 6-77, 7-81, 8-108, 9-119

Grove	10.1	3	29	1
K. Dollery	11	4	40	4
Weeks	8	1	24	1
Hollies	10	4	48	3

Umpires: L.Gray and E.Cooke

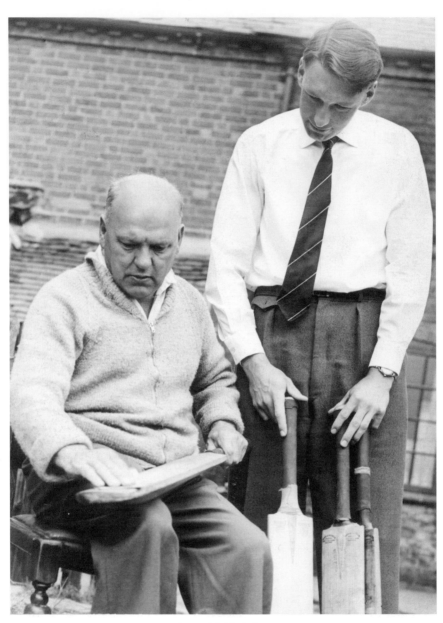

Tom with his father

Tom with his mother and sister Lily

CHAPTER 5

LANCE-BOMBARDIER CARTWRIGHT
1953 – 1955

For their next championship match after The Oval, Warwickshire picked the 27-year-old Norman Horner, a Yorkshireman unable to break into his own county's side, to take Tom's place, and Tom himself continued his education in the second eleven, coming back into the runs immediately with 82 at the Rothwell Town ground outside Kettering.

Tom was briefly back in the first team in July when Warwickshire gained a revenge victory over Surrey at Edgbaston, another match in which the condition of the pitch occasioned comment. "Surrey reckoned there was grit in the top dressing. I remember Stuart Surridge going out to the pitch before the second day's play. He collected all these bits of grit and chippings in a match box; he even came off with a broken cup handle that he said he'd found just below the surface. I also remember Peter May's bat leaning up outside their dressing room, and all the young players were picking it up because it was so heavy. It was two pounds six ounces, and at that time bats were two-two or two-three. Two-six seemed outrageous."

Tom also played in the first eleven at Northampton where the elegant Dennis Brookes hit an unbeaten 171.

"We thought Tom was going to become a batsman like Dennis Brookes," Jim Stewart says. "Or Jack Robertson. A classical batsman, playing in the V."

Brookes and Robertson, they were two yeomen of the county game. Jack Robertson of Middlesex had scored 2,000 runs in each of the seven post-war summers, Dennis Brookes of Northants in five of them. Yet, at a time when Hutton and Washbrook kept a firm grip on the opening batting positions for England, neither had Test careers of substance. Their runs, made with consistency and style, underlined the depth of quality in the English game.

"There was an assuredness about the way they batted," Tom says. "It was an art form. They didn't hit the ball, they caressed it, and they had the ability to control the pace of the ball off the bat so that they could run singles. Javed Miandad was like that years later. He had so much control of how he hit the ball that he could run it down to third man at Swansea and run two. That was the great art of his batting, and I can't think of anybody since who's played quite like that."

Unfortunately Tom's opportunity to observe the art of Dennis Brookes that day at Northampton owed much to his own incompetence. "He'd got 24 or 25, and I dropped him at mid-wicket. He'd got that sallow look under his cap, not much emotion, but, when I crossed over, I thought I could see a look of sympathy for me. That really registered. I've never regretted dropping that catch, because it was brilliant to see him get those runs. He was a lovely player to watch."

Tom was a keen, young cricketer, and he still recalls the thrill of his seniors' praise. "I loved fielding and, when we came off, if I'd had a good day, Tom Dollery would sometimes say, 'Well done, Tom, first class again today.' And that was like somebody giving you £10,000. Occasionally even Charlie Grove would come and say 'Well fielded'. He was a hard taskmaster, and from him those two words were worth volumes."

At the end of that second summer on the staff Tom – now turned eighteen – departed for two years of national service. "There was a war on in Korea, and I was expecting to go in the Royal Warwicks and be shipped out. All the blokes I was at school with were."

His cricket, however, saved him from the battlefront. During a Club and Ground fixture at RAF Innsworth in Gloucestershire, Tiger Smith was asked by the Squadron Leader if he had any good cricketers coming up for service, and he recommended Tom. Then a phone call came in to Leslie Deakins, the Warwickshire Secretary, from a Colonel Garthwaite at the Royal Artillery base at Shoeburyness in Essex, where Jim Stewart was stationed. The colonel was captain of the cricket team, and Leslie Deakins called Tom into his office to pass on his message: "He wants to know if you want to go down there. Go and have a word with Tiger about it."

"Jim tells me they've got a wonderful pitch," Tiger said, "and they play a lot of good club sides. And you'll get all the Royal Artillery matches as well. It's a long way away but, if I were you, I'd be inclined to go down there."

"It's ridiculous, isn't it? I'm going to do national service, there's a war on, and Tiger's advising me what's best for my cricket."

Before Tom left, Leslie Deakins – made aware that Tom had been earning less as a Warwickshire cricketer than he earned at Rootes – arranged with the chairman for him to be sent £25. The Edgbaston library retains three bulging files of correspondence relating to Tom, and in them are his letter of thanks and the secretary's reply to it. "Leslie was notorious for his letter-writing," Tom recalls. "If you thanked him by letter, he'd have to write back, thanking you for thanking him."

At one point it seemed that Tom would fail his army medical. At the start of the football season he had been sent on a month's trial from Aston Villa to Northampton Town, and in his first match – for the reserves at Rushden – he came up against the former Birmingham City centre-half Ted Duckhouse. "He was well past his best. I did this little shimmy and went past him, and he ended up crashing his head into the rail that went round the ground. He split his eye and, after they'd stitched him up, I was terrified for the rest of the game. At every set piece he was right behind me, whispering about this terrible injury I'd caused him. I was really glad when the whistle blew."

Two days later at British Timken he was less fortunate. "This big, cumbersome centre-half sat on my leg and pulled all the inside ligaments of my knee. I was in a terrible state. For six weeks I was catching the train every day from Coventry to Northampton for treatment with Jack Jennings, who was also the Northants physio. Just a heat lamp and his hands."

On the train with him was Alf Wood, the former Coventry goalkeeper whom Tom had watched as a boy – "a real icon in Coventry" – and he and the Northampton Town captain Ben Collins looked after Tom paternally during his days with them.

Despite the state of his knee, Tom passed his medical and was posted to the 63rd Heavy Ack-Ack Regiment, Royal Artillery, Shoeburyness. On the walls in the barracks there were water marks four or five feet up, a reminder of the floods earlier in that year of 1953, and he heard repeatedly from his new comrades about the rescue work the regiment had undertaken. "All the dead bodies they'd dragged out, they talked about it all the time."

There was square bashing: "I thought it would cripple me, but in fact it built up my knee." Then Gunners training: running with heavy gun parts above the head, assembling limber guns in quick time, doing bayonet drill. Six weeks in North Wales, setting large guns out to sea and firing 72-pound shells at sleeves drawn by planes: "Twelve of us on each gun. My job was to set the fuses, timing them so that the shell went off at the right moment. I used to think the pilots were very brave. They weren't far away from the sleeves." Then a spell on Salisbury Plain: "With the 3.7 gun, firing 56-pounders. You'd fire at static targets which you couldn't see, but you had somebody on an observation post, what Tom Dollery did in the war. That seemed a dangerous position, too."

With plenty of sport, it was not too arduous a posting. "In some ways it was a bit of a holiday camp. It had that reputation because all the officers and warrant officers had been in the same prisoner-of-war camps in Japan. I think there was a deliberate ploy to send them to Shoeburyness, to give them an easy time. When you did bayonet drill, it was always some slant-eyed individual you were sticking it into. It was very much the Yellow Peril that was obsessing people at the time."

In April the cricket began, and he found himself playing alongside not only Jim Stewart but also Malcolm Heath and Peter Sainsbury of Hampshire, Don Ward of Glamorgan, Bob Gale of Middlesex and a young officer Peter Croft who won a Cambridge blue and played hockey for England. The year after, Chris Greetham of Somerset joined them. Colonel Garthwaite had gone to the War Office, but his replacement – Colonel Lawson – also took on the captaincy of the cricket team.

Jim Stewart had landed himself the job of driver to the commanding officer and, when he was not required for that, he worked on the cricket ground, preparing beautiful practice pitches. There was a long fixture card – and nets in the evening when there was no match.

David Belchamber, an ex-public schoolboy doing his national service as a junior officer, remembers long hours of facing Malcolm Heath, Peter Sainsbury, Don Ward and Tom in the nets.

"I'd wanted to be posted to Germany. I was going up to Cambridge to study modern languages, and it would have improved my German greatly. Instead, I ended up working on my batting. I went from being a number eleven bat at school to opening the innings for Teddington in good club cricket in London."

In regimental matches Tom opened the innings with Jim Stewart, and so prolific were they, David Belchamber recalls, that in the second half of the summer the colonel started dropping them down the order so that the young officers could get more chance to bat. The colonel also tried to enforce more sense of rank by having the NCOs call them Mr Belchamber and Mr Croft, not David and Peter. "He gave us a real bollocking for being too familiar on the field, but I don't think anybody took any notice. In the end I think we dropped him from the team."

"We played Southend, Westcliff, Upminster, Colchester, all the best club sides in Essex," Tom says. "Then there were the Royal Artillery games. The great game each year was against the Royal Engineers. A two-day match at

Lord's. We had a dinner on the first evening in the Tavern, and there were so many top brass there, generals and brigadiers, and they laid out the table so we each had to sit between two of them. They called us by our first names. We were almost mates for the night."

His first encounter with the great Gubby Allen was less friendly. "Bob Gale had popped back to the dressing room, and I was waiting outside for him. Gubby saw me. 'I've told you kids before. Stop hanging around.' 'But … but.' And he just carried on. 'I'm not going to tell you again. Get out.'"

There were also Army games. "And, in my second year, the Army were running the Combined Services matches. They leaned towards their own, and I played against Lancashire at Old Trafford. Peter Richardson gave me a lift in his little car. He'd just had the invitation to captain Worcestershire the next summer. I think it was one of the last games I played. I'd go away for three weeks or so, and I'd come back to Shoeburyness and draw my wages. I'd spend a day there, then go off somewhere else."

OLD TRAFFORD, 25 AUGUST 1955.
SERGEANT P.E. RICHARDSON, CAUGHT AND BOWLED GREENHOUGH, 43.
LANCE-BOMBARDIER T.W. CARTWRIGHT, BOWLED COLLINS, 51.

All eleven of their Combined Services side that day played county cricket.

"It was very easy-going at Shoeburyness. My Battery Sergeant-Major was a lovely man called Harry Cavill. He used to have a wry smile when I'd go to see him. 'Is it all right, sir?' I'd say. 'I've just had an invitation to play for the Royal Artillery.' And he'd always agree.

"I played football for the regiment as well, but the standard wasn't as high. All the best footballers got sent over to Towyn near Aberdovey in Wales."

In any case Tom's football was on a downward path after his knee injury. At the end of national service he played for the Rootes work team and for Kenilworth Rangers, "but it gradually fizzled out."

However, he was still an important part of Warwickshire's cricket, and in May 1955, in his second summer at Shoeburyness, he managed to get away for six matches for the county, the first of which took him up to Sheffield for his first encounter with Fred Trueman.

"I was away from the garrison, and I got a phone call telling me to report to Grindleford, south of Sheffield, and they would fix it for me. I can remember arriving at the Grindleford Arms, not knowing if I was in big trouble because technically I was absent without leave."

The next morning they were preparing to bat first on a green pitch at Bramall Lane, and Alan Townsend remembers the discussion. "Dick Spooner and myself had a word with Tom Dollery. We said, 'It's not fair to put Tom Cartwright in against Freddie Trueman. He's only a youngster.'"

As a result, Tom was dropped down to number four – though the score had only reached 23 and Trueman was still bowling when he arrived at the wicket. As he battled his way to a personal score of 27, Tom's education took another step forward – though his main memories of that day are of Fred Trueman's histrionics and of the umpire Alec Skelding, now 68 years old, a man who, with the passing of the years, seemed more and more to be doing things his own way. Some bowlers of that time recall him whistling to himself as they ran in and delivered the ball – while Worcestershire's Martin Horton tells the story of how, as a green 18-year-old, he was put on to bowl at Skelding's end. Wanting to come round the wicket, he politely asked the umpire to step back a pace. "Don't worry about that," was the reply. "I'll stand over here." And he promptly took up position well to the right of the stumps.

"When I was 16," Tom says, "I went up to Bradford as twelfth man, and we stayed in the Alexander Hotel. The night before the match there was this old boy walking up and down in the lounge, reciting Shakespeare. I thought he must be an actor preparing for a production. Then I saw him at the ground in the morning. I said to Alan Townsend, 'There's that old bloke who was reciting Shakespeare.' It turned out it was Alec Skelding, and he was the umpire."

When Tom reached the wicket at Sheffield, Skelding was in more belligerent mood, looking to mix it with Fred Trueman and with the Yorkshire supporters.

"I can see Fred now," Tom says. "He swore and cursed all through; he was appealing a lot and he was snatching his sweater. And Alec held on to it and yanked it back. 'I'll clip his ear,' he said to me. The crowd was getting more and more worked up. There was always this noise from the bank on the football stand side, and Alec said he was going to sort them out. I thought he was joking, but the next moment he was over the fence. And there was this sudden hush. He came back and winked. 'I told you I'd sort them out.'

"When he was younger, Alec had been a heavyweight boxer, and he'd fought Bombardier Billy Wells. Tiger Smith used to say that, when they umpired together before the war at, say, Southampton, Alec was keen to get Tiger to have a few drinks in the dockside pubs and for the pair of them to sort out a few ruffians."

The world of county cricket was full of revelations for Tom. The beautiful flow of Joe Hardstaff's arms, the caressing touch of Dennis Brookes' bat, the intimidating throng of close Surrey fielders, the copperplate writing of the Flying Horse's head porter, the wartime talk of Tom Dollery, the cutlery at the House of Commons dinner, the advice of Eric Hollies – 'Be honest with yourself' – and Alec Skelding wading into the crowd at Sheffield. They were all fascinating elements of a way of life that he was still absorbing.

Tiger Smith

CHAPTER 6

TIGER

Eddie Branson, Tom Dollery, Tiger Smith. They were the three great influences in Tom's early cricket career.

"Eddie Branson taught me the basics of the game and the love of it. Tom was an inspiration as a captain. And Tiger's coaching, that was like going to university. I never speak to young kids without hearing Eddie Branson's voice in my head. I never go onto a field with my under-16s without hearing Tom Dollery. And I never go into a cricket net without hearing Tiger."

Ernest James Smith was born in Birmingham in February 1886. He was orphaned and left school at 13, going to work at the Bournville chocolate factory where he lost the top joints of three fingers in a machine. Despite this, he took up wicket-keeping and, though he never played for the Bournville first team, he was taken onto the county staff at the age of 18 and made his debut that summer against the touring South Africans.

They were hard times for the professional cricketer. "He used to tell me that he'd leave home about 4.30 to walk to the ground. He'd shoe the horse and roll the pitch, then he'd get called into the Secretary's office to be told he was playing. He was very tough. Very hard. And physically very strong. He was the amateur heavyweight champion of the Midlands, or something like that. And he became a soccer referee; he took charge in a lot of top matches."

Tiger Smith spent some years as under-study to the Warwickshire and England keeper Dick Lilley. Then, when he finally inherited the gloves, he was a key member of the county's championship-winning side of 1911 and spent the following winter in Australia. He was not picked for the first Test, which was lost, but he played in the last four, all of which were won. It was the series in which Jack Hobbs moved into the ranks of the greats with three big hundreds, but the victory owed as much to the new-ball bowling of Frank Foster, the young Warwickshire captain, and the legendary Sydney Barnes. Tiger stood up to the wicket to both of them.

"He talked a lot about Jack Hobbs who, he thought, was a genius. The greatest. And he had a very soft spot for Sydney Barnes. I remember in 1958, when Barnes was 85, he came to an old players' lunch, and he was slim, upright like a ramrod, beautifully turned out."

Tiger played till the age of 44 in 1930, scoring 1,000 runs in each of his last four summers. He umpired through the 1930s, standing in eight Tests, and was appointed Warwickshire coach in 1946 at the age of 60.

So, as Tom coaches the under-16s in Wales, he is talking to boys who may progress to county cricket and be playing in the 2010s and 2020s – and the voice they hear will contain a distant echo of Tiger, an echo that – though they do not know it – will take them all the way back to the Golden Age of the early 1900s – and Tiger in turn, joining the staff at Warwickshire when the club was only 22 years old, would have spoken with the sound of older voices in his head. "He would talk about Charlie Charlesworth, who he learnt from, and Billy Quaife, men who were playing before the turn of the century."

In Tom's early years at Edgbaston Tiger was the head coach, and he was a dominating figure in the nets, a disciplinarian looking to instil good habits in the young players.

"He was tough. God, he was tough. He wasn't domineering, but he had a physical presence, even when he was in his 70s. The chairman would knock on his door, poke his head round and say, 'May I come in, Tiger?' He was the boss. Nobody stepped into his domain without permission."

Tom travelled across from Coventry with Jim Stewart. If there was a first team match on the Saturday, as youngsters not in the side they had to be in the nets, changed, by 9.30. "I'd get the 7.30 bus to the railway station. We'd catch the 8.18 to Birmingham, stopping at all the stations. Then we'd rush across the Bull Ring and get a tram to Pershore Road. And, if we'd been held up outside Birmingham for the express to come through, we'd have to run like hell. Where there's a wall now at the ground, there used to be a fence with holes in it, where the knots had been knocked out, and you could peer through to see the nets. If we were late, we knew we were going to get it in the neck – but, if Tiger was in the net, that wasn't too bad. We could run and change and have the row when we got there. But some days he'd be pacing up and down the forecourt. 'What sort of time is this?' The members would be coming in, and we'd run off into the dressing room to change. And sometimes he'd follow us. There was a wooden floor, with a big sunken team bath, and you could hear him coming. When he was angry, he used to rattle the coins and keys in his pockets. Then he'd give us a chore for the day, like putting us on the scoreboard."

Jim Stewart was a different personality from Tom, and he did not respond well to such treatment. "Tiger handed me over to Derief in the end. Derief was more of an encourager. I was an excitable type of guy, wouldn't stand to be bullied. I'd say, 'Oh bugger it.'"

"Jim was a bit of a jack-the-lad," Tom says. "He'd played rugby for Coventry at 16, and the rugby culture's very different, isn't it? Tiger was very aware of that, and he was always looking to jump on him. But he never blocked Jim's path. He was always scrupulously fair in his cricket judgment."

'Tom Cartwright had all the qualities,' Tiger Smith wrote years later, 'but he lacked confidence and wasn't over-strong. My job was to be gentle with him, to persuade the committee he was a fine bowler as well as a good batsman and keep hoping his enthusiasm remained high.'

"He could be quite aggressive, in your face," Tom recalls, "but he didn't frighten me. He was daunting. He'd talk to you short and to the point. But he could be very fatherly; he was to me.

"The environment he created was like an academy of learning. You read about West Ham being like that with Ron Greenwood. It does happen occasionally in clubs, and it's usually down to one person. I've always said that, for nets to work properly, they've got to be fun, they've got to be disciplined and they've got to be a learning environment. You need the fun to inspire people, you need the discipline to make it happen, and you need the learning so that people will develop."

Tiger was well into his 60s, but he still had an observant eye – and, if necessary, he could still show how it should be done. "He was at Lilleshall one time, for a wicket-keeping night, and they wanted somebody to do a demonstration. He stood on a table, got them to throw balls from all corners of the hall, and one of two of the young wicket-keepers wouldn't do it afterwards. They didn't think they could follow him."

Finally Tiger stepped down as head coach at the end of the summer of 1955. He would turn 70 that winter, and the time was right to hand over to Tom Dollery, who had just finished playing.

But this was not retirement for Tiger. The new indoor cricket school was opening, and he took on the task of running it, assisted at first by Derief Taylor, then from 1963 – through the winter months – by Tom. The two were still working together six years later when Tom left Warwickshire. By this time Tiger was 83.

"I'd get in at two o'clock, and he'd always be there an hour before me, to open up. And, when I arrived, he'd be sitting there at his desk with a sheet of paper, solving mathematical problems that he'd made up himself. Or he'd be writing long letters to his daughter in Rhodesia. 'You've got to do something to keep your mind active,' he'd say. He'd stay right through the afternoon and evening and, when we'd closed up, I'd take him home."

Tiger was not somebody who instinctively let others into the secrets of his coaching ideas. "He used to say to me, 'When you're down in the net and you're talking to the batsman, and the other coach comes down into the next net, come out again. He's only come to listen to what you're saying.' I can understand that. Knowledge should be for sharing, but in some ways the other coach would change it and take away its value."

Tom, however, became a trusted companion, and Tiger opened up to him. "He taught me how to look at things. Sometimes he'd say to me, 'This is just for you.'

"He was way ahead of his time. I had some amazing afternoons with him in the indoor school before we started work. Just cricket. Nothing else. He sparked things that then occurred to me, opened up areas for me to grapple with.

"He'd talk a lot about psychology. 'There will be days when you don't know what's wrong,' he said. 'A player will look in good nick and keep getting out. And you can't put your finger on it. So what I do, I go in the nets and get the bowlers to feed them deliveries they're good at playing. Have 15 or 20 minutes of playing shots outside the off stump, or whatever. So they're doing something they know they do well. It's amazing how many times they then go into a game and blossom into a big innings.' It was psychology – getting somebody to believe in themselves again – though it's much easier with a batter than a bowler.

"He said that 80 to 90 per cent of all errors in batting come from the grip, stance and back-lift. If you go through the whole stroke, you'll find the root cause in grip, stance and back-lift. Every day I coach, that becomes more apparent to me.

"I'm an inside-out coach. I can only think of batting by looking from a bowling point of view, and vice versa. From the end to the beginning. Getting to the root. That's the way Tiger taught me.

"With bowling, he'd always talk about aiming with your head – because your eyes are in your head. If your head moves, it's like a camera, middle stump will become a blur and you'll find yourself not aiming straight. Coaches all say about keeping the head still, but they don't explain why and it's not obvious.

"Tiger always said, 'If you're coaching, you must be able to explain what you're saying – and they must be able to understand and to agree. It's only when you get that agreement that you can move forward together.' With some people, they have their own ideas or other people telling them different things – and you don't get that agreement. And if you don't get that agreement, you can work with them for a hundred years and you'll never progress."

At the end of 1969 Tom left Edgbaston, moving to Somerset where in time it fell to him to put into practice on his own some of his mentor's teachings, not least with the young Ian Botham.

"Ian was a classic example of what Tiger told me. We had a terrific agreement on almost everything, and his bowling always demonstrated the importance of the head."

Each year Tom would return to Edgbaston with the Somerset side. "Tiger had retired from the indoor school. But he had a car to bring him to the ground, and he was always at the games. He'd be looking out through his thick glasses, and he'd have his scorecard. And he'd flick it across the table at me. He'd have made notes. Kitchen, Virgin, comments on why they'd got out. 'Do you agree?' he'd ask. 'Of course I agree, Tiger.' He was on a stick by then, and he'd get up and use it as a bat. And, if what he'd written was something I'd spotted and I'd been working on with a player, I used to feel like somebody had given me a huge cheque."

Tiger Smith's book, written with the help of Patrick Murphy, was published some time after his death at the age of 93. 'No one will ever master cricket,' the last paragraph read. 'At my age I'm still learning, still writing in my notebook about certain players' qualities. It'll always fascinate me, and I'm happy that the small amount of common sense I ever had was used to play the wonderful game of cricket.'

Tom, though, is certain that Tiger had much more than 'a small amount of common sense'. He had worked out aspects of the game about which few of his generation had any knowledge.

"He understood how the body worked, all the parts and how they should move. He'd done a correspondence course in physiotherapy, and he knew the various muscles and joints by their medical names. Nobody in my life has spoken to me about cricket in the way Tiger spoke to me – until I was asked to go to Lilleshall a few years ago to meet John Harmer, the Australian biomechanic. We were talking and after a bit he said, 'You know what I'm going to say next, mate, don't you?' It was a magic day. All of it was coming back to me from Tiger forty years earlier.

"Biomechanics is hugely important, but you still have to treat each person as an individual. When you take away what's peculiar to the individual, you'll almost certainly take away what makes him a success. Today, with sports science, everything is geared to the perfect biomechanic movement. The people wielding the power try to force the bowlers into a template. And I don't think you can do that. That's not what Tiger did. If you take away what's natural, you take away what's successful. You end up with a lot of automated people.

"I think about Tiger, and I look at people in the game today. Compared to him, they pale into insignificance."

CHAPTER 7
CHANGES AT WARWICKSHIRE
1956 – 1957

In Tom's view Warwickshire in the early 1950s was triply blessed. Not only did they have an inspirational professional captain in Tom Dollery and a supremely perceptive coach in Tiger Smith but, away from the cricket itself, they had a forward-looking secretary Leslie Deakins, who in 32 years in post from 1944 to 1976 oversaw with great efficiency a remarkable transformation in the fabric and facilities of the ground itself.

"Three very high class people," Tom says. "In the three key positions, all at the same time. I've never seen that since."

Deakins was only 19 years old when in December 1928 he moved from a local law office to become Warwickshire's Assistant Secretary, working for Rowland Ryder who in turn had been at the club since 1896, the year after its admission to the county championship. Edgbaston staged occasional Test matches in the early years of the century, alternating with Trent Bridge as the Midlands venue – but, as a result of improvements at the Nottingham ground, Deakins' first years at Edgbaston saw it drop out of favour altogether.

By the time war was declared in 1939 the ground had not seen Test cricket for ten years. Deakins enlisted in the Royal Navy, and from aboard ship in 1943 he sent the club a blueprint for developing the ground when the war was over. He succeeded Ryder in 1944 and, when he eventually returned to dry land, he threw himself into trying to make a reality of his vision.

The big breakthrough came in 1953 when, copying a recent initiative at Worcester, the committee sanctioned the setting up of a Supporters' Association, whose main purpose was to raise money through a football pool. The weekly subscription was set at a shilling, and volunteers acted as agents to collect the coins from streets and factories all over the county. By 1956 there were 42,000 supporters; seven years later the figure had risen to 650,000. By the end of the 1960s so much money had been raised that the county even found themselves in a position to make an interest-free loan to Essex so that the near-bankrupt east coast county could buy their own ground at Chelmsford.

The money poured into Edgbaston, and year by year the improvements were made: new stands all round the ground, an indoor cricket school, a purpose-built press box, a pavilion suite available for winter hire for dinners and dances, even a new house for the groundsman.

"There was nowhere on the county circuit that grew at anything like the pace of Edgbaston," Tom says. "Every year, when we came back in April, they would have the forecourt up and there'd be some development going on. And they'd be painting the dressing rooms. It grew to be completely different from the ground that was there when my mother brought me over to see the New Zealanders in 1949, with the low bank all the way round and all the planks on stumps of wood. It was an incredible stage-by-stage transformation."

In 1957 the ground was awarded its first Test for 28 years, taking the place of Old Trafford where the previous summer Jim Laker had taken 19 Australian wickets on a controversial pitch. After that, with its claim to Test cricket reinforced by yet more development work, it became the equal of Headingley, Trent Bridge and Old Trafford when the out-of-London Tests were allocated.

Meanwhile the county built up a large playing staff. In 1946 there had been only seven professionals, and the team had been supplemented by a bewildering succession of amateurs, 25 in all. Eric Hollies carried the bowling, in action at one end for over 80% of the time they spent in the field that summer, and he had a fund of stories about the players who came and went. On one occasion, on the morning of the match, he was asked to go to the nets with the latest debutant Stanley Gobey, who – they were told – was a fast-bowling all-rounder.

"What's he like?" Peter Cranmer the captain asked Eric when he returned, and back came the reply, "He's slower than me."

In the match Gobey was only given two overs. Most of his balls were too wide of the off-stump for the batsmen to reach, and he took nought for nine. Then in his second and last appearance he played as a batsman and bagged a pair. And he was not the only one that summer to be out of his depth.

Things started to settle down in 1947. The New Zealand fast bowler Tom Pritchard, whom Tom Dollery had met in North Africa, had completed his residential qualification and he shared the new ball with the returning Charlie Grove. Later that summer Alan Townsend came down from County Durham for a trial.

In the immediate aftermath of war the process of identifying potential county cricketers was fairly chaotic. Alan Townsend had already had a trial the previous year with Glamorgan, his aunt in Cardiff having spotted an advert for cricketers which the county had placed in the *Western Mail*. He went down and played in a second eleven match against Gloucestershire on Barry Island where among his team-mates, also responding to the advert, was Vic Cannings, later to open the bowling for Hampshire.

"He got a few wickets, and I scored a fifty. And we hit it off straightaway. Then I was paid my expenses and told I'd hear by letter. And when the letter came – it was from Wilf Wooller – it said they were very sorry, I'd played well but they wanted bowlers."

When Alan arrived at Edgbaston for trial, he met up again with Vic Cannings, who in the meantime had signed for Warwickshire and was doing well in the first team. "I couldn't understand, if they wanted bowlers, why Glamorgan hadn't taken him on. And he told me they'd written him a letter, saying he'd played well but they wanted batsmen."

Tom Dollery had been a reluctant wicket-keeper in 1947, and Alan recommended his Durham team-mate Dick Spooner, who was on the verge of signing for Somerset. Warwickshire took him without even seeing him and, as a result, Harold Stephenson – another in the Durham team and also a wicket-keeper – offered himself to Somerset in place of Dick Spooner. There were so many openings as cricket tried to find its feet once more.

They continued to arrive at Edgbaston – Ray Hitchcock working his passage on a boat from New Zealand, Ray Weeks via national service from Cornwall, Bert Wolton from the Birmingham League, Fred Gardner from Coventry – and by 1951 Tom Dollery had fused them all into a championship-winning side.

In April 1952, when Tom arrived on the staff, he joined a club that had go-ahead plans off the field and was accustomed to success on it.

By April 1956, when he reported back after his two years of national service, there was more terraced seating around the ground, the pavilion had undergone a major reconstruction and the indoor cricket school was about to open. But on the field the county was about to have its least successful season for some years.

Tom Dollery had retired as captain and, as a stop-gap solution, it had been decided to offer the job to the ever-popular Eric Hollies. "It was a miserable year for him," Tom says. "He was reluctant to do it, and I don't think he enjoyed one moment of it. He'd always batted at number eleven, stood at mid-on and bowled; it didn't suit him at all to be captain."

They won an early game at Bristol, thanks to an extraordinarily generous declaration by the home team, but by mid-June only the perennial strugglers Kent were below them in the table.

"I was twelfth man for the game up in Liverpool, and I shared a room with Eric in the hotel in New Brighton. He was up most of the night, walking about; the captaincy had got right on top of him. He was full of fun usually, and that summer he got alopecia; his hair started to come out in patches."

Two years away from Edgbaston had set back Tom's position in the club. "When I left, Norman Horner was still fighting to make his way but, by the time I got back, he'd established himself as Fred Gardner's opening partner." Furthermore, in 1955 his fellow Coventrians Jim Stewart and Clive Leach had done well in the second eleven, and they were now pushing for places in the first team alongside Tom.

In that wet summer of 1956 Tom played 18 of the first team's 33 matches and managed a top score of only 50 and that against Scotland. "It was a bit of a disaster," he says. "I had a very poor year."

Nevertheless the senior players continued to nurture him – in their different ways. "Alan Townsend was like a father figure to me. I spent a lot of time with him on the bus, and I changed next to him in the dressing room. Above almost anybody else I ever played with, he was the perfect-natured man. He was the only man I've ever seen who, every time he got out, he threw his head up in the air and had a beaming smile on his face. He was a good batsman, a good partnership-breaking bowler and he caught the ball so brilliantly at slip. Tiger told me that at one stage he was close to going on a tour. Tiger got a call from Gubby Allen, asking his opinion about him, and he asked Alan how he would feel about being selected. But Alan was a real family man. 'I think I'd rather be home with Hilda,' he said."

Tom the apprentice slip fielder catches the ball at the third attempt,
to the great amusement of Dick Spooner and Alan Townsend.
In his years as an all-rounder, Tom also fielded in the slips,
taking as many as 32 catches in the summer of 1964

Dick Spooner was at the other end of the spectrum. He played seven times for England, five on the long 1951/52 tour of India and Pakistan, and behind the stumps he was a harsh and rather intimidating figure to the youngsters coming into the side. Clive Leach, a slow left-armer, had his first bowl for Warwickshire in May 1956, and after a few balls Dick Spooner – puffing his cheeks out, as was his wont – called down to Eric Hollies, "He's not spinning the thing, skipper. It's not turning."

"Dick was a bit of a driving force, a keeper of standards," Tom says. "If you played a bad shot, he'd let you know."

In front of a Whit Monday crowd at Derby that May, Tom was fielding in the covers to Eric Hollies, and the ball sped past him. "I was never going to get near catching it up. So, when I was about 25 yards from the boundary, I slowed right down. And I chatted with the front row of the crowd. Next thing, when I turned round, Dick Spooner was coming from one end and Eric from the other. I got a lecture from Dick in no uncertain terms. 'Never ever stop chasing. The bowlers expect it. Everybody in your team expects it. The message you send to the opposition is No Surrender.' I'd never seen anybody look so angry. … And I never made the same mistake again."

Tom was still scoring runs when he played in the second team, including an unbeaten 145 against Staffordshire, but, under Peter Cranmer's captaincy, he did not send down a single over. By contrast, in the first team he had a brief bowl in four games. His first spell – of one over against Combined Services – went for 15 runs. There followed largely uneventful four-over spells against Hampshire and Worcestershire. Then finally, on a wet, miserable August afternoon at Edgbaston, while Leicestershire were going through the motions in a game certain to be drawn, he had two more overs and took his first first-class wicket, the Australian Vic Jackson caught by Alan Townsend.

"At second slip," Tom recalls. "He stood there. I had to appeal. The umpire had to tell him to go."

One of the great bowlers of the post-war English county game had taken his first wicket – four years after his debut, in his 32nd first-class match.

Around this time Tom was among a group of Warwickshire players sent to Lilleshall to gain their coaching certificates, but the course did not end with success. "We went up to the pub one evening – Ray Carter, Alan Townsend and me – and we didn't get back till the early hours. We had a crate of beer with us, and we had to knock up the warden. We all got failed."

Tom would not return to Lilleshall to gain the qualification till he settled in Wales twenty years later. He had already spent several years as Somerset's coach.

Walking when you were out was expected in county cricket in the 1950s but in that summer of Eric Hollies' captaincy, when Tom played at Edgbaston against Worcestershire, he saw the other side of this arrangement. "Sam Pothecary gave me out when I hadn't hit it and, when I got back to the dressing room, Eric was furious. 'Why didn't you walk?' 'But I didn't hit it.' 'You'll go and apologise to the umpire afterwards.' 'But I didn't hit it.' 'Tell him you got in a bit of confusion.' In the end I didn't have to go and see Sam. He came off the field straight to our dressing room and gave me a huge bollocking."

Five years later Tom got involved in another such incident. "We were playing Somerset at Nuneaton, and I had a lazy lap at 'Langy'. I missed the ball, and it hit me on the bicep of my left arm. 'Steve' caught it, going down leg, and they all appealed. I was given not out and, because I hadn't walked, a lot of chuntering started in the field. I was furious. There was a big red ring on my shirt. And I got in a bit of a state. I hated being accused of cheating, and I was bowled soon afterwards.

"In the next game we played Sussex at Edgbaston, and I played forward to Ronnie Bell. I missed the ball, but my bat clipped the inside of my front foot and Jim Parks started to shout. Before I knew what I was doing, I was walking. Jim came in later: 'Why did you walk? You didn't hit it.' 'But you started to appeal.' 'Yes, but I strangled it. You hit your boot.' 'I'm sorry,' I said. 'I just couldn't face a repeat of what happened at Nuneaton.'"

Nuneaton, 16 May 1961. Cartwright, bowled Langford, 21.
Edgbaston, 19 May 1961. Cartwright, caught Parks, bowled Bell, 14.

The summer of 1957, when Test cricket returned to Edgbaston, was a better one for Warwickshire. Eric Hollies was happy to return to the ranks; his hair grew back and in his final season, at the age of 45, he took 132 wickets. The captaincy passed back to an amateur, the young Oxford graduate MJK Smith, who had been playing in his vacations for his native Leicestershire and who kept his amateur status at Edgbaston by being appointed Assistant Secretary.

"I got the idea I'd like to go into cricket administration," he says, "and I left Leicestershire because I thought I'd do better at a Test ground, which Edgbaston was becoming again. It was on its own at that stage, the only club in the country with money. I had no intention of turning pro and playing cricket as my main employment. I thought, 'I'll play for four or five years and get it out of my system. I'll regret it if I don't. Then I'll get down to a proper job.'"

Mike Smith had broken all records at Oxford, scoring centuries in each of his three Varsity matches, one of them a double, and – despite his spectacles and his rather diffident manner – he was also an outstanding rugby player, having won one cap for England in January 1956 as a fly half.

The easiest way for a young amateur captain to establish his authority in a mature county side was to show that he was a good player, and Mike

Smith made the worst of starts at Warwickshire, not getting beyond five in nine of his first ten innings that summer. The turning point came in a last-day run chase against Somerset at Edgbaston. 'He made a shaky start,' according to *The Times*, but finally he cut loose. His unbeaten 97 not only brought a thrilling victory but launched him on a summer of run-scoring that had him finishing up as one of only eight batsmen in the country to reach 2,000 runs.

In the following summer, the wet one of 1958, he passed 2,000 again, his aggregate second only to Peter May. Then in 1959 he topped the list with 3,245. In ten years from 1957 to 1966, summer and sometimes winter, he hit 25,476 runs and only Ken Barrington (with 23,573) came within 3,000 of him.

"You could never fathom Mike," Tom says. "When you meet him, he's vague, and you think he's having an off day or he's putting it on. But when you saw him with a bat in his hand, he was electric. The volume of runs he scored, I go out of my way to tell people. It's a great shame that people don't know.

"He played a lot on the on side. 'Why did you want to go on the sissy's side,' he'd ask, 'when there aren't so many people on the other side?' I upset him one day. They were rebuilding Edgbaston, and they'd got this new stand called Extra Cover. We were talking in the dressing room about it, and he squinted out. 'Where do you mean?' 'Extra cover,' I said. 'The part of the ground where you never hit the ball.'

"He started his innings the same way every day. He could be 200 not out, in cracking form, and he'd start again as if he had nought. He'd nudge it around and sometimes he'd look uncomfortable; he'd never start with a lot of flashy shots. He played an innings at Stroud that I'll never forget. We all thought we were going home on the second night. The ball turned square, it shot along the ground, it went over your shoulder. It was the most amazing pitch."

Stroud, 2 June 1959. M.J.K. Smith, not out 182.

"Mike is an enigma. He's never courted the glamour. It's not his style, and he's never had it. And therefore he's never had the recognition for how good a player he was. If somebody had said to me while I was playing, 'You can pick any team to win the championship next summer out of all the county cricketers you've seen', he would be my first name down. Without any question. Nobody played like he did on bad pitches. You got people who filled their boots on flat ones and then went missing or didn't bother too much when the going was tough. But not Mike. He always produced the runs."

After Eric Hollies' unhappy summer, Mike Smith's captaincy brought about a great improvement. "Mike was a nice bloke to play for. He appreciated other people's abilities, and he let them get on with it. His teams were always happy."

Tom with the Yorkshire-born leg-spinner Eddie Leadbeater (left) and Shirley Griffiths

"Eddie used to give me his money to look after. He'd go home to his wife in Yorkshire, and he'd leave me with all these notes. I didn't even have a bank account. I remember Tom Dollery saying. 'He obviously trusts you.'"

There were other fresh faces, among them Billy Ibadulla from Lahore, Shirley Griffiths a local bus conductor from Barbados and the Cambridge blue Swaranjit Singh. With the half-Indian Clive Leach and the Jamaican Derief Taylor, the club was multi-ethnic long before such words were used. "They were just blokes," Tom says. "I shared a room with Billy for years. He was bright; he came from an intelligent, professional family. It never occurred to me to think that he was different."

Swaranjit Singh was different if only because he wore a turban. "He'd change it two or three times a day, and he'd get people to help him with it. I remember walking into the showers once in his early days and seeing this big bob of hair and thinking it was a woman. It was quite a shock."

As a left-handed batsman Swaranjit Singh played the amateur way, never frightened to hook. "He liked to put bat to ball. He got a lot of runs against Fred Trueman one year when he was at Cambridge. He said Fred was trying to knock his turban off with bouncers, and he kept hitting him over the top. He was a lovely bloke. Very entertaining, very social."

There were misunderstandings, however – "He was a dreadful runner between the wickets, an absolute nightmare" – and they all still talk of the day at Eastbourne when he did twelfth man duties. "It was unusual for somebody like him to have to do it, and at tea-time he didn't get in the list of drinks for close of play: the Guinnesses, the pints, the ciders. Then, when we all came off, he arrived in the dressing room with a tray with twelve gin-and-tonics on it. Lovely. Only somebody like him would do that."

Under the young Mike Smith's captaincy they were happy days, and Tom was still getting plenty of opportunities in the first team. In 1957 he played 18 of the 33 matches, as he had done in 1956, and he hit two fifties, albeit only against Oxford University and Scotland. With the ball his ration of overs increased to 58, and he took his second and third wickets, one against Scotland, the other against Notts in his longest yet spell of 14 overs. At this stage of his career, aged 22, he had played 53 first-class matches, bowled 71 overs and taken three wickets for 227 runs.

Tom Dollery, however, had taken over as captain of the second team, and he began to give Tom more bowling – and Tom repaid his confidence with three wickets at Loughborough and four at Newport in Shropshire. But his greatest triumph was reserved for the final day of the season.

In mid-September 1957 Warwickshire Seconds travelled to Scarborough to play Yorkshire Seconds in the Minor Counties Challenge Match. It was a three-day game, Yorkshire only needed a draw to be declared champions, and a combination of rain and dour batting by the home team meant that, at the end of the second day, Warwickshire were still only 92 for four in reply to Yorkshire's first innings total of 217. On the final morning the Yorkshire fast bowlers David Pickles and Mel Ryan soon finished off the visitors' innings for 112, and Warwickshire returned to the field.

Shirley Griffiths and Ray Carter took the new ball, but after only three overs Tom Dollery decided to switch their ends and, to achieve this, he put on Tom for an over. "I was bowling very gentle in-swing," he says, "but there was a sea fret drifting across the ground and the ball really did move about. I think at one stage it got so foggy we came off."

With his fifth ball he had Phil Sharpe caught, and he was kept on, taking the wicket of Doug Padgett in his third over. With Brian Bolus and Jack Birkenshaw also falling to him, he dismissed four future Test cricketers on that damp day, and he finished with figures of 26 overs, 17 maidens, 19 runs, 7 wickets.

Just as in 1952, when as a 17-year-old he had made 82 at Trent Bridge and immediately gone back to work at Rootes, so in 1957 Tom had saved his best for the last day of the summer and again he went back to work, unable for eight months to move forward from his success. "All winter I really wasn't sure if my bowling at Scarborough was going to have any influence on things the next summer."

Now he ponders whether it might never have happened if the circumstances had been different – "if the bowlers hadn't switched ends, if there hadn't been a sea fret, if Tom Dollery hadn't been captain. There's so much chance in cricket."

CHAPTER 8

BOWLING AT LAST

1958 – 1959

The distance between Coventry and Edgbaston is twenty miles, but for Tom there were more than miles to be travelled when he moved back and forth, summer and winter, between his two worlds: the noisy car factory, with its vigorous working-men's conversations, and the suburban county cricket club, with its well-spoken committeemen and members.

"I was very nervous when I started at Edgbaston, almost silent, watching other people, trying to fathom what the conversations were about. The formal education I'd had was very different from other people's. I'd see the odd *Times* newspaper, and at home we had the *Daily Mirror* and the *Sunday Express*. I'd look at the financial pages, and the language was entirely different. I didn't understand it, but I understood it was different.

"Back home my sisters would pump me all the time about what had happened that day, and they used to get angry because I wouldn't talk about it. They wanted to know every detail, and I wouldn't tell them. It was something I left behind when I came home."

He was entering another world, a world outside the one in which he had grown up, and his parents could not do enough for him. He was their only son, their youngest born, and he had a talent that offered him the chance of a life beyond the car factories.

"When I was in the army," Jim Stewart recalls, "I used to come home each Saturday to play rugby for Coventry, and every Sunday without fail I used to go for tea with Tom's mum and dad – and I used to pick up the parcels of goodies to take back to him. They thought the world of him; they used to run around all over the place for him."

The Cartwrights were a close-knit family, and Tom continued to live at home when he returned from national service. In the winter of 1957/58 he was back making cars, this time on the night shift. On the evening of Thursday 6 February, while Tom was upstairs getting ready for work, his sister Sheila and their mother heard on the radio the chilling news of the Munich air disaster that wiped out half of the Manchester United football team – and, as always, his mother's first thought was for her son. "Don't tell Tom till he's had his tea," she told Sheila.

The workers in the car factories were bound together in common interest, whether they were ensuring that the track moved round smoothly or joining in trade union action to improve their pay and conditions. Their culture was one of collective solidarity. By contrast, the world of professional cricket was to a much greater extent based on individual aspiration.

"You play as a team and you have team spirit, but lurking in the background all the time is the fact that you are in competition with each other – to survive, to stake your claim. And to survive in cricket, you've got to be selfish. That's forced on you. I don't know anybody in cricket who's been successful who hasn't – for a period in their life – been selfish. If they're a batsman, they'll be trying desperately to move their batting average up, rather than playing for the team. And if they're a bowler, they won't be as ready to catch the captain's eye when the going gets tough."

So, in the years when Tom was in his prime, does he think that he was selfish in this way? "Not as a batsman. I didn't care that much about preserving my wicket in my later years. But as a bowler I always wanted the ball in my hand, and that was terribly selfish. I really didn't want to stop. I wanted to bowl all the time."

Tom loved the life of the county cricketer, but he also had a deep loyalty to his roots – and there were times when he struggled to reconcile the two. The dressing room had its various strands of conversation: "Some people were interested in horses and betting, and they'd be quoting figures and odds to the nth degree. Some would just sit and do nothing. Jack Bannister would talk about the cricket; he would talk so intelligently about bowling, and I learnt a lot, listening to him. Then we started to get the people who'd been to university: Mike Smith, Alan Smith, Bob Barber. I used to sit and listen a lot.

"There would be odd comments about strikes, and I would be seething – because those were the people I went home to every night. But I never really said anything, because I didn't know how to. There's a general assumption in county cricket that everybody's Conservative, that the whole way of life is how it should be. They'd often moan about things, but they'd never challenge anything."

At the end of the summer of 1957 Tom got involved in a contractual dispute. "The meal money for playing away in a first team match was more than in the second team, and I thought – in my ignorance, I suppose – that that was totally wrong. For one thing, the people in the second team weren't on such high salaries, and also they were young people who were hungry. We had a little meeting in the dressing room, and we all said yes, we'd refuse to sign unless it was changed. It was the end of the season, and eventually I got a letter offering me a contract – I had 18 contracts in the 18 years I was there – and I wrote back to Leslie Deakins, saying that it was wrong and would they reconsider it, something like that. Then I got another letter, asking me to a meeting at Edgbaston with him and the chairman, a man called Alec Hastilow, a bit of an autocrat but a good chairman. I got there late in the afternoon and, when I walked in the office, they were sitting there and there was a bit of an atmosphere. It wasn't unfriendly. 'Sit down, Tom. Have you decided you can't accept this?' I said, 'Yes.' 'That's very odd,' they said, 'because all the others have returned their contracts.' I can't remember the outcome after that. They might have said they'd review it. It was my first clash with the establishment."

Tom started the summer well in 1958. Early runs in the second team saw him promoted back to the first, and against Kent at Edgbaston he made a major breakthrough. "Only days before the game, Tom Dollery had said to me, 'Tom, you're just about right now; you're going to get your first hundred.' And I did."

EDGBASTON, 18 JUNE 1958. CARTWRIGHT, LBW PETTIFORD, 128.

'Although it may not have been exactly a sparkling innings,' ran the report in the *Birmingham Post*, 'it had qualities of courage and concentration that were much to be admired.'

Edgbaston was a placid batting wicket, and Tom was more comfortable against the fast bowling of Fred Ridgway there than he had been when they had previously met on Dover's lively, green track. "He bowled a nasty bouncer. He was very short, and it skimmed at you throat high. I remember I kept trying to cut everything, and he asked the batter at the other end if they called me Gillette."

His maiden century, alas, did not open the floodgates to further success, and he became one of several young players – Billy Ibadulla, Clive Leach, Jim Stewart and Shirley Griffiths among them – whose performances in the first team were the cause of disappointment. The county had won its first championship match in early May, but there then followed three months without a second victory and gradually the team slipped down and down till on the evening of 22 August it occupied the foot of the table. Warwickshire was a go-ahead county, once more enjoying Test match status. It had won the championship seven years earlier, and this was not what was planned.

In mid-August the team travelled down to Portsmouth, and they stayed at the Bear in Havant, a well-appointed hotel that was a welcome improvement on their lodgings during their visit two years earlier. Sid Harkness, assistant secretary, had joined Edgbaston in 1946, having served in the navy with Leslie Deakins. It was his job to book the accommodation, and he did not always place the team in hotels as pleasant as the Flying Horse in Nottingham or the Portland Arms near Lord's. Eric Hollies nicknamed the worst of them Harkness Specials. 'There was one at a seaside town," he wrote. 'It was built as near to a railway line as any place could be without getting in the way of the trains. We slept by the timetable.'

"It was the same at Peterborough," Tom says. "The hotel was almost in the marshalling yard. But the one at Portsmouth was even worse. The Ship. The pub had the same name as a hotel, and we reckoned he'd booked us into the wrong one." Tom was from a working-class background, but he had seen nothing like this. "It was right on the docks, really rough, no lounge or anything, just a bar. Once you went in at the end of the day, you just went into your room. You didn't come out unless you had to."

The Bear, Havant, was altogether different – though Tom had less experience of it than most of his team-mates. By this stage of the summer he had met and fallen in love with Joan, a schoolteacher in South Wales. She was on a family holiday in Weston-super-Mare, and on Sunday Tom decided to drive across to see her, taking Jim Stewart and his fiancée Fran with him for a happy day out.

They were late starting back to Havant and, as midnight approached, somewhere near Warminster Tom's Morris Oxford ran out of petrol. "In those days the petrol stations were often shut on a Sunday, and we were driving across country where there weren't many, anyway." A passing taxi driver gave them some fuel – "It wasn't petrol, but he thought it might be OK" – and the engine started to splutter and backfire. Somehow they made their way through the New Forest where several times they were flagged down by other cars out of petrol – "courting couples who'd got stuck" – and, after dropping Fran at her hotel, they reached The Bear at nearly three o'clock to find it thoroughly shut up.

"We were very young, and we were terrified. We drove off and found a quiet place. The car had a bench front seat, and I slept on that; Jim went in the back. And it was freezing. We hardly slept a wink. Then we went to a transport café and had some breakfast, and we bought a paper. *The Sketch*, I think. And it had this article, 'Strife in the Warwickshire Camp'. Some dispute, and there were several players quoted. We were obviously in big trouble. So we rushed off to the ground, made sure we got there before the others and, when they arrived, we were changed and having some fielding practice."

The article had arisen from a piece in the *Birmingham Argus*, written under the by-line of Field-Mouse by a young reporter Tony Stratton-Smith, who would later make his fortune in the music business with his own record label Charisma, discovering the Bonzo Dog Doo-Dah Band and Genesis.

"The chairman came rushing down from Birmingham. He interviewed us in the dressing room, and we all denied everything."

It was that jumpy time of year when decisions were about to be made about contracts for the next summer, and Jim Stewart recalls how brutal the process could be: "We'd turn up at Edgbaston, and on the wall, as you came through the door, was an old-fashioned green board with sealed letters clipped to it. You'd take the one for you, go into the toilet and open it. And you'd come back smiling. And others would have a little tear in the eye."

That summer marked the end for Clive Leach and Shirley Griffiths, but there were still high hopes for Tom – and, in the last fortnight, for the first time he strung together a series of substantial scores.

Against Yorkshire he hit a top-scoring 36 and a vital 55 and took the good wickets of Phil Sharpe and Doug Padgett. Against Somerset, when he was awarded his county cap, he hit a top-scoring 44, bowled 46 overs in the match and, in a thrilling run chase that brought them victory at long last, he hit an unbeaten 62. Then in a rain-ruined contest at Southend he hit 33.

The season ended at Lord's, where he hit 37 and 89. At that stage of his career he had never taken more than two wickets in an innings in a first-class match. But on the final day of the season's final match he bowled 22.5 overs and took five wickets for 49 runs. It was hot and hazy that day at Lord's and, according to *The Times*, 'Cartwright worried the batsmen into inexplicable mistakes with his medium-paced in-swingers.' His swing even 'baffled Spooner the wicket-keeper, who conceded 21 byes out of the total of 146.'

'Warwickshire End A Mediocre Season On Winning Note,' ran the headline in the *Birmingham Post*. 'The spirit of the side, under Smith's captaincy, has been given a fillip.'

"I loved Lord's," Tom says. "I could always swing the ball there, the pitch was helpful, and the sense of occasion always seemed to bring something out of me. Even walking through the gates inspired me; I still get that feeling when I go there now.

"In that match Frank Lee was umpiring, and he was so kind and helpful to me. 'Stick it out,' he kept saying to me when I was batting. And when I was bowling at his end, he encouraged me all the time. He was a very nice man. In those days there was such a good relationship between the umpires and the players."

It was Tom's 76th first-class match, and his career tally of wickets jumped from 15 to 21. For the third time in his short career he had reached new heights in his last match of the season.

After several wet summers, 1959 was long and hot, with more hours of sunshine than any before it in the twentieth century. Tom was an established member of the Warwickshire side, playing all 28 championship matches, and for the first time he passed 1,000 runs.

He started the year at number three in the order, occasionally opening, but his bowling – though used more often than previously – did not at first yield outstanding results. By the morning of Saturday 13 June, when he took the field against Worcestershire at Dudley, he had scored 568 runs, including a century against Somerset, but he had taken only ten wickets at a cost of 48.4 each. In his eighth summer of first-class cricket, he was still a batsman who bowled a bit.

Then came the moment that, in Tom's view, changed the whole course of his cricketing life.

"As a kid at school I'd bowled all out-swingers. Then when I came to Edgbaston I didn't bowl much, only in the nets, and I went in the army, grew a bit, and by the end of it all I could only bowl in-swing. But that day at Dudley it was sultry. I was in the middle of an over, I just ran up and the ball swung away. It was the first time I'd done it since I'd left school.

"The miracle was that I knew exactly what I'd done. I didn't want anybody to talk to me as I walked back. I just wanted the ball, and I did it a second and a third time."

Although Eric Hollies as a leg-spinner was a very different bowler, his advice to Tom now proved crucial: 'Know yourself. Be in control at your end.' "I knew the shape of my hand when I let the ball go. I could see it in my mind's eye. And I retained the shape after I'd delivered the ball."

For two overs he bowled only out-swing. Then, when he was confident that he knew how it was happening, he started to mix in some of his usual in-swing. And the wickets fell to him.

CARTWRIGHT, 22.3 OVERS, 11 MAIDENS, 36 RUNS, 5 WICKETS.

"It was all down to the hand position. In time, by varying it, I found I could bowl an out-swinger with a pronounced in-swing action and an in-swinger with a pronounced out-swing action, just by varying the hand position. I demonstrated it on an NCA Advanced course."

In the next month his bowling spells grew longer and the wickets came thick and fast: six in an innings three times. Yet he was still batting at number three, and against Gloucestershire at Edgbaston he was run out by John Mortimore, inches short of his second hundred of the summer. "I played it to leg, and I knew when I touched down after the 99th run that Morty was approaching the ball with the speed that would encourage me to run. It was like a challenge. I knew he was setting me up, and it all happened in a flash. I took him on, and he sent in this incredible throw. The bails had just left the stumps when my bat crossed the line."

Tom followed his 99 with career-best figures of six for 48 the next day, and the newspapers started to speculate about higher honours. 'Cartwright Makes Bid for England Cap,' read one headline in the scrapbook his mother lovingly kept. 'Watch this man, England. He could be just the all-rounder to fill Trevor Bailey's old job.'

The opening pair ahead of him in the Warwickshire line-up was usually Fred Gardner and Norman Horner. "Fred was one of only three people I played with – Barrington and Boycott were the others – where I was always surprised when they got out. When they went out to bat, they seemed so solid and I'd always think, 'We're going to get a big score.' But Norman would be playing his shots in the first over, even if there were only a few minutes till close of play. Sometimes he'd come off with 30 not out, but other times he'd have a flash and get out in the first over. There were days when I was at number three when I'd come off the field, having bowled 20 or 30 overs. I'd have a quick dry rub with my towel, change my shirt and, before I'd even padded up, I'd hear this scream go up. 'He's out.' I'd rush out, and I wouldn't even know who was bowling."

As the season went on, however, and Tom's bowling became more and more vital to the team, he moved down the order to five or six.

It was a much better summer for Warwickshire. On 22 August in the previous year they had been at the foot of the championship table. Now on the same date, in a wide-open title race, they were at the very top, and only defeats at Clacton and Hove prevented them from repeating their 1951 triumph.

It was also a great summer for Tom. He had become a genuine all-rounder, scoring 1,282 runs and taking 80 wickets, and he was selected for the Players against the Gentlemen in the prestigious annual fixture at Lord's. In a contest dominated by the batting of Mike Smith, who scored 79 and 166 for the Gentlemen, Tom's testing medium-pace upstaged Fred Trueman and Les Jackson among the Players' bowling. Altogether in the match he bowled 41 overs for 86 runs, taking the prize wickets of Raman Subba Row twice, Mike Smith, Ted Dexter and Peter May.

"Fred was full of it," Tom remembers, "and Mike took him apart."

'Nothing ruffled Smith,' *The Times* wrote, 'no one really exercised him, and when the loose ball came along he dismissed it to the boundary without fuss.'

The Players at Lord's, 1959
Back row (left to right): John Murray, Ken Barrington, Ray Illingworth, Geoff Pullar, Tom Cartwright, John Edrich *Front row:* Fred Trueman, Brian Close, Dennis Brookes, Les Jackson, Gilbert Parkhouse

Captain of the Players was the serenely magisterial Dennis Brookes, a Yorkshireman who had settled in Northampton in 1933 and who was coming to the end of a long and distinguished county career. His Players team included Brian Close, Ray Illingworth and Fred, and after the match the three of them were the last apart from Tom and Dennis to leave the dressing room. "When they'd gone, Dennis sat back and sighed. 'Thank God for that,' he said. 'Don't they talk a lot, those Yorkies.'"

The next day Tom and Mike Smith were at the unpredictable Ind Coope ground at Burton-on-Trent, where the previous year the Derbyshire-Hampshire match had seen 39 wickets fall in a day. "Mike got given lbw in the first innings, and he was very angry. The wicket was like concrete, and Derbyshire had Les Jackson and Harold Rhodes. Harold was young and very lively, and Les was always a handful. They really did steam in. And in the second innings Mike got a big hundred, even more magnificent than the one at Lord's."

Burton-on-Trent, 18-21 July 1959.

H. L. Jackson, seven for 35 and five for 80.

M.J.K. Smith, lbw Jackson, 0, caught Morgan bowled Rhodes, 142.

In the first three weeks of July Mike Smith had scored more than 1,000 runs, and he was summoned to Old Trafford to the fourth Test, where he scored another century. Alongside Hutton, Hammond and Grace he remains to this day one of only four batsmen ever to score 1,200 runs in a calendar month.

Tom, meanwhile, received a letter from MCC. Along with 28 others, he was asked if he was available to tour the Caribbean that winter. In the event he was not selected, but it was a mark of how far he had come in twelve months. As the Warwickshire yearbook said of their 24-year-old all-rounder, 'The game's highest honours are within his grasp.'

Warwickshire's seven century-makers of 1959
(left to right)
Billy Ibadulla,
Alan Townsend,
Bert Wolton,
Mike Smith,
Tom Cartwright,
Jim Stewart,
Norman Horner

Tom and Joan
A marriage that has lasted

CHAPTER 9
CRICKETER AND FAMILY MAN
1960 – 1963

Joan Rees had grown up in the village of Skewen, near Neath, and, when Tom first met her, she was back living there, teaching at the infant school she had herself attended. And she was mad on cricket, had been since that day in August 1946 when the Indians had come to St Helen's, Swansea, and she had gone with her classmates from Neath Girls' Grammar because there was a group going from the boys' grammar school. "I was hooked," she says, "I thought it was wonderful."

Her childhood was a hard one. Her father had been a doubler in a tin plate works, and she remembers walking past and seeing him in front of the fierce furnace. "He wore a big white apron and had these tongs to double the plate into various shapes and sizes. He had big hands and strong arms, and I thought it was all tremendously important."

The works closed, and there were years of hardship. At one stage they went to an aunt in Birmingham, and her father walked the streets of the city in search of work. Often she would stand with him in the dole queue: "It was soul-destroying. The people looked so unhappy, with their drawn faces, worrying how they were going to get through the week. Sometimes, when the milkman came, my mother made us hide under the kitchen table."

Eventually he got a job on top of the colliery at Onllwyn. "They called him a railway plate layer, but he was just a common labourer. He worked out in the open in all weathers. It was 14 miles away, and he had to catch a bus at half past five in the morning. I used to sit in the window and watch him going off in his hobnail boots."

"At lunch they had to sit under the trucks to eat," Tom adds. "There was an old shed, and they asked the boss if they could have their food in there. He agreed, but he didn't put any seating in for them."

An intelligent man, Joan's father worked till he was 70 and he was Labour through and through. "He was so interested in geography," Joan remembers. "He was always reading newspapers, and he used to talk about wanting to go to Nassau in the Bahamas. I suppose it seemed like an exotic place to him. But he never went. He only got as far as Llandudno and Weston-super-Mare."

Joan's mother was English, but her father was very Welsh. "He would speak to me in Welsh sometimes, and my mother would say, 'What's he saying?' He'd slip into it because it was a natural language to him – though in his day, when he was at school, you were smacked if you spoke Welsh."

He had been left a house by his father, but there was a heavy debt to pay off and he spent the rest of his life struggling to clear it. "Every Saturday morning I had to go up to Mrs Evans the butcher's wife with this little white envelope. He always told me never to buy a house. 'Why do you need one?' he'd say."

The world of first-class cricket – with its vast green spaces, its healthy men all in white and "its leisurely, gentlemanly way of life, so different from the local rugby club" – opened up new horizons to Joan, and she fell in love with the game. In August 1948 she was on the 5.30 workers' bus to Swansea to join the tens of thousands queuing to see the Australians. And she idolised Glamorgan's opening batsman Gilbert Parkhouse: "I could watch him bat all day. He was so elegant. Off the field as well. Where the others would go to the pub, Gilbert would sit in a restaurant and drink wine. We thought he was really something." She called her first cat Compton; then, when he ran away, she had another and called him Parkhouse.

For a while she decided to go by her middle name Morwen – "I was stupid; I thought Joan Rees was very common" – and she won a place at teacher training college in Barry. "We had a lady principal who was very Welsh and very, very strict. We had to be in by half past seven in the evening in winter, five to eight in summer. If you were a minute late, you were gated for three weeks. We weren't allowed to talk to boys or wear make-up. And in the summer, when you went out, you couldn't just wear sandals, you had to wear socks as well."

Her first teaching position was in Birmingham. "You didn't get a job in Wales unless you'd taught for a year. They wanted more experienced teachers. So any pitfalls, the English had to put up with them." She lived in Handsworth with her uncle and aunt, and she taught in Perry Barr. "Birmingham was a good authority, but I had 49 in my class. I had an untrained lady to help me, but a lot of the time you were a glorified nursemaid. You had to tie all their shoe laces, and it would take half an hour to get them ready."

She became homesick – "the Welsh are dreadful travellers" – and returned to Skewen, where she once more went to watch Glamorgan. "School finished at a quarter past three and, if there was cricket at St Helen's, my friend and I would rush down to the bus stop on the main road and catch the Swansea bus. Then we'd walk to the ground, quite a walk, and we'd be there by tea."

In 1957 she had met Tom in the clubhouse at Cardiff at the end of the day's play, then in June 1958 Warwickshire came down to Swansea and they met again, this time at a Saturday evening party in the Mumbles.

"She was incredibly knowledgeable about cricket," Tom remembers. "She still is. She used to do the crossword in the back of the *Cricketer* magazine. She'd do it really quickly, and I didn't have a clue."

They met up when they could, and they became engaged the following year. "He likes to tell everybody that I chased him all over the country," Joan says.

It was an engagement that brought Tom into conflict for a second time with the Warwickshire club. "There were about four of us who were engaged, and several others had girl friends. Every year at the start of the season the Supporters' Association used to put on a pre-season dinner, and they invited wives. So I said, 'What about people with girl friends and fiancées?' We had a meeting, and we all agreed we wouldn't go. And, just like with the meal money, on the night of the dinner they all went without their girl friends and fiancées, and I was the only one who stayed at home. They were probably thinking, 'It's him again.' The next year and ever since, though, they've invited everybody."

Tom and Joan married in Skewen on 24 September 1960, with the Glamorgan batsman Bernard Hedges the best man. On the field of play it had been a disappointing season for Tom. He had missed half the matches with intercostal injuries, and his bowling in particular did not reach the heights it had reached the previous year.

They moved into a flat above an ironmonger's shop in Longford Road, Coventry. "Next to the canal," Tom says. "Across the road from the Chapel of Rest. Three pounds a week, fully furnished." He spent the winter on a capstan lathe at Courtaulds, making laminated gears, while Joan ran a remedial class at the school beside Keresley Pit where, by a happy coincidence, Tom's old teacher Eddie Branson was now working. "I had about fifteen eight- and nine-year olds; they couldn't read or write so I started with them as if they were just starting school. It was a lovely year, the best year of my teaching life."

Tom was growing in confidence, a married man and an established county cricketer, and he was starting to have an influence in the dressing room. "I used to take Joan with me to away games when she wasn't teaching in the summer. Then, when the kids came along, we'd bring them, especially to the South Coast or the West Country. And of course that didn't go down well with some of the senior players. There were chunterings; they thought I was a young upstart. But if you're away all the time, there's not very much you can do except things you probably shouldn't. You can get a drink culture – and all the other things. But eventually seven or eight of us were taking away our wives and girl friends, and there was a lovely atmosphere in the hotel."

In 1961 Tom had a glorious summer, scoring 1,668 runs and taking 77 wickets, but as usual he failed with the bat in his two games in front of his own people at Coventry. In the first of the two games, he might have hoped for better, having inadvertently managed to get the umpire Harry Baldwin on his side.

"Joan and I went out for Sunday lunch at the Bull's Head in Meriden, and little Harry was sitting there on his own in the foyer. 'I'm waiting for Jim Stewart,' he said. When we came out from lunch, he was still there – 'the bugger's let me down' – so we took him with us to Hampton-in-Arden cricket club and we finished up in the White Lion there. It was a county set pub, full of young deb types, and after about half an hour Harry was entertaining the whole bar lounge area. When I went off to buy him his third pint, he slapped Joan on the leg. 'You can tell him to get the lot in front tomorrow, my dear, he'll be all right.' And I had a feeling that he meant it, too."

COVENTRY, JUNE 1961. CARTWRIGHT, CAUGHT MILTON BOWLED BROWN, 4,

CAUGHT CARPENTER BOWLED BROWN, 10.

Tom made a century against Lancashire at Edgbaston, but the highlight of his summer came in August when the touring Australians visited Birmingham. "It was a strange day. Joan had to go into Coventry Hospital to have some growths removed, and she insisted that I went and played. So I was playing in this game, all the time waiting to hear the results from the hospital."

Alan Davidson and Ron Gaunt took the new ball for the Australians, and Warwickshire were soon struggling on 22 for three. Then Tom joined Mike Smith, who hit a quick fifty. Wickets fell in the afternoon but Tom batted on, reaching 93 at tea out of a Warwickshire score of 191 for six. 'A tall, elegant stroke player,' *The Times* called him. 'Displaying a wide variety of shots, he batted with supreme confidence.'

Only once in the history of the county had a Warwickshire batsman hit a century against the Australians – Fred Gardner, eight years earlier – and now Tom was set to become the second.

"They had this bloke Quick, a slow left-armer, and I swept him and I swept him. Neil Harvey was their captain. We came out after tea, and he put him on again straightaway. And I thought, 'Brilliant.' And instead of milking seven singles, I swept him again. The very first ball. Ron Gaunt was at short fine leg, he was quite tall, and he reached and caught it."

EDGBASTON, 9 AUGUST 1961. CARTWRIGHT, CAUGHT GAUNT BOWLED QUICK, 93.

Joan's growths were not malignant, but there were major changes ahead in their married life. The previous winter Jack Bannister had coached at the Wanderers club in Johannesburg, and he had recommended Tom to succeed him. It would be the first serious coaching Tom had done – but "let's go," Joan said and she handed in her notice. Then, when she discovered she was pregnant, they decided to stick with their decision. On their first wedding anniversary, they set sail on the *Windsor Castle*, arriving at Cape Town two weeks later.

Little can they have imagined that seven years later, faced with another invitation to South Africa, Tom would find himself at the centre of an international storm, a storm that would lead to a boycott that would outlaw such sporting visits.

"We had a whole day in Cape Town before we caught the train," Tom says. "I wanted to go to the loo, and I dashed across to this public toilet, one of those street ones where you go downstairs. I stood there having a pee, and the only people there were black and they were all looking very oddly at me. I felt very uncomfortable – 'What had I done?' – and then I realised I was in a 'non-whites only' toilet. I pondered that most of the day."

The Wanderers Club, situated in the suburbs of Johannesburg, was the largest amateur sports club in the southern hemisphere, with more than 10,000 members, including Test cricketers such as Johnny Waite, Sid O'Linn and Peter Carlstein. Its imposing Test match stadium, built like a modern bull ring, had been opened five years earlier, and there were also three beautiful cricket ovals and a practice field, the Cabbage Patch, where the nets were. In addition, there were tennis courts, bowling greens, squash courts, a golf course and a swimming pool.

Nine teams played each Saturday in various leagues, but "I wasn't allowed to play," says Tom. "I had to watch all the matches and go to the selection meetings. My only cricket was on Sundays with a team called the Nomads, a bunch of more elderly players with a family atmosphere."

Tom had had only two or three summers as an established county cricketer.

Now he was on the other side of the world, adjusting to very different playing conditions, and he was required to coach and pass judgment on the players. "It made me watch the game closer than I'd ever watched it before. Subconsciously I think I was taking in an awful lot."

Joan's pregnancy developed. She worked her way through eighteen cricket books while they were out there, and so knowledgeable did she seem on cricket that, according to Tom, "when we first got to Johannesburg, they thought she was a coach as well."

Most English cricketers enjoyed their winters of coaching in the South African sunshine, and for Tom it was a welcome contrast to his long hours on a capstan lathe at Courtaulds. Yet there were aspects of the privileged life that disturbed Joan and him.

"We lived in a service flat in Hillbrow, and we had a young cleaner Franz who was a Zulu, and he asked if his cousin Sophie could come in and do the washing. They were really lovely people, but their standard of living was so low – and you do get caught up with your emotions when you think about things like that. So we used to give them extra money. They would show you two hands when they took it. Zulus will always do that to show they haven't got a knife behind their back. And one day somebody was picking us up, and he saw me. 'What are you doing? Don't give them extra. We've got to live here after you've gone.'

"You'd go into the post office and you'd find a counter with whites at one end, non-whites at the other. The queue for the non-whites was back out through the door – and, if you walked in, the man would leave them and come and serve you. I found that very difficult. You could see this empty look in the faces of the blacks, the complete acceptance of the inevitable, that they had no rights, that they had no way they could complain."

For Tom, with a job to do, he learnt to hold his peace – but Joan was less inclined to be diplomatic. "A lot of people invited us to dinner, and they all had their servants. Often the ones serving the food would be wearing a white suit with a red sash and gloves, like chocolate soldiers, and to me that was degrading. Joan took total offence at it all. She would dive in and ask all kinds of questions – about apartheid and their feelings about it, and how they treated their servants – and I would be kicking her under the table. They had this system of 90-day house arrests, and you couldn't always be sure about the other people in the room – so people didn't express their views. I'd say to her, 'For God's sake, we're here. Whether we agree with it or not, I've got a contract to fulfil.'"

Back at Edgbaston Leslie Deakins received a letter from Joan, asking if he could send out to the Wanderers a film of the Australia-West Indies Test series of the previous winter: 'Tom feels the showing of any film concerning the West Indian cricketers can only foster good relations in a country where colour has caused such a problem in sport as in everything else.'

Two further letters were sent but, alas, the film was in constant demand from cricket clubs in the West Midlands and was never sent.

Before the winter was through, they were faced with a choice: whether Joan should have their baby in South Africa and stay there till Tom returned the following winter or whether they should both fly home early. "We'd made some very good friends out there," Tom says. "The Bonnells and the Wilcocks, they were some of the kindest people you could come across. In a way they were as helpless as the blacks to do anything about what had overtaken the country. They really wanted Joan to stay, and I'd have had no worries if she'd had the baby there with them. But there's no way we would have done that."

Instead, they returned to Wales. They had given up the tenancy of their flat in Coventry, and Joan decided to stay with her parents in Neath after baby Jane was born. Throughout the summer Tom would drive down each Saturday night and return to wherever he was playing on Monday morning. If he was playing at Edgbaston during the week, he would spend his nights with his parents in Coventry.

It was a punishing schedule, and it was made more demanding by the fact that Jane cried through the night and it was Tom's job on Saturdays and Sundays to look after her and to allow Joan two good nights of sleep a week.

It was 120 miles from Edgbaston to Neath, and Tom could enter Wales north of the river Severn. But from places like Folkestone, Colchester and Hove it was in excess of 200 miles of cross-country 'A' roads, and there was no Severn Bridge, only a ferry between Aust and Beachley. "On Monday morning I used to get up early to catch the first ferry. I used to be so petrified that I'd miss it that I'd drive down the slope, leap out of my car and count all the cars in front."

All this travelling might be sandwiched between two demanding days of cricket, such as the weekend of 23/24 June when on Saturday at Hove he scored 73 in a partnership of 199 with Mike Smith, then on Monday bowled 28 overs. As if that was not enough, the fixture list had a habit of zig-zagging them from one end of the country to another, never more than in the run-up to the Test at Edgbaston when there would be several away games in succession. In three weeks in early 1962 they moved from Cambridge to Nottingham to Swansea to Sheffield to Folkestone to Hinckley.

Yet despite it all, and despite a broken finger that kept him out for six matches, Tom became the first Warwickshire player since the amateur Frank Foster in 1914 to complete the double for the county, with 1,176 runs and

106 wickets. And the highlight of it all came on Friday 5 July at the Griff and Coton ground at Nuneaton.

It was a time when the counties took their cricket out to the people, setting up their temporary stands here, there and everywhere. Kent played on nine grounds in the course of that summer, Glamorgan on eight, Essex and Yorkshire on seven and Somerset on six.

On such out-grounds the game had great variety: from the exhilarating day at the little Hinckley ground when Jim Stewart, in the form of his life, blasted a quick-fire 182, despatching John Savage for 23 in one over – "Sav wasn't a bad bowler, but Jim murdered off-spinners; he just hit them a long way over long-on" – to the slow-moving day at Swansea when the little left-hander Alwyn Harris ground out a five-hour century: "He's the only player I've ever seen who's practised padding up at the non-striker's end. He was doing it most of the day, even while the bowler was walking back to his mark; I'm sure he was winding us up. Jack Bannister came in at lunchtime and said we shouldn't worry about him, he couldn't play, and he was still there in the evening, still padding up."

Warwickshire, having spent so much money at Edgbaston, were not so inclined to venture away from their headquarters. They staged two matches each year at the Courtaulds Ground, Coventry, and from 1960, as a result of some sustained lobbying, they agreed to a third trip into the county's industrial south-east with a match at the Griff and Coton Sports Club in Nuneaton.

There on a bitterly cold Wednesday in early July 1962 Middlesex battled against accurate seam bowling to make 280 all out. Then in the closing overs of the day Alan Moss and Don Bennett ran in with great hostility to reduce the home team to 38 for four. "The top of the surface was demolished on a length," Tom remembers. "Batting got very difficult."

The next morning two more wickets had fallen by the time the score had reached 67, and Tom was left with Alan Smith, the cheerful wicket-keeper-batsman, to rescue the innings ahead of the tail. Warwickshire were top of the championship table, starting to wonder if this was to be the year they would repeat their 1951 triumph, but it was looking unlikely that they could salvage anything from this match at Nuneaton.

"Once the top of the pitch had disappeared totally, batting started to get easier. In the end it was like playing on a strip of dust."

In the words of the *Birmingham Post*, 'Cartwright took every opportunity to demonstrate his artistry through the covers. ... His cutting and driving left the field helpless. ... Slowly the seemingly impossible became possible.'

At the other end Alan Smith passed his highest Warwickshire score of 54. "I know it sounds silly," Tom says, "but, if you were going to look for somebody to stay with you, he was as good as anybody you could drum up – because he was such a trier, such a fighter."

Tom reached his hundred shortly after lunch. According to *The Times*, he displayed 'a fine repertoire of shots, all of which would be found in any textbook.' Alan Smith fell with the score on 311, six short of his century, but by tea Tom had passed 200. 'He found gaps in the covers where none apparently existed,' the *Post* wrote, 'and when this venue was closed he swept and on-drove with equal disdain.' 'He never seemed to be in trouble,' reckoned *The Times*. 'On this form he can have few equals.'

NUNEATON, 5 JULY 1962. CARTWRIGHT, BOWLED BENNETT, 210.

A double century. The highest score of his career was higher than any ever made by his captain Mike Smith. He even had time before close of play to take a wicket. The match was eventually drawn but, when the first-class averages appeared in the papers on Saturday morning, Tom's was the one name to be found in both the batting and the bowling lists. He was a genuine all-rounder.

"Just like 1951," one Nuneaton spectator beamed to the *Post* reporter as he left the ground that day – but in the end the championship was not won. With seven batsmen scoring 1,000 runs and three taking 100 wickets, maybe it should have been.

Perhaps the square at Edgbaston was too easy to bat on: "You win championships by bowling people out. I didn't mind bowling there, because I could get it to swing and I did get a little seam movement, but it was pretty flat and not terribly pacy. A lot of games were drawn."

Perhaps, also, Mike Smith was a little too easy-going as a county captain: "He was a very intelligent cricketer, but I'm not sure he had the same ready wit as Tom Dollery had, at making things happen on the field. Sometimes with Mike it drifted a bit."

And perhaps they lacked a high-class spinner: "We'd had Basil Bridge the previous year. He'd been the first slow bowler in England to 100 wickets. And he lost it completely."

Ask Basil himself, and he will tell you that an internal injury, undiagnosed, threw him off course, but Tom has a different theory. "He came out to South Africa with us on the *Windsor Castle*, and in that fortnight on the boat his personality changed. He was a shy boy, living at home with his parents and never really saying anything to anybody, and he latched onto Bob Berry, who was a very funny bloke. Suddenly he felt he had to become this loud extrovert.

"Bowlers who get the yips, it's often because their natural lifestyle has changed. I've seen it a few times. And poor Basil, he didn't just bowl full tosses; he bowled balls which went over the wicket-keeper's head. Even in the benefit games, when he was under no pressure, he was the same. It was very sad. Warwickshire were kind. They arranged hypnosis and all sorts. But it was like he was walking down a road, trying to find his way home. And he never did find it."

In any case, perhaps winning the county championship was not that important. "It wasn't a big thing. It was only if you were in the running in July that you started looking at the fixtures and the members and the press began to talk about it. Most of the time the spectators came because they wanted to see particular people bat and bowl. They were looking for something artistic, something of real class. It wasn't a question of 'Will my team win or not?' The expectancy is different now. There's much more hype; people are talked into looking for excitement all the time. In those days I think people were looking for a deeper meaning."

Tom's double of 1,000 runs and 100 wickets brought him a gift of £50 from the county, money he spent on a sideboard that he and Joan put into the house in Shirley where they moved the following spring. Bert Wolton had vacated it, retiring from the staff to take a pub, and the Supporters' Association lent Tom the money at 6% interest on the understanding that, when his benefit came round, he would clear whatever debt was still outstanding.

Tom's role at Warwickshire was changing from year to year. He had started as a specialist. He had become a batsman who bowled occasionally, then a genuine all-rounder. Now he would become a bowler who batted a bit. The Lancashire batsman Bob Barber had been recruited by Mike Smith, and promising young batsmen like Dennis Amiss and John Jameson were beginning to appear in the first team. Never again would Tom come close to 1,000 runs in a summer.

But his bowling was entering its golden period. Established as the county's regular first-change bowler, he opened the 1963 season with eight wickets on the first day and was never out of the national averages all summer.

On the morning of Sunday 2 June he was hoovering the dining room, preparing to go out with Joan and Jane to a benefit match that was being staged for Ray Hitchcock at the little club ground of Stockingford, near Nuneaton.

"There was a hatch into the kitchen where Joan was, and she had the radio on. And I suddenly became conscious that they were reading out the twelve for the first Test. And, when it finished, Joan's head came through the hatch: 'Did you hear something daft?' And I said, 'I was going to ask you the same thing.' Nobody rang or anything. And we really weren't sure. We had to stay at home for another hour to get the next news flash."

The twelve names were read out again, and there between Barrington and Close was the one they thought they had heard: Cartwright.

CHAPTER 10
A TEST CRICKETER ... EVENTUALLY
1963 – 1964

The first Test of 1963, against the West Indies, was at Old Trafford and, as the press had predicted, Tom was the one asked to be twelfth man. He spent two days on the balcony, then returned to Warwickshire to play at Nuneaton.

The Test was a disaster for England. The bowlers took only six wickets in ten hours, then the batsmen failed twice, leaving West Indies to score only one run for a ten-wicket victory. The press cried out for changes to the team and, with the next match at Lord's, where for several years the pitch had given great help to medium-pace seamers, Tom seemed likely to win his first cap.

On the first day of the first county match that summer Tom had taken eight for 45 against Hampshire at Coventry, and in the evening Derek Shackleton, a bowler in the same mould of medium-pace accuracy, had responded with a spell so wayward that, he admitted in later life, he had lain awake during the night, wondering what had gone wrong, wondering if at the age of nearly 39 his long bowling career was drawing to its end.

Tom laughs. "He was probably thinking, 'How on earth did that little twerp take all those wickets for Warwickshire?'"

Shackleton soon recovered his metronomic accuracy. In the week before the Old Trafford Test he was at his best at Hove, repeatedly troubling the England captain Ted Dexter. Then he took seven for 71 in 48 overs against a Kent team that included Colin Cowdrey. So, when the twelve for the second Test at Lord's was read on the radio, there was no longer a Cartwright between Barrington and Close. Instead, between Parks and Stewart, came the name of Shackleton, resurrecting a Test career that had seemingly ended twelve years earlier. 'The old man of the South,' John Woodcock called him in *The Times*. 'It was less a recall,' Ian Wooldridge of the *Daily Mail* wrote, 'than a resurrection from the mothball fleet.'

Aided by the Lord's surface, Shackleton took seven wickets in as dramatic a draw as Test cricket has ever seen, and he retained his place in the England side for the rest of the summer. Tom, meanwhile, had only one encounter with the West Indians, for Warwickshire at Edgbaston when he was twice bowled out cheaply by the fast bowler Charlie Griffith.

"On both occasions I'd been in a little while, and I saw Frank Worrell at mid-on nod at Charlie. So I knew I was going to get a bouncer or a yorker. He bowled from so wide on the crease, as wide as anybody I've seen, and he leaned even further back as he propelled the ball. The ball seemed to be well wide of the off stump, it was full-pitched so I tried to hit him past cover's left hand and I finished up being bowled middle-and-leg. The stumps went flying."

Between his two brief innings, however, Tom had used the overcast conditions to great effect, and his first nine overs against the tourists brought him four top-order wickets – Hunte, Nurse, Kanhai and Solomon – for the cost of only six runs. 'His varied swing mystified the West Indies,' *Wisden* reported.

"I remember Charlie coming up to me at lunchtime. 'I'm going to bowl like you,' he said. 'Run off a few paces and make it move around.' And he started gesticulating with his hand. He was a lovely bloke, but I still don't know if he meant it as a compliment or if he was taking the mickey."

Charlie Griffith was the most feared fast bowler in the world, taking 32 wickets in that summer's Tests, and England longed to find bowlers of a similar pace, bowlers to succeed Trueman and Statham. For the winter tour of India, they turned to David Larter, John Price and Jeff Jones – but not to Tom.

Colin Cowdrey later wondered if this dedication to pace was always the right policy. 'At certain times it is easier to play in Test cricket than in county cricket,' he wrote. 'Lord's during those years was a seamer's paradise and had England picked Jackson of Derbyshire, while he was still playing, plus Shackleton and Cartwright, I wouldn't have backed a visiting Test team, whatever its reputation, to make above 200 more than once in twenty attempts. The trouble was that we never had the courage to come to terms with the power of seam bowling.'

"I'm not surprised Colin wrote that," Tom says. "He was quite a deep thinker about cricket. So many people at that time thought pace was everything. They do now. It's like they can only see the part that's glaringly obvious. Pace and spin are easy to understand. But the middle ground, the medium-pace swing and seam, requires a lot more thinking. It's a bit tongue in cheek, but I've always said that there's more mystery in swing and seam than there is in spin."

Tom was becoming one of the best bowlers in the country, a master craftsman who would be consistently high in the national averages for the next ten years, but there were plenty of people who were looking for ways to make life harder for bowlers like him. The MCC Secretary, Billy Griffith, called for a law preventing the polishing of the ball, the BBC commentator Rex Alston wanted to have only one ball per innings, and the *Times* correspondent John Woodcock called for a change in the top dressings that were creating green pitches and lush outfields: 'Seam bowlers are a diligent lot, and skilled in their way; but oh! how oppressive they become.'

"They saw seam bowling as negative," Tom says, "and that infuriated me.

All my fielders were attacking. I hardly ever bowled without two slips, a forward short-leg and a leg slip. On Sundays, when the Sunday League came along, I often bowled with a forward short-leg as well."

Mike Brearley confirms this. "Tom wasn't negative at all. He had no fine leg, no third man, because he bowled so straight."

"The people running the game have always been batsmen," Tom says with a chuckle. "The bowlers are just the workers. Whenever they get on top, the laws are changed. Yet nearly all the best days of cricket you'll have seen, the ball will have had the edge over the bat – and one or two batters will have done something exceptional."

By 1963 Tom was thinking of himself primarily as a bowler. He had dropped to six or sometimes seven in the order, and his summer's tally of runs continued to fall: from 1,668 in 1961 to 1,176 in 1962 and now to 687. "Concentration was a huge part of his bowling," his Warwickshire team-mate Jack Bannister says, "so his batting went backwards."

Tom was still in the selectors' thoughts, however, and in October 1963 he was in a twelve-man MCC party that flew out by Comet to East Africa for a five-week tour. The player-manager was the 43-year-old Willie Watson, himself a selector, the ever-cheerful Mike Smith was captain, and they packed in 25 days of cricket as they travelled about Kenya, Tanganyika and Uganda.

"It was a magic tour," Tom says. "It was like exploring with your school atlas. We went up to the Murchison Falls in Uganda, I think it was 170 or 180 miles out of Kampala. The first thirty were tarmac, but after that there was murram, just that red dirt they have the safaris on. We were literally driving through the wilds of Africa. It was brilliant."

The party included several young players in whom the selectors were interested, among them the leg-spinner Robin Hobbs, the fast bowler David Larter and the larger-than-life batsman Colin Milburn. "There wasn't one person who was a nuisance or didn't fit," Tom says. "It really was a happy tour."

The purpose of the visit was for MCC – in Tom's words – 'to fly the flag', and they mingled readily with the host community and attended functions wherever they went. "Willie Watson was such a good manager, very calm, very good at receptions. He used to say to us, 'If you're getting an ear-bashing, tug on your ear and I'll come over and rescue you.'

"He was a real father figure – and still a wonderful player. So stylish, so elegant in everything he did. Young Richard Langridge had to bat with him in one game. He was a left-hander as well, and you couldn't help but see the difference. It was very hard on Richard."

MCC tour of East Africa 1963
Standing *(left to right)*: Jeff Jones, Robin Hobbs, Richard Langridge, David Larter,
Tom Cartwright, Colin Milburn, Laurie Johnson
Sitting: John Mortimore, Willie Watson, Mike Smith,
Micky Stewart, Peter Parfitt

The batsmen – in particular Peter Parfitt, Micky Stewart and Mike Smith – were soon scoring runs, but the bowlers took a while to adapt to the matting pitches. "If you bowled a good length, the ball would go over the top of the stumps." In due course, however, David Larter and Tom found themselves taking plenty of wickets, though not as many as Robin Hobbs who advanced his reputation both on and off the field. Robin was the ideal tourist, full of fun, and that trip to East Africa marked the start of a friendship that remains one of Tom's most enduring in his life in cricket. "I sat next to Hobbsy on the plane going out. We got talking, and he told me he was never going to get married. We had a bet on it. I said he'd be married within five years."

"The furthest I'd been on holiday was Southend," Robin says, "so you can imagine how excited I was. I remember, when we got to Nakuru, we saw this lake all covered in flamingos, a wonderful sight, and on the news recently they were showing how they'd all died off from pollution. We were visiting all these places, long before the days of organised safaris. And the cricket was great fun; I had a terrific time on the jute matting. The ball bounced like a tennis ball. It was a fabulous few weeks – and we got paid eighty quid!"

Colin Milburn was another who looked to live life to the full: "In one of the games," Tom recalls, "he hit the first five balls of an over for six, and the sixth was caught in front of the sight screen." But his heavy bulk was not ideally suited to the conditions: "In Dar-es-Salaam he came off the field with heat exhaustion. I can remember walking into the dressing room at the end of the session, and he was laying naked on top of a big wooden box. There were rivers of perspiration running down his body; the box was going black with the water. 'How are you feeling, Colin?' 'Rough.' That's all I could get out of him. 'Rough.'"

They played against Derek Pringle's father Don, who ran a market gardening business in Kenya, but the most talented cricketers they faced were Asians, notably the Kenyan Basharat Hassan and the Tanganyikan John Solanky, both of whom played for the East African Invitation XI in the three-day match at Kampala that brought the tour to a close.

"The mat was damp at the start, and it developed these invisible indentations where the ball was landing. We had David Larter and Jeff Jones bowling, both very quick, and it was nasty for the batsmen. They were getting hit in the ribs and going off, then coming back. At that time it was considered that Indians couldn't cope with fast bowling – they hadn't faced up very well to Fred in the early '50s – but they were very brave. This little lad John Solanky took a bit of a peppering, and he hit a fifty."

Tom was the most successful of the bowlers, taking five wickets, and the MCC batsmen prospered once the mat had dried out, building a large enough total to achieve an innings victory – though Tom's lasting memory is of the tall David Larter coming out to bat and the little John Solanky, a gentle medium-pace bowler, running in from the boundary. "I can see him now. They had this chap de Souza, and John ran up to him. 'Let me bowl, captain, let me bowl.' I think he wanted to bounce him."

In Test cricket David Larter was an under-achiever – "A nice lad; I was never really sure how bothered he was at the time" – and another with great talent on the tour was the wicket-keeper Laurie Johnson, who for years understudied Keith Andrew at Northampton: "A fine keeper, but he was very laid back. He always seemed contented with his life. Somewhere along the line his burning ambition to play in the first team got dowsed."

The tour was a great success in playing terms, with seven victories and four draws, and *Wisden* reckoned the behaviour of the players 'was impeccable both on and off the field.' But there were only small crowds at the matches, making it a financial disappointment, and in Kenya in particular there were weightier matters on the minds of the local population.

"It hadn't been all that long since the Emergency," Tom says. "When we were playing at Nakuru in the Rift Valley, Peter Parfitt and I stayed several miles away on a big farm that was growing coffee, and all the fortifications were still there from the days of the Mau Mau. From pillar to pillar on the verandahs of all the farmhouses were thick mesh and big galvanised steel doors. The Kikuyu were all round there. If they hadn't taken the oath of allegiance, I think they were slaughtered."

During the tour the Kenyan Prime Minister Jomo Kenyatta was in London, negotiating Independence with Duncan Sandys, the Commonwealth Secretary, and the talks looked at one stage as if they would break down.

"In one match we were introduced on the field to a man called Murumbi, a big, big man who was the next in command to Kenyatta. Then, while we were playing one of the games in Nairobi, he called a meeting at the football stadium. People were coming in from all around, packed on these lorries and beating their skin drums, and Mister Murumbi was going to speak to them, tell them what would happen if they didn't get their independence. I can remember quite clearly standing in the field and hearing all these drums coming from many miles off. Then we saw all the lorries going by."

So how did the white people feel? "There was a lot of unease. They were very guarded in what they said."

And the reaction when Independence was granted? "Relief. I think Mister Murumbi was a man of action."

The summer of 1964 started well for Warwickshire. At the end of June the county, still under the benevolent captaincy of Mike Smith, was top of the championship table and had progressed to the semi-finals of the Gillette Cup.

Mike Smith had taken part in two winter tours of the Indian sub-continent when several of the leading England players had made themselves unavailable but, despite their strong showing each year in the championship, no Warwickshire cricketer had played in a full-strength England side in the last three years. Tom had done the double in 1962, his bowling had developed further in 1963, he had impressed in East Africa, and now in the first two months of 1964 he was the leading wicket-taker in the country. He was, according to the *Daily Express*, 'the man the England selectors have consistently ignored.'

At the end of June Warwickshire were playing Glamorgan at Ebbw Vale, and Tom and Joan – together with two-year-old Jane and their new baby boy Jeremy, were staying with Joan's family in Skewen. Tom had bowled

34 overs on Saturday, taking four for 44, and he was fast asleep when news of his selection in the twelve for the third Test came on the radio. 'Wakey, Wakey, Tom!' ran the *Daily Mirror* headline. Amid speculation that the second spinner Norman Gifford would compete for the twelfth man role with either Colin Cowdrey or Ken Barrington, several of the newspapers declared that the Warwickshire seamer was certain to play on the grassy Headingley pitch.

Tom arrived on Wednesday and got the firm impression from Ted Dexter the England captain that he would indeed be in the final eleven. But Colin Cowdrey withdrew with a bad back, Ken Taylor was summoned from Yorkshire and on Thursday morning Tom found that, for a second time, he was twelfth man.

Once more he sat on the balcony. He watched as England, thanks to Dexter and Parks, made 268 on the first day. And he was sitting with Walter Robins, chairman of selectors, after tea on the second day as Australia, five wickets down, moved within 100 runs of England's total. "'Wouldn't it be great,' he said to me, 'if we could get a wicket now with the new ball coming up?' 'Yes,' I said, 'it would be rather nice.' And Fred Titmus took two in quick succession."

ENGLAND 268. AUSTRALIA 178 FOR SEVEN.

"Then Ted took the new ball. Peter Burge was still in, but the other end was wide open. Ted was pilloried afterwards, but it was what the chairman of selectors wanted and I should think 99% of the people on the ground would have done the same."

Trueman and Flavell, in a display of aggression, opted to bowl short. But they were men well into their thirties, they had not the fire they once had, and Burge despatched them with such freedom that all England's advantage was lost in a matter of overs. Burge, with his strong forearms, had been on 33 when the seventh wicket had fallen, and he reached his hundred in the day's final over. "It was the best exhibition I've ever seen of hitting short-pitched bowling," Tom says. "Burge was a magnificent player of the pull and hook shots, and he murdered them."

Tom left at close of play on Friday. "I played 26 years of first-class cricket," he says, "and that's the only time I've been on Headingley cricket ground in my life."

On Saturday he was at Edgbaston, taking part in a memorable victory in which the tall Barbadian Rudi Webster – arriving from Edinburgh, where he had just finished his year's study of radiology – destroyed the reigning champions Yorkshire.

R.V. WEBSTER, 12.4 OVERS, 7 WICKETS FOR 6 RUNS; 27 OVERS, FIVE FOR 52.

"He was a very good bowler, not fast but accurate and coming from a great height. He wasn't a West Indian who was poor, shy, almost withdrawn like Viv Richards was when he first came to Somerset. He was a bright, confident chap. He just strolled in and took it all in his stride."

For Tom it was part of the joy of county cricket that so many different characters played the game. "Rudi was a real romancer. He was a 440 champion in athletics, he used to tell us. He also reckoned he was an expert limbo dancer – till we got down to Bournemouth at the end of one season and we were in the Great Western. All the wives and girl-friends were there, and we tied our ties together to make this rope and got Rudi to try to fulfil his boast that he could get down under two feet or whatever it was. But of course he couldn't. He ended up in a heap every time he tried."

The victory over Yorkshire kept Warwickshire at the top of the championship table, and it took Tom's attention away from the Test where on Saturday morning Burge went on from 100 to 160, punishing Trueman so severely that he was removed from the attack after only two overs. 'I have seen the sad sight of a great fast bowler in complete eclipse,' wrote Denis Compton. 'Fred has been one of the all-time greats in the game, but now it is all over. His pace has gone – and his menace too.'

Australia won by seven wickets, and for the fourth Test at Old Trafford the selectors shuffled the pack dramatically. The headline writers concentrated on the dropping of Fred Trueman and of Colin Cowdrey, but in fact only Fred Titmus survived of the Headingley bowling attack – with call-ups for John Mortimore of Gloucestershire, John Price of Middlesex and Fred Rumsey of Somerset.

Fred Trueman was only three wickets short of being the first man in Test history to reach 300, and he did not take the news of his dropping well. "I'm not done yet," he growled to the *Daily Express* reporter Crawford White. "Let's see how this southern shower go on."

Tom was for the third time in the twelve, and he travelled up to Manchester on Wednesday with Mike Smith, who at long last was recalled. It was Tom's 29th birthday, and during the Wednesday afternoon he was in the Old Trafford nets. There he was joined by the 46-year-old Alec Bedser, who had retired from the game four years earlier and was now an England selector.

"Alec got changed and came to bowl in the same net as me. I was always in awe of him, from that day at The Oval in 1953, and suddenly, to find him in the net, still a great bowler, with his sweater on, with the crown and three lions, it was a bit daunting. To be honest, I was thinking, 'What am I doing here? Why isn't he playing?'"

Perhaps there was a lineage of quality seam bowling that ran across the generations from Bedser to Cartwright. Certainly there was a mutual respect and, according to the writer Denzil Batchelor, 'I understand Alec Bedser has been urging Cartwright's selection for four years.'

It was a time of uncertainty in the England team. A tour of South Africa was scheduled for that winter and, with the dropping of Trueman and Cowdrey, it seemed that few in the team could be sure of their selection. They spent Wednesday night at a hotel in Lymm, and Tom travelled into Manchester on Thursday morning with Ken Barrington.

"Kenny was desperate to go to South Africa; he hadn't been there, and he seemed to be worried whether he'd go. I was amazed. If somebody had said to me, 'Put a team down', his would have been one of the first names on my sheet of paper. I really liked him; he was a nice bloke to have around. But he was a real worrier. 'I'm concerned,' he said. He never took anything for granted."

Tom went into the nets again as they awaited news of the final eleven. "I can still see Walter Robins beaming at me from forty or fifty yards away. 'I told them there's no way that you were going to come here again and not play.' He shook hands and said, 'I'm delighted.'"

To the surprise of many, England played an extra bowler and Mike Smith was named as twelfth man.

It was a dull morning, and the coin rolled a long way on the dark-looking pitch before the Australian captain Bobby Simpson broke into a smile and opted to bat. So, just before half past eleven, Tom stepped onto the Old Trafford turf and finally became an England cricketer.

More than 200 miles away his eldest sister Joan was on holiday with her family in Weymouth. "We'd just gone down to the beach and I said, 'The Test match is on today.' My husband Ken said, 'Don't you worry. Tom won't be picked.' But I went back to the hotel, and I stood in the door of the television lounge, where a few people were sitting, waiting for play to start. And Tom was in the team. 'He's playing,' I said. 'I'm going home.'"

They drove back to Coventry, stopping in Solihull to see Joan, Tom's wife, whose father was up from Skewen, and they decided to travel together the next morning to Manchester. So that evening she rang the hotel at Lymm. "I got the receptionist. 'Can I speak to Tom Cartwright, please?' I said. And she passed me over to this man. 'Who do you want? … No, dear, you've got the wrong hotel.' 'I don't think so,' I said. 'I'm his sister.' 'Oh, are you? He's had half a dozen of those already today.'"

They were at the ground bright and early the next day: sister Joan and her husband Ken and wife Joan and her father. "Tom left the tickets on the gate for us," his sister remembers. "And guess who brought them? Alec Bedser.

101

He was lovely. 'I know who you are,' he said."

It was the only time in his life that Joan's father attended a day of Test cricket, and he too was overawed by the faces around him. "Look who's behind us," he said at one point – and it was Len Hutton. Then at another stage of the day they saw a group of famous faces from *Coronation Street*.

They were days of great pride for Tom's family – but not just for his family. Back in Coventry his old schoolmaster Eddie Branson celebrated, his protégé recognised at last. So too did the car workers in the Rootes factory; they might be alarmed by the news that the American firm Chrysler had bought a stake in their company, but one of their own, their very own, was playing for England. Tom was Coventry born and bred, the first from the city ever to play for England.

At Edgbaston Tiger Smith was quietly proud, too, though he did not show it. "He didn't let you know how he felt," Tom says. "It would have destroyed his image. Not like Derief Taylor; he would have been full of excitement. One of his 'yutes' playing for England – he'd have been so excited that people would have been keeping out of his way." Nevertheless, years later, Tiger Smith wrote of his 'thrill of seeing a boy make the grade after being under my wing. I've been more elated at seeing men like Tom Cartwright play for England than anything I've done in my own playing career.'

Tom had made his way from schoolboy to county cricketer and, by turning in good performances week after week for several years, he had forced the selectors to pick him ... eventually.

'We're all delighted,' the Warwickshire secretary Leslie Deakins told the press, 'that a local product, a man born and bred in Warwickshire, should have come right through to the top.'

CHAPTER 11

FIVE TESTS AND A TOUR
1964 – 1965

Has a bowler ever had a first day of Test cricket like it?

On Thursday 23 July 1964 Tom took the field at Old Trafford, watching with anticipation as the Australian openers Bill Lawry and Bobby Simpson negotiated the new ball bowling of John Price and Fred Rumsey.

There was no Trueman, no Statham, no Tyson, no Loader. A great era of English fast bowling was coming to an end, and suddenly there were opportunities for newcomers. John Price approached the wicket on his long, snaking run and off the last ball of his first over, bowling to the left-handed Bill Lawry, a great appeal went up for a catch down leg, only for the batsman to look unmoved and for the umpire Syd Buller to walk briskly to his position at square leg.

At the other end the left-armer Fred Rumsey was fast and accurate. Three years earlier, kept out of the Worcestershire team by Flavell and Coldwell, he had written to nine counties, offering his services, and he had been rejected by every one of them. Now he was a Somerset man, the first from that county to play in a home Test for 25 years. "He was a good bowler," Tom says. "He had plenty of skill and intelligence. A lot of the top batters in England didn't like facing him. But he was a big man and, with his size, he did struggle physically at times."

It was not a day to be a fast bowler with a big frame. "It was the greatest batting wicket I ever played on in my life," Fred Rumsey says. "Then or since. I've never played on a better track. And the first two new balls we had, neither of them swung at all."

Neither Lawry nor Simpson took risks, being happy to push the ball into gaps and scamper singles in which, one observer wrote, they were 'like mechanical men set in motion by a penny dropping.' Price bowled five overs from the City end, then Ted Dexter turned to Tom and off only his third ball Bill Lawry – legendary for his defensive technique – swung him away for a great six over square leg. "That was a statement," Tom says. "I never doubted that. Australians play like that. They like to get on top of you straightaway. I knew I had to take that on and assert myself."

Tom was soon switched to the Stretford end and he did indeed assert himself, as Denis Compton's report made clear: 'Cartwright, moving the ball both ways off the seam, beat Lawry around the off-stump three times with successive balls. He had set to work on the left-hander's weakness, and continually he beat Lawry's forward stroke – but with no luck.'

Simpson glanced a ball from Tom fine to leg, and Jim Parks – standing back and moving late, according to Compton – could not hold the ball in his gloves. After that, there were no more chances till the score reached 201 and a sharp piece of fielding by Ted Dexter found the two batsmen at the same end.

Lawry, run out, 106.

In the last half hour Ian Redpath pushed forward to Tom, was beaten by seam movement and was given lbw, the only wicket to fall to a bowler in 122 overs in the day. At close of play Australia were 253 for two, with Simpson – completing a maiden Test century – on 109 not out.

Tom's first day of Test cricket was over, and he left the field with figures of 43 overs, 17 maidens, 76 runs and one wicket. He had bowled more overs than Price and Rumsey combined, more overs than the spinners Titmus and Mortimore combined.

The great West Indian Sir Learie Constantine was impressed:

> As one who feels he understands the game, I am puzzled why it has taken the selectors so long to cap Cartwright. He moved the ball in, he moved it away, and at all times in Ted Dexter's apparently excessive use of him he never allowed the batsmen to relax for a second. It was a wonderful effort, and it left me to imagine what might have happened on a wicket that gave him some assistance.

John Woodcock in *The Times* was also impressed:

> His was as good an exhibition of seam bowling as one could wish to see. A dozen times or more he beat the bat, and hardly a single stroke of positive assurance was played against him.

Also Charles Bray in the *Daily Herald*:

> Considering the conditions, I thought his was some of the best bowling I've seen for many years. The track gave not the slightest assistance to any bowler. Yet by some almost miraculous persistence and skill, he managed to make the ball beat the bat every now and then. Forty-three overs in the day was a heavy stint for any bowler, but for one who bowls medium pace from a fair run-up it was a giant's task.

"I was going for under two an over," Tom says, "so I never felt under any pressure. In fact, I rather enjoyed it. It wasn't that hectic a day. They didn't make us rush about in the field. It was just a long grind. I remember Alec Bedser came and sat with me in the dressing room afterwards. He did it each day. He just sat and talked with me, like a father almost. Then he took me across to the tent for a drink. He was so kind and helpful. 'I wouldn't drink a lot of beer,' he said. 'Have some Beaujolais, that's what I do.'"

Tom was back in action soon enough the next morning. "I was lucky," he says. "I don't know if I had a slow heart rate or what it was, but I always had a good recovery rate." By lunch he had bowled another 17 overs.

In his first four sessions as a Test cricketer Tom had bowled the astonishing total of 60 overs. In the modern game, when teams struggle to complete a minimum of 90 overs in a scheduled six-hour day, it would barely be possible for a bowler to reach such a total by lunchtime on the second day of a Test – and then only if he sent down every single over from one end. Moreover Tom was not a slow bowler, coming off three or four paces to the crease. Every delivery was born of great physical effort.

England were one down in the series, needing to win both the remaining Tests to regain the Ashes, and Bobby Simpson, ignoring the intermittent slow handclaps among the crowd, was remorseless in making sure that all possibility of an Australian defeat would be eliminated. On and on he went with little change of tempo. Records tumbled, and by the close he had made 265 out of a total of 570 for four.

"The Ashes do get people excited," Tom says, "but at times they can also bring about some very negative cricket."

Tom's share of the work decreased as the day went on. He bowled 'only' 34 of the day's 120 overs, conceded 42 runs and captured a second wicket, that of Peter Burge caught at square leg.

John Woodcock thought that, when Australia passed 500 at 5.15, 'Cartwright's step was scarcely less sprightly than when he started' though Denzil Batchelor saw it differently: 'Poor Cartwright by this time had sunk to something slower than medium medium-pace, but his bowling retained in full measure its nagging accuracy.'

After two days of Test cricket Tom had bowled 77 overs, 32 of them maidens, and had figures of two wickets for 118 runs. It was the hardest-working debut of any bowler in the history of Test cricket. If only he had made his debut elsewhere, he can have been excused for thinking: on 'the seamer's paradise' at Lord's or even at Headingley.

Look up Tom's statistics, and you'll find 13 grounds where he bowled more than 250 overs in his career. His favourite was Weston-super-Mare where his 77 wickets came at only 9.75 each, followed by his home ground Coventry with 74 wickets at 14.28. But at the other end of the spectrum was Worcester, with 26 wickets at 22.50, and – far beyond that – Old Trafford, where in 12 matches he bowled 337 overs and took only 18 wickets at 35.72 runs each. Such was his luck to have to make his Test debut there. "It was never a ground where I had much success. I do remember thinking about that at the time."

The Australians went for quick runs on Saturday morning. Simpson's maiden century turned into a triple but four wickets fell in the helter-skelter, two each to John Price and Fred Rumsey. But, after his two days of hard work, Tom was given no opportunity to gather any easy pickings. "I was a bit disappointed not to get on. I was looking all the time, but Ted never saw me."

Australia declared on 656 for eight. Then England, fired up by a fiercely determined Ted Dexter, set out to match the Australian effort. Dexter himself led the way with 174, and Ken Barrington, with an 11½-hour 256, secured his place on the boat to South Africa. It was Barrington's tenth Test hundred but remarkably his first in England.

Any prospect of one or other side winning was long dead and at one stage, one journalist reported, six senior members of the press box were asleep – though such was the fascination of this match of records that the London telephone number UMP, which gave out the up-to-date score, was engaged solidly throughout the last two days, as the *Cricketer* magazine reported:

> The great British public wanted two things. As Australia had scored 656, they wanted England to score 657; and as Simpson had scored 311, they wanted Barrington to score 312. The result did not matter. They wanted those two things more than anything since they wanted Sir Gordon Richards to win the Derby.

JL Manning in the *Daily Mail* called it 'the worst Test match ever played in England', but a leader-writer in his own newspaper had other ideas:

> If this isn't cricket, who do they think keeps dialling UMP? You couldn't even dial VICtoria because so many people were dialling UMP. Windows of TV shops were besieged. You heard nothing else in pubs.

"It's very difficult for me, looking back, to see anything terribly wrong with the game," Tom says. "The weather was good all five days, and it was my first Test, a very special occasion in my life. And if Bill Lawry had been given out early on, or Jim Parks had held that catch, or some of the playing and missing had taken the edge, we could have been batting on the second day – and it would have been a very different game. There were a lot of intriguing possibilities in that match. I can never look back and see it as being boring."

The debate about the match, alas, tended to obscure the skill of Tom's contribution on the first two days.

Then on the Wednesday, following straight on from the Test match and still at Old Trafford, Tom found himself caught up in another game that created a great furore.

Lancashire were at home to Warwickshire in the semi-final of the Gillette

Cup. In its second year, the knockout competition was still a novelty, attracting big crowds, and many of the counties had not yet worked out the different requirements of the format. In the first year the winners had been Sussex, whose captain Ted Dexter – ever a free-thinking theorist – had realised quickly that it was more important to restrict runs than to take wickets, setting defensive fields almost from the first over.

In Sussex's very first game in that first year they played Kent at Tunbridge Wells and, with the home team keeping slips and gullies in place throughout their 65 overs in the field, Sussex made 314 for seven. Then, when Kent batted, according to Sussex's Alan Oakman, "After about the third over the second slip went to mid-wicket, gully went into the covers, and we blocked off their shots." Peter Richardson scored 127, but he could not keep up with the rate required and he became ill-tempered. "If this is the way you play it," he said, "you can stuff this knock-out cricket."

It was a radical departure – a cricket match where you could bat first and win without taking wickets – and the players' differing expectations came into conflict dramatically at Old Trafford in July 1964.

A crowd of 21,000 – mostly ardent Lancastrians – packed the Old Trafford ground, with hundreds sitting on the grass, and in the morning they watched a dashing display by the Warwickshire opener Bob Barber who only two years earlier had been one of their own. In his years at Old Trafford he had been a cautious batsman, weighed down by the cares of captaincy and dispirited by the rumbling politics of an unhappy club. Now, rejuvenated by the happy atmosphere at Edgbaston and told by Tiger Smith to stand tall and swing his arms, he was as attractive an opener as any in England and he raced to 76 in the first 25 overs.

Mike Smith weighed in with a brisk 58, followed by some uninhibited hitting by Ray Hitchcock and Tom, and Warwickshire's 60 overs brought a total of 294 for seven, 74 more than any team had successfully chased in the short history of the competition.

Yet the pitch was as true as the one used for the Test, and the Lancashire openers David Green and Duncan Worsley began with a blaze of shots, hitting 60 off the first 10 overs from Jack Bannister and Rudi Webster. Green, in particular, was hitting the ball hard, causing John Woodcock in *The Times* to compare him with 'Dexter at his best' and to talk of his playing for England soon. For those who had grumbled about five days of Simpson and Barrington, here was a very different fare. 'There was high excitement and a cup tie atmosphere. We heard more cheers than in any of the previous five days at Old Trafford.'

Warwickshire, however, had learnt from Sussex's success the previous summer. "The first year we'd been knocked out in the first round," Alan Smith says. "We batted too extravagantly and were eight or nine wickets down by lunch. And one or two people, Jack Bannister in particular, paid attention to Sussex's tactics. So our approach in '64 was different."

Billy Ibadulla was brought on to bowl his darting seamers, and Mike Smith stationed six fielders on the boundary. Tom took over at the other end, the light grew murky and – with Warwickshire bustling quickly through their overs – Lancashire rapidly lost their way. By the time their keeper Geoff 'Chimp' Clayton – one of county cricket's less deferential characters – came to the wicket, they were five wickets down and needed a near-impossible 134 in only 20 overs.

"We could hear the Lancashire team high up on the balcony," Tom says. "They were very unhappy about the fields Mike was setting, and Chimp came in, obviously to make a point. Harry Pilling was getting one run off the first ball of every over, and Chimp was blocking the other five."

John Kay described the scenes in *Playfair Cricket Monthly*:

Clayton, smarting at the turning down of his appeal against the light, senselessly stone-walled and even refused to answer the willing Pilling's calls for easy singles. Slow hand-clapping developed into stormy booing and, amid a welter of unpleasant barracking, the match fizzled out into a disgraceful exhibition of bad cricketing manners.

"Bob Barber was loving it," Tom recalls. "He'd just left Lancashire, and he ran up to Mike Smith. 'Let me bowl,' he said. 'Let me bowl.'"

So, with Lancashire needing seven and more an over, their former captain bowled eight overs of flighted leg spin for just 19 runs.

"A bloke in the crowd came out onto the field, right into the middle. He went up to Chimp and took his bat off him – and Chimp just gave it to him meekly. He played some big swipes – 'That's the way it's done, lad' – gave the bat back and went off."

Lancashire finished on 209 for seven, with Clayton's 20-over stay bringing him a score of 19 not out. Most of the crowd had streamed out long before the end, and the players returned to a pavilion full of angry members, among them Lancashire's cricket manager, the formidable disciplinarian Cyril Washbrook.

"We went up the spiral staircase, and Washy was stood at the top with his arms folded. Chimp went to go in the Lancashire dressing room, and he said, 'Not there, Geoffrey. In there.' And he pointed to his office."

Lancashire were in the midst of their centenary celebrations, but by the end of the year they would have lost their secretary Geoffrey Howard to Surrey, sacked Geoff Clayton, captain Ken Grieves, Jack Dyson and Peter

Marner and seen their committee overthrown by a vote of no confidence. Warwickshire, meanwhile, were in the final of the Gillette Cup.

Alas Warwickshire's season ended in disappointment. Their challenge for the championship faded in the closing weeks, leaving neighbours Worcestershire to raise the pennant for the first time, and at Lord's in the Gillette Cup final they opted to bat first on a hazy autumnal morning and were humbled by the veteran Sussex medium-pacer Ian Thomson.

The final Test at The Oval was ruined by poor weather, but there was time for Tom to impress a second time, bowling 62 overs and taking three wickets for 110 runs. 'Cartwright bowled splendidly,' was the Australian Jack Fingleton's judgment. 'He seems to be in the Test side for years to come.'

Simpson, not out 311 at Old Trafford
caught Dexter, bowled Cartwright 24 at The Oval
"As Ted caught it, he threw it up and said, 'That's about bloody time.'"

The other highlights were a maiden Test century by the young Geoff Boycott and the return of Fred Trueman, replacing poor Fred Rumsey after the Old Trafford ordeal and looking for the three wickets for his 300. He seemed unlikely to achieve the feat when, with Australia on 343 for six, he was still wicketless – but, on the stroke of Saturday lunchtime, he took two in two balls and The Oval buzzed with excitement as the afternoon session began.

Neil Hawke survived the hat-trick ball, and it was some while before the great moment arrived. "I was fielding at forward short leg," Tom remembers, "and I was convinced I was going to get a bat-pad catch. I suppose I was looking for a spot of glory for myself."

In the end it was Colin Cowdrey at slip who took the vital catch, and Fred was in every headline, even going to the Black and White Minstrel Show that night and being invited up on stage.

"I was having a bath in the hotel, trying to shake off my stiffness," Tom says. "It was quite late, and Fred came in. He'd been feted quite a bit all day, and he sat down for about ten minutes. I suppose he was looking for somebody who was still up, and he just sat there quietly, as if he was trying to take it all in. It was an emotional few minutes. It was obvious that it meant an awful lot to him."

Fred's other ambition was to go to South Africa that winter, a tour he had never done, but the selectors decided against taking him. "He desperately wanted to go, but I think there might have been a feeling in some quarters that with a five-month tour, if he wasn't playing in the Tests, he might have created some distraction."

Instead, England selected John Price and Warwickshire's young David Brown for pace, with support from Yorkshire's Tony Nicholson and Tom. And, when Nicholson pulled out, the selectors remembered the Gillette Cup final and turned to Sussex's 35-year-old Ian Thomson, who was two years older than Fred Trueman.

*

Tom was to spend five months away from Joan and the two children, with the tourists scheduled to depart on Thursday 10 October, Polling Day in the General Election. With Ted Dexter in Cardiff, busy trying to capture James Callaghan's seat for the Conservatives, the MCC party was captained by Mike Smith, though he had not played in a Test all summer, and managed by the Assistant Secretary of MCC, Donald Carr.

"Donald had a lovely way with people," Tom says. "He was a terrific bloke. If criticism was needed, you'd get a sharp word, though not too sharp from him. If somebody said to me, 'You're young again and you're going on tour; pick the people to go with,' he would be my manager without a shadow of doubt. And with Mike as captain, it was a very good tour."

They were to travel to Africa by plane. "It was the first time MCC had flown out for a tour, and they put us in two different planes. I think they still had the Munich air crash in mind."

Tom was in the second group, waiting on the pavement outside Lord's when the Conservative candidate for the constituency of Marylebone, Quintin Hogg, drove past, blaring out his message through a loud hailer.

Tom was a Labour man. He had played first-class cricket for thirteen summers, and every one of them had been under a Conservative Government. So even on his best behaviour in his MCC touring blazer his reaction was instinctive. "We were by the Red House pub at the top of Baker Street and, as his car went past, I waved a fist and shouted something. And there was Michael Brearley beside me, and he was doing the same."

"I remember that moment," Mike says. "I could never vote Conservative, and Tom could certainly never vote Conservative. Somehow we knew that about each other straightaway. So there was an immediate pleasure in each other's company."

It was not a successful tour for either of them.

The 22-year-old Mike Brearley seemed to have the world at his feet: he had shone academically at Cambridge, come top in the Home Civil Service examination and had been the third highest run-scorer in England that summer, with 2,178. Already, *The Times* reported, he was being groomed as a future England captain.

"He was playing really well at the start of the tour," Tom remembers. "He looked a very good player, and Geoff Boycott didn't seem to be in as good form as you might have expected. But Geoffrey got the nod on the basis that he'd got a ton in the last Test at The Oval, and he got 70-odd in the first Test and didn't look back. So Michael went weeks without getting into the middle."

111

Mike Brearley

"He was a very fine young player, but he went off to lecture at Newcastle and he missed several seasons. You have an initial period in cricket when you're forming and developing your game, then you consolidate – and Michael missed out on the consolidation. It was a terrific achievement to come back like he did and to captain England. Only somebody with his mental ability could do that. It was almost similar to the people who went away in the war.

"When I was at Somerset, he came down to see me on a flying visit. 'Tennis players have personal coaches,' he said. I picked him up from the train at Bath and drove him to Taunton for a net. I talked to him about back-lift and I said, 'Look, there's a man who knows a lot more about this than I do. If you get the chance, go and talk to Tiger.'

"Michael was always very keen to learn. He was younger than me, but I felt comfortable with him – except I used to say to him, 'Don't start analysing me.' He found it very difficult not to do that. It's very disconcerting when you're talking to somebody and you know they're analysing you.

"He had so much humility. That was the key to his success. It came from a genuine caring."

"I was immature when I went to South Africa," Mike says. "I got tenser batting, flaws got into my technique, and I got very bored with having to watch the cricket all the time and having no role. I fooled around, stayed out too much, went to parties. And I played worse and worse."

During the first Test at Durban he was batting badly in the nets, with Robin Hobbs and David Brown bowling to him, and he became aware of an elderly man standing behind the net. "He was wearing a trilby hat and looked a bit yellow; he obviously wasn't well. 'Could I have a word with you?' he said, and he told me that I had to relax; my hands were too tight on the bat, especially my left hand. I listened politely and took bugger all notice."

The man, who was he? "It was Wally Hammond. I'm ashamed to say that I knew who he was. And he was absolutely right. It was another ten years before I did anything about it. Tom told me to speak to Tiger Smith, and it's what he told me. And it's what Botham told me four or five years after that. Botham showed me his batting glove; he held the bat so lightly, it was hardly marked at all.

"Tom tried to help me with my batting on that tour. I wish I'd listened to him. So many people came up with pieces of advice, all different, and Tom would have been the one to listen to."

Tom's own tour started well. His runs and wickets on a grassy Durban pitch played an important part in a morale-boosting victory over Natal, the champion state side for the previous four years. But he bowled 60 overs in that match, and perhaps – having bowled nearly 1,200 in all cricket the previous summer – it was too much for his body. He had a bruise on the joint of his big toe, and he altered his bowling to take the pressure off it. As a result he suffered a fracture of a metatarsal bone – "It's what they call a march fracture; people who do a lot of marching get it" – and he did not play between the Natal game in mid-November and the end of the third Test in early January. Instead, he became one of the tour's extras, along with Mike Brearley, Robin Hobbs and David Brown.

"Our physio didn't have ultrasound so, when we were in Cape Town, I used to go off round the coast to Frenchoek for treatment. It was quite a way, and I was taken by this driver Joe, who was what they called a Cape Coloured. A nice man, very bright. His wife was a schoolteacher. He would ask me all these questions about England. He'd got a sister in Blackpool who wrote and told him all about things, and he couldn't believe it. 'Would I really be able to get on the same bus as you? And stand in the same queue?'

"There was a little fishing village, Kalk Bay, and they were moving all the people there, mostly coloureds, about twenty miles away into an estate of new township housing, leaving Kalk Bay free for the whites to move in. You had people in their nineties who'd lived there all their lives, and suddenly they were having to move to some dustbowl. And the fishermen, imagine what happened to them. I found that very difficult to understand in any way at all.

"Joe had a mother and an uncle, her brother, who were both designated white. When he took his mother to her brother's hotel in Paarl, he had to drop her at the front and go round the rear entrance himself. That was mind-boggling to me, how people could be so inhuman. It was a country without any human dignity at all.

"Doctor Verwoerd came and had tea with us in Cape Town during the Test, and that was a strange feeling, to be in the pavilion, eating nicely cut sandwiches and cakes, with this man sitting with us. He looked, for all intents and purposes, a lovely old man."

Christmas Day fell halfway through the Johannesburg Test, and Mike Brearley was invited for a family meal with his Cambridge University team-mate Ray White, taking Geoffrey Boycott and David Brown along with him.

"Ray's sister Jill was married to a barrister, and they were left-wing. He'd been in prison under the 90-Day Act, and she was extremely loud-spoken. Their father was a businessman, a decent sort of chap, and he said we should all drink to absent friends, and we went round the table. Boycott said somewhere up in Yorkshire, I said Ealing Broadway and it came to Jill – and she said 'Pretoria Central Gaol'. She was talking about this man who was due to be hanged; he'd set off a bomb in Johannesburg Station, and somebody had been killed."

The man, a young schoolteacher who had studied at Oxford University, was hung the following April. His parents were not allowed to attend the cremation where a family friend, a fifteen-year-old boy called Peter Hain, stood up uninvited and read from *Ecclesiastes*: 'A time to kill and a time to heal … A time to every purpose under heaven.'

"There she was at the table, benign and friendly in the middle of a Christmas dinner, and suddenly this thing comes down into the middle of it."

"Michael and I," Tom says, "would discuss things that you wouldn't discuss with too many of the others. He asked me if I'd go round a Ford motor company plant in Port Elizabeth with him. The manager took us round. I felt almost at home in some ways, all the bustle of the track and the cars being put together, and they looked after us well, gave us a nice tea afterwards.

"But Michael got this notebook out, and he kept asking these questions – questions that I was hoping he wouldn't. He was asking what they were paid – the coloureds, the blacks – and he'd turn to me. 'What would they get in Coventry at Rootes, Tom?' Then he'd write it down."

"I was a bit earnest probably," Mike admits now.

England won the first Test at Durban. Having seen the England seamers – Tom among them – destroy the Natal side in the earlier match, the ground staff opted to prepare a different surface for the Test. "When we arrived," Mike Smith says, "there were two lads on a hand mower, and they were creating havoc. They'd obviously decided that they were going to take off all the grass. And that suited us because the greatest difference between the two teams was that our spin attack – Titmus, Allen and Barber – was in a different league from theirs. In a way, Tom's injury solved a problem. It sorted out our selection dilemma."

The England spinners took 15 wickets as South Africa went down to an innings defeat, a result that also looked possible at one stage of the second Test at Johannesburg – till a Colin Bland hundred secured a draw. For Tom, the highlight of this second Test was an innings of 172 by Ted Dexter.

"I liked Ted. This image people had of him – Lord Ted and all that – was totally wrong. I think he was a very shy person, very unsure of himself. I can remember him turning up in the hotel in Salisbury, when he'd just flown in after losing to Jim Callaghan. Ian Thomson and I were going out to dinner and, after a while, he said, 'What are you doing tonight? Do you mind if I come along?' I thought, 'This bloke is not as flamboyant or as pushy as people think.'

"The tragedy was that he finished just when he was becoming a great player. At Old Trafford against the Australians and again at Jo'burg, he batted brilliantly. I thought, 'This is a bloke who's maturing into something very different.' But he wanted to do so many things with his life."

The Johannesburg Test ended on Tuesday 29 December. On Wednesday they took the 3½-hour flight to Cape Town. Then on Friday they started the third Test, a high-scoring draw in which rumbling ill-feeling between the teams, on the subject of walking, came to a head.

"In the first Test," Tom remembers, "the South Africans reckoned that Boycs had been caught off his glove, and Roy McLean had kept their blokes in the dressing room afterwards. He wasn't captain, but he insisted that nobody walked. When he batted, our boys reckoned he was caught three times at bat-pad and didn't go."

There were further incidents at Johannesburg, but matters really boiled over at Cape Town in front of a newly-arrived party of MCC dignitaries that included a trio of Old Etonians: the ever-influential Gubby Allen, the President Dick Twining and the President-Designate General Sir Oliver Leese, Montgomery's second-in-command in the war.

On the first day Eddie Barlow, the South African opener, hit 138 out of 252 for one – but, when he was on only 41, he played a ball from Fred Titmus down, apparently onto his boot, and it lobbed away to slip where Peter Parfitt held the catch.

With so few state matches, the South African umpires were less experienced than those in England, and John Warner – never a first-class cricketer himself – was standing in only his ninth first-class match in eight years. He turned down the appeal, and at the end of the over angry words were exchanged between Titmus and Barlow. When Barlow passed 50 and 100, there was no clapping from the England fielders, though they did – in the words of one writer – 'indulge in an absurd display of congratulations' when Barlow's partner Tony Pithey reached 50.

"Donald Carr made Fred go into the South African dressing room and apologise," Tom says. "He told him he'd be on his way home if he didn't."

The MCC dignitaries tried to calm the atmosphere. Dick Twining called it 'a storm in a teacup' while Gubby Allen surprised everybody by saying that in his day the custom was not to walk until you were given out.

Alas, the arguments began again during the England innings when Ken Barrington on 49 edged a ball to Denis Lindsay behind the wicket – with John Warner again the umpire. Tom was away in Frenchoek, having treatment on his foot, but he recalls going to the cinema and seeing it on the Pathé News. "The camera was right behind the batsman. Kenny hit it, there was a big roar, and he just stood there. And you could see the umpire shaking his head. Then Kenny turned, put his bat under his arm – as he used to – and walked off."

The crowd applauded his sportsmanship, happy that the spirit of cricket was triumphing above the earlier pettiness, and several journalists joined in. Denys Rowbotham in *The Guardian* called it 'a refreshing piece of chivalry'; Crawford White in the *Daily Express* said it was 'one of the finest acts of sportsmanship I have seen in Test cricket.' But others, in the confused atmosphere, saw it entirely differently. JL Manning in the *Daily Mail* said it was 'too ostentatious …it smacked of "we chaps know how to play the game, even if you lot don't"' and, according to Tom, "a lot of people said Kenny did it deliberately to make a fool of the umpire."

Barrington later wrote that he had no such intention; he had hesitated because he had been wrestling with his own conscience. Meanwhile Fred Titmus, later in the innings, found himself walking when he had not touched the ball. "I'm in such a state with it all," he said in the pavilion. "I don't know what to do."

As the dust settled on all of that, Tom returned to fitness. Mike Brearley was a lost figure on the tour, all out of sorts, and he remembers the day Tom, his foot better, reappeared in the nets. "I went in to bat, and he ran up for his first ball. He'd been out for six weeks with a bad foot, and it landed on a perfect length and hit the top of my off stump. It didn't take much doing to beat me by that time, but he found it very humorous. I think I did, too, in a chagrined sort of way. It was somehow so right about Tom, that he'd come in like that and bowl you the perfect ball straightaway."

Tom played in the next match against Border at East London. There he made a century, surviving – thanks to the umpire Harry Winrow – a mighty appeal for a stumping when he was 98. He also bowled 35 overs, and he was selected for the fourth Test at Johannesburg, at the Wanderers ground where three years earlier he had been the coach.

The pitch was expected to be green, and Tom took the place of the off-spinner David Allen, who had been the leading wicket-taker in the first three Tests. "Tom came up to me before the match," David remembers. "He said, 'They're wrong. You should be playing, not me. It's not as green as they think it is.' There aren't many people who would have said that."

The pitch, in fact, did not especially help any of the bowlers, and the match became another that did not quite catch the imagination. "I put them in," Mike Smith says, "and that turned out to be a rubbish decision. Then John Price broke down, and we struggled."

Once more Tom was the workhorse, sending down 55 overs for 97 runs in the South African first innings, but the game took too long to move forward and, with stoppages for rain and an obdurate 76 by Geoff Boycott, it ended in another draw, the most notable feature of which was a century – his only one in 41 Tests – by the South African captain Trevor Goddard. When he was on 99, he played the ball just wide of Tom and set off for the sharpest of singles. "I picked up the ball," Tom says, "and I threw it side on at the wicket and I missed by a whisker. I almost ran him out for 99 – and forever I've been glad that I didn't. He was such a nice man. I'm glad he got a hundred."

Before the final Test there was a match against a South African Invitation XI at Cape Town, and for a while it looked as if the MCC tourists might be forced to follow on. Needing 288 to avoid this, Tom found himself at the wicket with number eleven Robin Hobbs, with 24 more to be scored, and they added a flamboyant 62, a triumph for two of the tour's neglected men.

'Each man batted attractively and well,' the South African writer Charles Fortune wrote. 'Cartwright always looks a good batsman but, bowling as much as he does, he tends to let his concentration wane.'

"I could still bat when the situation required it," Tom says. "But bowling so much, I wasn't selfish in my batting so I didn't get as many runs each year as I might have done."

Robin Hobbs had spent most of the tour on the sidelines, but he had not wasted his time, finding a South African girl, Izzie, whom he would soon enough marry, losing the bet he had placed with Tom on the plane flying out to Kenya. "I can still see her the first time he brought her back," Tom says, starting to describe what she was wearing – "dark slacks, a dark top" – before a thought causes him to break off: "Now I think of it, he's never paid up, you know."

"I don't know about that," Robin retorts, fighting back his laughter as he recalls the lack of success of their later association in Wales. "I think, after being persuaded by him to go down to Glamorgan to captain them, he owes me a bloody fortune!"

A young Barry Richards, playing for the Invitation XI, hits Tom for four
Later he was lbw Cartwright, 25

In the Invitation XI's second innings at Cape Town, Tom's knee flared up again, the remnants of his old football injury, compounding an injury crisis in which John Price, David Brown and Bob Barber were already doubtful for the final Test that was starting in three days' time.

The Invitation XI set MCC an improbable 428 for victory and, with three hours of playing time remaining, the tourists were on the verge of defeat at

100 for seven when Tom stepped out to join Mike Smith in the middle. 'It is always exciting to end the unbeaten record of a touring side,' John Woodcock wrote in *The Times*, and 'the Invitation XI played unquestionably the better cricket in this match – but Warwickshire held them at bay.'

CAPE TOWN, 9 FEBRUARY.

MCC, 205 FOR SEVEN. MJK SMITH, NOT OUT 78. TW CARTWRIGHT, NOT OUT 42.

'Cartwright played well enough,' wrote John Woodcock, 'to suggest that, even if he is unfit to bowl at Port Elizabeth, he might win a place with his batting. Not for a long time has he played so well.'

In the event England opted to open the batting with the reserve keeper John Murray and to call up Somerset's Ken Palmer, who was coaching in Johannesburg. The Test ended in a fourth successive draw, and the tourists returned to England unbeaten. The cricket had not always been exciting, but they had mostly had a good time.

"It was a happy tour," Tom sums up. "A happy bunch of people. Good management. Good captain."

Mike Brearley stayed in Africa. He had met up with Sir Cyril Hawker, Chairman of the Standard Bank and a future President of MCC. Both were old boys of the City of London School, and Hawker took the young man under his wing, happy to debate with him the political situation in South Africa.

"He believed in gradualism. He had this theory that British business would open things up and that democracy would come that way, and I said that I didn't believe it. So he said, 'I'll put a car and a driver at your disposal at the end of the tour, and you can go wherever you like, meet whoever you want to. And see if you don't agree with me afterwards.'"

For three weeks Mike Brearley travelled across the country. He met Nationalist MPs; he met radicals. He visited Swaziland, Basutoland and the Transkei. He visited a township – "It was illegal, I think. I do remember getting scared of all the dogs barking" – and he had lunch with Alan Paton, author of *Cry My Beloved Country*. "We talked about future tours, and I said something about not knowing the consequences, how one can know whether the impact will be for the better or the worse. And eventually he said – and I always remember this – 'You can never know the consequences of what you do. Sometimes you have to do things because you think they're right – or because you think it's wrong to do the other thing.' It was a good lesson."

"At that time," Tom says, "I held the same view as most people in cricket. I thought it was good to go out there, to make contact with people, to make them aware of what the rest of the world was like. I'd met a lot of people on my two trips there, and I thought that was important. It was only in 1968, with all the things that happened with the selection for that tour, that I changed my view."

The world moves on

Tom and Joan in Neath, enjoying the company of their local MP and his father

The summer of 1965 was a mixed one for Tom. It was the first time two touring teams had shared the Test match schedule, and Tom played in one Test against each of them. In late May he was in the England team that overwhelmed the New Zealanders at Edgbaston, but an injury the following week saw his place for the next game at Lord's go to a young John Snow. When he did return to county cricket, Tom made a quick hundred against the New Zealanders and bowled as well as ever, maintaining his position high in the national averages. So in early August, when the selectors anticipated a damp seamer's pitch at Trent Bridge for the second Test against the South Africans, he was recalled – and on the first day he enjoyed the highest point of his brief Test career.

The dampness, caused by torrential rain a few days earlier, seemed to have dried out when Peter van der Merwe, the South African captain, opted to bat first – but, under an overcast sky, his early batsmen struggled as soon as Tom took over from David Larter. 'His first two overs were maidens,' John Woodcock reported in *The Times*. 'In his third he had Lance leg-before with a ball which came back from the off and Lindsay caught at the wicket with the one that goes the other way.'

That was 16 for two. Then Tom had Barlow caught at slip, Parks stumped Bland off Titmus, and at one o'clock the South Africans were 43 for four – with 'Cartwright threatening total destruction.'

There followed one of the great Test innings, played by the 21-year-old left-hander Graeme Pollock, cautious at first and even edging Tom between keeper and slip early on, then after lunch unleashing shots in every direction and drawing comparisons with the great Frank Woolley. 'There is no one who holds Woolley in greater esteem than myself,' EW Swanton wrote, 'and I believe that he would have been proud, at his best, to have played as well as Pollock did this afternoon.'

'He held dominion where others foundered,' wrote John Woodcock. 'It was inspiration, as much as batting. I can think of no innings played against England since the war which was so critical and commanding. I can think of none more beautifully played.'

Pollock hit 125 out of the 162 runs scored while he was at the wicket, falling eventually to a slip catch off Tom, and was applauded loud and long as he returned to the pavilion.

For Tom the purist, there were too many balls hit in the air through gaps for it to be an outstanding innings technically – "I thought he had a shade of luck on his side" – but he has no doubt that, in its context, it was a truly great innings: "He was in a position where it was hit or bust, the challenge was there and he met it. Cricket is about imposing your will on the man 22 yards away, and that confrontation between him and me that day was really brilliant. In a way it's why you play cricket, to have the excitement of challenges like that. It's like people who climb mountains; they always want to climb a higher one. And that challenge, it was a high point in my life. You get a real tingling feeling from moments like that."

After Pollock's dismissal, Richard Dumbrill hit the ball hard back to Tom. "I dived for a caught and bowled, and I didn't quite get it. And I dislocated my thumb, the one I used as a rudder with the ball. I pulled it back into place, but the nerve made an involuntary movement and it leapt out again. So I pulled it a second time, and I held it for a couple of minutes. It was very painful, but there was no way I was going to go off."

In due course Tom took two more wickets, finishing the innings with six for 94 off 31.3 overs, but immediately he was driven to hospital by Doug Insole, now chairman of selectors. His thumb was by now badly swollen, and an x-ray revealed a double fracture. He had bowled his last ball in Test cricket.

The tour that winter was to Australia, and many thought that Tom's style of bowling would be ineffective out there. In any case, he did not want two winters in a row away from his family. "When I'd been in South Africa, Jane had been ill, and it was a lot to do with my not being there. I'd had a great deal to do with her in her first weeks, because Joan was ill from the birth, so we were very close. I remember driving with Mike Smith to the Test at Trent Bridge, just when the possibilities of the tour were looming. And I told him I didn't want to go. I'm not sure I'd have been picked, anyway."

England at Trent Bridge 1965

Standing *(left to right)*: Fred Titmus, Peter Parfitt, Bob Barber, John Snow, David Larter, Tom Cartwright, Geoff Boycott, Dennis Amiss (twelfth man)

Sitting: Jim Parks, Colin Cowdrey, Mike Smith, Ken Barrington

Tom had made his Test debut twelve months earlier on a batting paradise at Old Trafford. His tour of South Africa had been plagued by injury. Now at Trent Bridge he had found conditions to his suiting, and he had returned his best Test figures – in a contest with one of the greatest batsmen of the post-war era.

T.W. Cartwright, five Tests, 15 wickets at an average of 36.26.

Now it was back to twelve more years on the county circuit.

"I really loved playing county cricket. I loved everything that went with it, the interaction with the other players, the warmth of the people who came to watch and their love of the game. I was always happy in the county game, and to get paid to do it was incredible.

"It was an achievement to play for England. It was something I set out to do, and I would have liked to have played more – not for the glory of winning Test caps but so that I would have experienced more challenges like that one against Graeme Pollock. Something like that, it takes you up to a real high and it's hard to come down from it afterwards."

ENGLAND v SOUTH AFRICA

Trent Bridge. 5, 6, 7 &9 August 1965

SOUTH AFRICA WON BY 94 RUNS

SOUTH AFRICA

E.J. Barlow	c Cowdrey b Cartwright	19	(4) b Titmus	76
H.R. Lance	lbw Cartwright	7	c Barlow b Snow	0
D.T. Lindsay +	c Parks b Cartwright	0	(1) c Cowdrey b Larter	9
R.G. Pollock	c Cowdrey b Cartwright	125	(5) c Titmus b Larter	59
K.C. Bland	st Parks b Titmus	1	(6) b Snow	10
A. Bacher	b Snow	12	(3) lbw Larter	67
P.L. van der Merwe *	run out	38	c Parfitt b Larter	4
R. Dumbrill	c Parfitt b Cartwright	30	b Snow	13
J.T. Botten	c Parks b Larter	10	b Larter	18
P.M. Pollock	c Larter b Cartwright	15	*not out*	12
A.H. McKinnon	*not out*	8	b Titmus	9
Extras	lb 4	4	*b4, lb 5, nb 3*	12
		269		**289**

1-16, 2-16, 3-42, 4-43, 5-80, 6-178, 7-221, 8-242, 9-252, 10-269
1-2, 2-35, 3-134, 4-193, 5-228, 6-232, 7-243, 8-265, 9-269, 10-289

Larter	17	6	25	1	29	7	68	5
Snow	22	6	63	1	33	6	83	3
Cartwright	31.3	9	94	6				
Titmus	22	8	44	1	19.4	5	46	2
Barber	9	3	39	0	3	0	20	0
Boycott					26	10	60	0

ENGLAND

G. Boycott	c Lance b P. Pollock	0	b McKinnon	16
R.W. Barber	c Bacher b Dumbrill	41	c Lindsay b P. Pollock	1
K.F. Barrington	b P. Pollock	1	(5) c Lindsay b P. Pollock	1
F.J. Titmus	c R. Pollock b McKinnon	20	(3) c Lindsay b McKinnon	4
M.C. Cowdrey	c Lindsay b Botten	105	(6) st Lindsay b McKinnon	20
P.H. Parfitt	c Dumbrill b P. Pollock	18	(7) b P. Pollock	86
M.J.K. Smith *	b P. Pollock	32	(8) lbw R. Pollock	24
J.M. Parks +	c & b Botten	6	(9) *not out*	44
J.A. Snow	run out	3	(4) b Botten	0
J.D.F. Larter	b P. Pollock	2	(11) c Merwe b P. Pollock	10
T.W. Cartwright	*not out*	1	(10) lbw P. Pollock	0
Extras	b 1, lb 3, w 1, nb 6	11	*lb 5, w 2, nb 11*	18
		240		**224**

1-0, 2-8, 3-63, 4-67, 5-133, 6-225, 7-229, 8-236, 9-238, 10-240
1-1, 2-10, 3-10, 4-13, 5-41, 6-59, 7-114, 8-207, 9-207, 10-224

P. Pollock	23.5	8	53	5	24	15	34	5
Botten	23	5	60	2	19	5	58	1
McKinnon	28	11	54	1	27	12	50	3
Dumbrill	18	3	60	1	16	4	40	0
R. Pollock	1	0	2	0	5	2	4	1
Barlow					11	1	20	0

Umpires: C.S. Elliott and J.F. Crapp

123

CHAPTER 12

ON BOWLING

Bowlers can only operate in the conditions which they are given – and in county cricket in the 1960s and early 1970s, played over three days on uncovered pitches, with lighter bats than today and longer boundaries, Tom was a supreme operator.

He bowled at medium pace – not more than the low 70s on today's speed guns – and he did enough in the air and off the wicket, both in to the batsman and away, to pose problems wherever he bowled. He was an English bowler, but then they were English conditions in which he was asked to bowl.

The bowler with whom he is most commonly compared is Hampshire's Derek Shackleton, who took 100 wickets in every season from 1949 to 1968, a man of metronomic accuracy who seemed happy to bowl all day. John Arlott's description of 'Shack' could equally be of Tom:

> It does take a cricketer fully to appreciate his bowling; certainly every worthwhile batsman in England recognises it. 'Shack' does not make an instant, spectacular impression on the casual watcher by immense pace, violent spin – nor by extravagant gestures or posing. He gets on with the job of beating and deceiving batsmen, or – at worst, on an absolutely plumb wicket – of keeping them on a tight rein.

The similarities were many, but there were significant differences, too, as Mike Brearley saw clearly from the batsman's end:

> Shackleton floated up to the wicket and seemed not to do very much, he just sort of waved his arm, whereas Tom came up with a much more determined stride and you would see the effort that went in. He really hit the bat, high on the bat. Shack seemed to caress the ball, and the ball seemed to caress the pitch, whereas Tom seemed to hit the pitch, hit the bat. Shack ran in a little canter, whereas Tom bounced in and meant business from the start.

The wicket-keeper Brian Timms moved from Hampshire to Warwickshire and kept to each of them:

> Shack was brilliant. His record speaks for itself. But he just bowled line and length; he didn't think about it that much. He might vary his angle to the crease, but he would always bowl with the seam up. Tom, though, would change his grip, drag his hands across the seam to bowl a leg-cutter or an off-cutter. He had the wrist action, and he'd really dig it in. He would give you more on a wicket that was slower. He was more of a thinking bowler than Shack.

Alan Smith was Tom's regular wicket-keeper for most of the time he was a bowler at Warwickshire:

> Tom was the finest bowler of his type in England. He was quicker than Derek Shackleton, and he made the ball bounce more. He hit the bat high up. And he was hitting the seam all the time. Even on flat wickets he could make the ball deviate a bit off the seam. His action was a model one, and he was very accurate. But he was no great pace, and he didn't bowl bouncers. He might have bowled three all the time we played together. It's hard to think of a bowler like him these days. A slower version of McGrath, perhaps.

Jack Bannister observed at close quarters how Tom's bowling evolved within county cricket, where the batsmen all tried to find ways to outwit the emerging bowlers:

> It was like a game of chess. People like Eric Russell and Brian Bolus worked him out for a while. But Tom developed such control of the hand action that he could alter the position of his feet and bowl the away swinger from chest on. He learned how to drop his feet in all sorts of positions.

Tom never took the new ball, preferring to come on after men like Jack had had an opening burst:

> We'd go down to somewhere like Swansea, bowl on a white strip, and they'd be 58 for one with bugger all happening. Then Tom would come on. He'd be nidging away for about 20 overs, and he'd finish with five for 31.

The figures were sometimes more impressive than that.

SWANSEA, 9-11 AUGUST 1967.

BANNISTER, NOUGHT FOR 12. BLENKIRON, NOUGHT FOR 16.

CARTWRIGHT, 29 OVERS, 12 MAIDENS, 50 RUNS, 8 WICKETS.

SECOND INNINGS:

BANNISTER, THREE FOR 40. BLENKIRON, NOUGHT FOR 11.

CARTWRIGHT, 17.3 OVERS, 4 MAIDENS, 39 RUNS, 7 WICKETS.

Bill Blenkiron was a brickyard labourer's son from near Bishop Auckland, seven years younger than Tom, and at this stage he was still trying to establish himself in the Warwickshire side:

> Tom was my idol. Everybody else used to bowl. Then Tom would come on, and it was a different game. He didn't have a long run-up, and he wasn't that quick, but he did so much with the ball. He hit the seam regularly, that was the secret, and he had a very high action. Hand grenades, he used to bowl.

Peter Roebuck watched Tom at Somerset towards the end of his career:

> The ball moved two ways. That was the problem. It might swing a bit away, not violently, then come back off the seam, or it might come in and go away. Only two or three inches. But it meant that you couldn't line him up. That's why great attacking players like Kanhai and Sobers couldn't take him on, because the odds weren't there. The only guys who could take him on were village hitters, because they didn't know anything about odds.

He recalls a Sunday League match at Taunton in August 1971, when Somerset were top of the table, dreaming of their first trophy, and Nottinghamshire – captained by Gary Sobers – were the visitors:

> Sobers came in at number three; they needed runs, and he just played Tom out. Then he whacked the other bowlers around. Sobers was a truly great batsman, but even he didn't try to take Tom on. That sort of thing happened week after week.

TAUNTON, 8 AUGUST 1971.

G.S. SOBERS, NOT OUT 73.

CARTWRIGHT, 8 OVERS, 4 MAIDENS, 11 RUNS, 1 WICKET.

> Tom would work the batsman over. Patiently, over a long period of time he'd set him up, move him around the crease, just little things here and there, very subtle. McGrath is a bit like that. Dravid said of McGrath that he makes you play the game on his terms. And that's what Tom did to a great extent.

> And if he got on a broken wicket he was lethal. The seam would be so high and he'd be hitting the pitch so relentlessly, ball after ball, that he'd make his own worn patch. Then he'd bowl into it, and the ball would go all over the place.

Some people have said that such bowling is dull and negative, but Mike Brearley agrees with neither sentiment:

> It isn't dull, if you know what you're watching: to see the batsman reduced to not knowing whether to go forward or back, not knowing whether to play the leg side or the off side, fretting to see how he's going to score his next run. What's boring is if the batsman is hitting every ball defensively in the middle of the bat, when there isn't a problem. Cricket can be boring if the batsman's in charge. In my view, as a spectacle, it's less boring if the bowlers are on top.

> And Tom wasn't negative at all. He bowled with his own particular field. He had no fine leg, no third man, because he bowled so straight. But he had one or two short-legs, two or three slips and a gully. And

you felt you could never get him away – or get away from him.

It wasn't easy batting against him. He hit the seam, he swung the ball and, if you made half a mistake blocking it out, you got a thin edge onto your pad and you were caught. Most great batsmen don't like being pegged down like that.

Brian Langford:

It's all about pressure. To create pressure, you've got to have disciplined bowlers – and with Tom you always had that at one end. One hundred per cent.

Alec Bedser, writing in 1968:

To many eyes, unless you bowl fast, with a cordon of often wasted slip and leg fielders, or spin with the wrist, you are not considered an attacking bowler. Tom, given the conditions, is most certainly a fine attacking bowler – and a very economical one, too.

Mike Smith, also writing in 1968:

Had he turned in the same performances as a spinner, he would have been praised to high heaven. But for me he will usually have shown more artistry than the spinner – and certainly more ability.

Mike Smith, now:

You can't consider it a negative form of attack if a bloke's bowling with four close catchers beside the wicket-keeper. And sometimes he would have five.

Vic Marks:

Tom would often bowl with nobody on the boundary at all. He was landing it in the right place, time and time and time again. That's not negative. That's skill. I used to think Curtly Ambrose was an extension of Tom, taller and speeded up a bit. He had a classical action, and he didn't strive for pace. He had the same metronomic quality.

It wasn't Tom or Shackleton who created dull cricket. On uncovered pitches you had to have that accuracy; you needed to be a machine. And in the modern game the bowlers have lost that.

Peter Roebuck:

He wouldn't find it so easy if he were playing today. Every bowler struggles more than they did then. The batsmen might try to play him differently, because they might try to take their life in their hands more – as modern youth do – but he'd have a lot of good ideas. There's no reason to suppose that he wouldn't trouble great players still. He was a master craftsman, and they're few and far between in this age. What else is McGrath? And Pollock? They understand the mechanics of movement, and movement is still the key to bowling.

Vic Marks:

I'd love to see somebody like Tom bowling today in the one-day internationals, bowling the middle overs that people like Collingwood bowl. He wouldn't take one for 15, he'd take more like four for 40; but he'd still get wickets.

Mike Brearley:

In Test cricket there's always been a bias in favour of pace. I thought Tom should have played for England a lot more.

Vic Marks was at the Rose Bowl, Southampton, for a Twenty20 match in the competition's first summer, and the umpire Merv Kitchen – an old Somerset team-mate – was wired up to the Sky Television commentator David Lloyd to add an extra dimension for the viewers:

The ball was jagging around on the pitch, and David Lloyd said, 'Merv, who do you think would bowl well on this?' Hoping he'd say somebody like Flintoff or McGrath. It's 20-over cricket, you're looking for the young audience. 'Oooh,' Merv said in his broad Somerset accent. 'Tom Cartwright.'

*

"If you want to learn how to bowl," Tom says, "you've got to learn control. Because it's only when you're in control that you develop the peripheral vision, the peripheral awareness, to understand what's happening and to learn from it. If you're in control, you can recognise what you're doing and what the batsman's doing – and you can teach yourself. If you're only striving for control, you can't do that.

"If you're not in control, your first two overs can go for a lot of runs, and you can spend the rest of your spell trying to redress that, literally trying to mend something that you've broken. So you'll be bowling deliveries to repair what's gone before, not to attack and take wickets. If you've got the thing right in the first place, if you're in control, then you're in a far better position.

"If you have a skill, it's not sufficient to produce it now and then. You have to repeat, repeat, repeat. Success is repetition. Some bowlers will bowl an unplayable ball, but they can't repeat it. They don't know how it's happened. The trick is to read your mind's eye, know your hand position, that's the key.

"Jack Bannister was one of the driving forces in my development, being conscious of how much he put into thinking and talking about bowling. It sparked it off in me. You can be in dressing rooms with all kinds of people and, if there's somebody who has a gift to talk like that, you can either walk away or you can listen. And if they can make you see things that are happening, then you can get a better idea of what it means to be successful.

"In the end I could change my hand position and bowl an out-swinger with a pronounced in-swing action and an in-swinger with a pronounced out-swing action. And of course once my reputation grew, people treated me differently.

"Cricket is about imposing your will. You've got a batter, you've got a bowler, and halfway you've got a gain-line. If you're bowling, you have to impose your will beyond that gain-line. And the batsman is trying to do the same. And you don't do it by sledging, you do it by body language and by the sheer ability to be in control of what you're doing. If people have that understanding and they have the ability to impose themselves, they're going to get to the top.

"It's not defensive to bowl with control. The person who can control his skills can be more attacking, more devastating than the other type of bowler.

"I do believe that every bowler has an optimum speed and, once you go above that, you lose control. You have to discover your optimum speed. If you can find that, you can develop.

"There's so much emphasis on speed now, and more and more bowlers are not bowling the ball; they're running up and hurling it. So they haven't learnt control. Somewhere along the line people have got to put their hands up and say, 'We brought this on ourselves.' I think it came from the great West Indian team of the 1980s. We became obsessed with finding fast bowlers. And also from this flaming machine that measures speed. You've got bowlers all trying to bowl at 90, 95 miles an hour. And if you watch them, they're hurling the ball; they're not getting up there and bowling it.

"I think bowlers should bowl as much as possible. That's how they'll learn. I feel sorry for the young bowlers today. There are no short cuts or easy ways. They need to be bowling, out in the middle in matches.

"I don't think they should do weight-training. You want long, loose muscles, not short, fat ones. Wes Hall used to say, 'You don't need to be strong to bowl fast; you need to be loose.'

"An hour in a gym isn't the same preparation for bowling as a nine-hour day working on a farm field or down a mine or even in a heavy-industry factory. You may have a similar energy output, but you don't build up the same core strength – so you haven't developed the ability to keep your concentration when the body is starting to get tired, when the physical stress it can exert is in decline. There's an important relationship between physical stress and concentration. It's difficult in the modern world to replicate the preparation for bowling that people had when they walked everywhere and there was more manual work. Doing a lot more bowling is part of what's needed, but it would be hugely beneficial if young bowlers went off and spent winters doing hard, physical work. It would build their core strength, and that's irreplaceable by anything else.

"We brought sports science into cricket. It's like sponsorship and marketing. It started out as a welcome element of support, and it's come to dominate. People are afraid of science. I am in some ways. They're afraid to question it; you can get slaughtered in an argument if you oppose it. So something that may have a worthwhile place takes over, and everything gets turned upside down."

Tom has spent a lifetime in cricket. He has received the wisdom of generations before him – from Tom Dollery and Eric Hollies who played before the war, from Tiger Smith who played before the first war – but his views are somehow of little worth alongside the latest scientific theory. "If you're arguing from experience, it's only an opinion. But when they're arguing from science, they're always on safer ground.

"About twelve years ago there was a study at Alsager College about mixed actions, bowlers who they believe have developed bad backs from not having their shoulders and hips properly aligned. There are so many people doing these sports studies courses and, when they get employed, because they're not confident of their own background, they feel they have to justify their jobs. So now we've got a situation where every Tom, Dick and Harry who turns up on a coaching course is told about mixed actions, and they go back to their clubs full of it. They see a kid bowl, and the first thing they're looking for is a mixed action. 'You can't bowl like that, son,' they say. 'You've got to bowl chest on.' It's good to be knowledgeable, but I think you should start by saying to the lad, 'Let's get a bit higher in the action' and see if he can land sideways. There are huge benefits to being side on. If he can't do it, then go back to the midway.

"More and more bowlers are bowling chest on. You can't get as close in to the stumps, the front arm doesn't disguise the bowling arm at all, and you lose the body action which creates lateral movement. It's much easier as a batsman to pick up the rhythm from a bowler bowling chest on.

"If you watch people when they land sideways on and their foot lands parallel to the crease, there is a cushioning effect. It's almost like a car suspension; it absorbs. When you're chest on, there's no give because your back foot hits and you're straight over.

"The change in the no ball law had a huge effect. When fast bowlers landed on the back foot, and they dragged it forward, there was quite a long gap between the two feet landing. The body had time to open up and turn in the air before the front foot landed – so there was time for it to align itself better.

"I can't believe what goes on. At the Somerset Academy they had people they stopped bowling for a whole winter. There have always been people with indeterminate actions. Lindwall and Trueman were classical, but most people have been halfway. It's not something that's just come about. My belief is that it's not the actions that cause the problems; it's bowling above optimum speed."

Hardly has Tom spoken his mind about modern bowling than the Ashes series starts in Australia. Steve Harmison is given the new ball, not having bowled in a first-class match for three months. He runs in, straining for extra pace, delivers the ball chest on, and it hits second slip.

"What can you say?" Tom says wearily. "What a way to start!" Then he breaks into a chuckle. "Can you imagine what would have happened if he'd been a Formula One driver? He'd have demolished the grandstand."

CHAPTER 13
SIXTY WICKETS IN A MONTH
1966 – 1968

The years of 1966 and 1967 saw Tom settled into a rhythm of life: summer on the county circuit, winter in the Indoor School with Tiger Smith. There were no calls from England, and there were no significant injuries.

In 1966, in a summer in which only the bowler was allowed to polish the ball, he took 100 wickets for the fifth successive year, and he was in the Warwickshire side that played against Worcestershire in the Gillette Cup final.

Tom with Peter the Lord's cat on the eve of the final
(left to right): Tom Cartwright, John Jameson, David Brown, Alan Smith,
Rudi Webster, Dennis Amiss, Eddie Legard, Ray Hitchcock

Only the previous day Worcestershire had narrowly missed out on winning their third championship title in a row, and on a sunny morning they sought to put their disappointment behind them by batting first. Their captain Don Kenyon opened with Martin Horton, and they had reached 33 without alarm when misfortune struck.

"Don pulled a ball from Rudi Webster for four," Tom says, "and, after he'd finished the shot, he slipped onto his wicket. They kept changing the law on hit wicket, whether it was out or not if you had completed your shot, and he stood for a second or two, then walked. He was at the pavilion end, I was at slip and, as he reached me, he said, 'I'm not sure I should have walked for that.' I said, 'It's a bit late now.' It was an important wicket for us. He was a good player when he got going."

Tom came on to bowl, and his 12 overs went for 16 runs. He bowled Martin Horton, had Alan Ormrod caught behind and, in his final over, the last before lunch, took the vital wicket of Tom Graveney, caught bat-pad by Ibadulla: "Billy dived to his left and took it one-handed." Worcestershire were 88 for six and, though Norman Gifford hit a few blows, the game never quite came to life after that. Bob Barber led the way to victory with a well-judged 66, and he won the Man of the Match award from Peter May, who was now an England selector. "I'd have given it to you," his fellow selector Don Kenyon told Tom.

"Winning the Gillette Cup wasn't a huge deal," Tom says. "I'm not sure people valued it that much; they had a more balanced view about cricket then. It reminded me of when I was playing in Coventry. We had a league game on Saturday; then one evening in the week we'd play a 20-over match and it was just a bit of fun."

The summer of 1967 was Mike Smith's last as captain, and the county struggled, particularly with its bowling. Rudi Webster was no longer available, Jack Bannister was 37 in August, David Brown was sometimes playing for England, sometimes injured, and Bill Blenkiron did not progress as quickly as had been hoped. Among the slow bowlers Ronnie Miller had not been re-engaged, Bob Barber was only playing occasionally and the West Indies' off-spinner Lance Gibbs was still completing his residential qualification.

More than ever, the county relied on Tom, and on the morning of Wednesday 9 August, taking the field at the St Helen's ground in Swansea, he was – as he always was in these years – high in the national averages. So far that summer, despite a new regulation which allowed no-one at all to polish the ball, he had bowled 811.1 overs and taken 86 wickets at an average of 17.10.

At Swansea Tom took 15 wickets in the match, equalling Sam Hargeave's Warwickshire record, set in 1903. Kevin Lyons, later to coach with Tom, was a fresh-faced 20-year-old, trying to establish himself as a batsman in the Glamorgan eleven, and he remembers how the senior players prepared him for his first encounter with Tom. "They were all saying, 'You're not going to get a run off him, he never bowls a bad ball.' And you're thinking to yourself, 'This is some sort of monster who's dropped out of the sky.' But when I got out to the middle, it was easy to appreciate what they were talking about."

Curiously the former Worcestershire wicket-keeper Hugo Yarnold was umpiring in that match, just as he had been umpiring at Nuneaton when Tom made his 210 and at Weston-super-Mare when he turned in his best-ever innings figures of eight for 39.

Hugo was a great admirer of Tom, as he made clear in Tom's benefit leaflet the following summer:

> Tom Cartwright is a modest man. ... His modesty is linked with his happiness on his good days – for he is a sensitive man who feels keenly anything which could be regarded as a failure – and the kicks are met with unusual courage which makes him more than unflinchingly kind and honest. ... First-class cricket reveals a man to his fellow players, and it would be hard to find a player who is better liked and respected than Tom Cartwright.

And Tom was very fond of Hugo: "He used to make me laugh a lot. He was always talking about football. He was a very small man, and he'd tell us he'd been a centre-forward and how he used to jump up in the box and nod the ball in. Also I think he'd been a bit of a rebel in his time. He fell out with Worcestershire at the end; when he left, he sent them back his wicket-keeping gloves through the post."

The wickets at Swansea were the start of an extraordinary 24 days for Tom:

			First innings				Second innings			
August 9-11	Swansea	Glamorgan	29	12	50	8	17.3	4	39	7
August 12-15	Edgbaston	Hampshire	20	6	46	1	9.4	7	6	5
August 16-18	Edgbaston	Yorkshire	32	15	46	3	25	16	26	4
August 19-21	Chesterfield	Derbyshire	21	10	31	3	34	11	85	0
August 23-25	Edgbaston	Somerset	31	9	76	6	33.5	10	63	5
August 26-29	Dover	Kent	41	19	103	7	16	3	60	3
Aug 30-Sept 1	Middlesbrough	Yorkshire	43.5	15	95	6	29	7	85	3

In seven matches Tom bowled 382.5 overs and took 61 wickets for 811 runs. He ended the season as the leading wicket-taker in England, with 147. His efforts in August leave him to this day as the last bowler to take 60 wickets in a calendar month.

"I always reckoned I was more likely to get people out late on in a season, when batters had got a few runs in the bank and were starting to play a few more shots. They were more adventurous, a little looser. So I would come with a bit of a rush from about halfway."

Those 24 days came at the end of a long summer of non-stop cricket and travel, with no week more tiring than the last one: Tuesday in Dover, where Kent beat them with just two minutes to spare, followed by Wednesday in Middlesbrough.

"It was very hot at Dover, we'd fielded all day, it was a hard slog and we lost the match right at the end. Somebody set the showers off, and we just ran through them. It was like a day at school, when the kids all run through the showers. We were throwing on our shirts and ties. I can see us now getting into taxis to the station, and they held the train up. We were half-dressed."

"It was Bank Holiday Tuesday," Alan Smith remembers. "There were all these people coming back from the continent. It would have been impossible to have created a worse journey for us."

"We had to go across London and up to Darlington," Tom says. "We stayed the night there, opposite a night club that was still going strong at four in the morning. Then we had to get up early to catch the train to Middlesbrough, then get in taxis to take us to the ground.

"David Cook had opened the bowling in Dover. The last of the amateurs. He'd gone off on his own in his two-seater sports car. And, when we got to Middlesbrough, we got this message that he wasn't feeling well and had gone home."

Warwickshire lost the toss. Tom, who had bowled the last ball at Dover the previous day, was forced to bowl the first ball of the morning to Geoff Boycott and on a slow, turning pitch, against a Yorkshire team pressing for the championship title, he sent down 43.5 overs in the day. 'His length was immaculate,' AA Thomson wrote in *The Times*, 'and his power to lift the ball uncanny. Every ball needed lynx-like attention, and such is the smooth economy of his action that he looks capable of going on forever.'

In fact, by this stage of his career, Tom had developed a chronic shoulder problem. He could bring the arm over to bowl without difficulty but, when he raised the same arm out sideways, he could not get it above the horizontal. Perhaps, in his desire to bowl, he had over-worked the joint. Whatever the reason, he would hit more serious problems with it the following summer.

The match at Middlesbrough was played against the backdrop of another controversy in English cricket. A fortnight earlier Yorkshire, led by the England captain Brian Close, had been at Edgbaston and, in the closing minutes, a young John Jameson looked like leading the home team to victory in an exciting run chase. If Yorkshire could somehow prevent the victory, they would get two points for the draw, points that might prove vital in the final championship reckoning and, with no requirement to bowl a set number of overs in the final hour, their play grew slower and slower. The ground was damp, there was drizzle in the air, and vital time was spent drying the ball, engaging in long consultations, resetting the field and walking slowly back to the bowling mark. Fred Trueman made his final over last six minutes, and it contained two no balls and three bouncers. 'In the end,' *The Times* reported, 'even some of the Yorkshire side seemed to be hanging their heads in shame.'

"The ball was taking an age to get back to the bowler," Tom says, "but it was the sort of thing that was going on in other games at that time. They probably carried it a bit further – but not that much. There was a game the next week against Somerset, and I remember sitting in the dressing room, thinking it wasn't that dissimilar."

YORKSHIRE 24 OVERS IN 98 MINUTES OF PLAY: 14 OVERS 4 BALLS AN HOUR.
SOMERSET 42 OVERS IN 170 MINUTES OF PLAY: 14 OVERS 5 BALLS AN HOUR.

"It wouldn't have happened in the days of the amateur captains. They were more independent from the committees; there wasn't the same pressure on them to get results."

The Yorkshire match ended in a draw, with John Jameson on a run-a-minute 36 not out that included a massive straight six off Tony Nicholson. "It was such a pity that John's innings got overshadowed. He was young, he took them on and he deserved a better ending."

To add to the rumpus, there was a kerfuffle in front of the pavilion. A member attempted to obstruct Brian Close and, in the words of Tom, "Fred weighed in as the saviour of all things, the peace-maker." The man in question, a businessman Alf Myers, had distinctive black hair; another man at the match, with similar hair and sitting upstairs, was Tom's first second-eleven captain Cyril Goodway, who was now a Vice-President. "When Cyril was driving home, this car came up tight behind him, another one swerved in front and a photographer jumped out and started taking pictures. When the story was splashed all over *The People*, they had all these pictures of Cyril."

By the time of the return game at Middlesbrough the England captaincy had passed back to Colin Cowdrey. "Closey wouldn't have been everybody's choice as England captain. I suppose, if it had been a spook programme on television, you'd have said it had been set up deliberately."

There was no ill feeling between the teams at Middlesbrough. Brian Close hit a gutsy 98, and Yorkshire's victory led to a championship title that was won by a larger margin than the 'two dishonourable points' at Edgbaston.

Tom had a break of only three weeks before he was back in action. Warwickshire had organised a four-week tour of East Africa, and a party of 45 – including wives, girl friends and supporters – flew out. Among them were Tom and Joan, who had left Jane and Jeremy with Tom's family in Coventry.

Tom has many happy memories of the trip:

Of Mike Smith the captain and tour manager: "We had a pre-tour meeting at Edgbaston where he went through the itinerary. And he seemed to be reading from the back of an envelope. He was peering at it, turning it up one way, then the other. Then, when we got out there, he kept scribbling the arrangements on bits of paper and losing them. But of course it all ran without a single problem. He was almost an invisible manager – and, when you look at all the people they have now on tours, it does make you wonder."

Of the match against an African XI at the Logogo Stadium in Kampala:

"There was a downpour in the night. When we got there, we thought there was no chance of playing. The murram was like mud. But they poured kerosene over it and lit a match. A great plume of cloud went up, just like an atom bomb. They put down the mat, and we played the game. They didn't have much in the way of equipment, and we left them bats, boots, all kinds of things."

Of his stay in Uganda with the Harbottles, whom he had got to know on his previous visit: "Moira worked at Makerere University, and we met up socially with some of her African students. It was obvious that Uganda was much more advanced in integration than Kenya. The relationship between the Europeans and the Africans was very different. It was such a pity when that idiot Idi Amin came into power, and it all went wrong."

Of bowling in Kenya: "Mombassa on the coast was like Durban. You could get it to swing when the tide was right. But Nairobi is several thousand feet up, and the air is very rarified. You could throw the ball in from the boundary, and it would travel much further. But it still swung when you bowled."

Of the long journeys: "With the MCC we flew from Kenya to Uganda, but this time we went everywhere over land. We did a long coach journey – I can still see John Jameson on the roof, tying all the luggage down – then we split into small groups in mini-buses. Our driver was John Three; he was always hustling us and Billy Ibadulla got annoyed with him. He'd learnt a bit of Swahili, and he called him 'a cheeky fupi'."

Of Roger Edmonds, the off-spinner who had as much success with the ball as Lance Gibbs: "He was a quick off-spinner, a bit like Don Shepherd. A good cricketer. He never really got the opportunities at Warwickshire that he should have done. Probably I was to blame. He needed to bowl a lot, and perhaps I was bowling some of his overs. But he had a very successful career as a teacher, and he went out to Kenya at one point. So the tour must have set him off on something that was good for him."

Of camping in the foothills of Mount Kilimanjaro: "There were monkeys above you in the trees, and you could hear all the roars and trumpetings all round. We had a biggish tent for a dining room, and there was a fire outside that was kept going all night, to keep the big game away. You got the odd clown outside your tent, making growling noises – David Brown was the main suspect – and I remember Lance Gibbs. What did he say?" Tom pauses to get the accent right. "Dis tent, man, will be biscuits and cheese to dem elephants."

And of his 123 in the three-day match against Kenya: "Charlie Elliott had come out with us to umpire, and we were five wickets down for not very many. He looked at me rather seriously. 'Somebody has got to take responsibility here, Tom.' That was my Test match hundred."

*

Tom, having won his county cap in 1958, was awarded a benefit in the summer of 1968 – and what a summer it turned out to be!

He was approaching his 33rd birthday and, in the view of most of the national press, his short England career was over. But, as Mike Smith wrote in Tom's benefit leaflet, this did not reflect the opinion of Tom that prevailed among those playing on the county circuit:

> Some players are described as *cricketers' cricketers*, the ones the players would pick in their sides. It would be interesting to know how many current players would have Tom in the England side this summer against Australia – a very high percentage I would suggest.
>
> His performances speak for themselves. What is not shown is the number of times he has played the vital part in an innings – the one who has dismissed the good players or broken the big partnership. In this day and age of denigrating the medium-pace seamer his ability has not received its true recognition.

Mike Smith had retired from cricket, passing the Warwickshire captaincy to the wicket-keeper Alan Smith, whose team included not only Lance Gibbs, his residential qualification completed, but also Gibbs' West Indian team-mate Rohan Kanhai, signed under a new regulation that allowed counties to play one overseas player.

In April of that year Enoch Powell delivered his 'rivers of blood' speech, heightening racial tension in the West Midlands. But, for Tom, there were no such problems in the world of cricket. "People used to talk about the good-natured Brummie. People get put off by the accent, but there's a genuine warmth there, and Lance and Rohan were very popular players. The disappointment was that we didn't get the West Indians into the ground to watch their fellow countrymen."

Alan Smith was a popular character on the county circuit. He was a good enough batsman to hit three first-class centuries, two in the same match, and his 1,201 runs in 1962 helped to win him a place on the boat to Australia where improbably he became England's first-choice keeper.

For purists who expect the keeper to be neat and unobtrusive, he was not a pretty sight: "I remember him standing up to me one day at Worcester," Tom says. "The ball was getting up a bit, and he always had difficulty turning his hands round. So it was hitting him in the chest and all sorts. You could hear his bones rattling. We had to keep standing him up and dusting him down. But he was a real trier. He had deficiencies in technique, but he had lots of courage and he put in so much effort. You could never fault him for that."

Alan Smith was also a handy medium-pace bowler. Twice on the East

African trip he took five wickets in an innings, and once at Clacton, when Rudi Webster was injured, he completed a hat-trick. Essex were going along easily at 28 for no wicket and, jettisoning his gloves, he took four wickets – Barker, Smith, Fletcher and Bailey – before he conceded a run.

As one contemporary put it a little unkindly, "As a batsman who bowled a bit, he wasn't a bad wicket-keeper."

A soccer blue at Oxford, he was an all-round sportsman with a good brain, though he and Tom were not of like mind politically. "In the early days he had a car to carry the bags in, and I used to go with him. He said, 'I've got to make a call at the Young Conservative Club. Do you want to come in?' I said, 'No, thanks. I'll sit in the car.'"

There was a fresh tactical edge to Warwickshire under Alan Smith's leadership, and Tom was soon among the wickets: taking five in an innings four times before May was out – though not at Middlesbrough, which this time involved a journey only from Chesterfield. Geoff Boycott hit an unflustered 180 not out, and Tom's 37 overs brought him no wickets for 54.

"I didn't mind bowling at him. He was a great battler, but he didn't take you apart. I talk a lot about bowlers having an optimum speed, but batters also have an optimum power. If they go above that, if they try to hit the ball too hard, it's fatal – and Geoff never did that. He was a master of himself. He played long innings, he learned while he was playing them and he came to know himself. And once you know yourself, you can deal with so much."

Yorkshire won by an innings, with Ray Illingworth returning match figures of ten for 71 in 38 overs. Meanwhile Lance Gibbs, who in time would pass Fred Trueman's record of 307 Test wickets, bowled 34 overs and took one for 91. "Illy was an English-type off-spinner, bowling to build pressure as Fred Titmus did, as all our bowlers did, but Lance had the mindset of a West Indian Test cricketer. He had a lovely high action, he spun it and he was full of variation and experiment; he was as likely as not to bowl a leg-break fifth ball of the over. In Test cricket that was fine – but it wasn't in county cricket, not on turning pitches like Middlesbrough. He never did come to terms with the need to be miserly, but it's probably better that he didn't. He might have been a duller person. I've played with a lot of lovely blokes in my years of cricket, but he really was special. He made it so much fun to play."

The following week at Edgbaston Tom took eleven Surrey wickets for 109 runs in 63.2 overs, and – to the surprise of the press more than his fellow players – he found himself, at the age of nearly 33, named in a fourteen-man England squad for the first Test against the Australians at Old Trafford.

CHAPTER 14

PICKED FOR SOUTH AFRICA AGAIN

1968

It was a difficult summer for the England selectors.

'At one time,' the Australian Bobby Simpson wrote, 'national selectors chose what they thought were the twelve best players in the country and sent them along to the venue. Once there, after a cursory glance at the wicket, they omitted one player. A simple procedure, and one that has worked since cricket began, but I am afraid that in this present computer age, where every move must be analysed to the most minute detail, this process was too simple for the England selectors. The answer to confuse everyone – and I am sure the players themselves – was to announce that they would take a squad of fourteen players to Manchester and announce the eleven on the morning of the match.'

John Woodcock in *The Times* offered a more sympathetic explanation for the large squad: 'Amiss is included in case Barrington, whose back is troubling him, should be unfit. Cartwright will get a game if the pitch is green, Underwood if it looks like being wet.'

When Barrington's back did not improve, however, Bob Barber was summoned to Manchester. Now a businessman playing cricket part-time, he had appeared in only four matches so far in the summer, with a yield of 54 runs and three wickets, and he insists that he only turned up on the understanding that he was not going to play. "Alan Knott asked me to bowl to him in the nets," he remembers, "and I said, 'I don't feel like it.' He told me afterwards that he thought I was a very strange character. Then half an hour before the start, Alec Bedser said, 'You're playing.'"

The three men left out were all bowlers, Derek Underwood, David Brown and Tom, leaving an attack of Snow and Higgs with the new ball, Pat Pocock for off-spin and Basil D'Oliveira and Bob Barber, neither of them front-line bowlers.

"It was an extraordinary decision not to play Derek," Tom says. "He was such a potent bowler at that time."

"I'd been haymaking on my smallholding in Cheshire," Bob says, "and I'd got bad sunburn on my back. So I didn't change with the others in the changing room. And I had flannels that were all creased. My wife was quite upset about it; somebody hinted that she couldn't iron. Before long I was bowling to Bill Lawry. I think I got him to hole out off a double long hop."

The selectors that summer were Doug Insole, Alec Bedser, Don Kenyon and Peter May, supported by the captain Colin Cowdrey. May later explained their thinking that morning at Old Trafford: 'We were concerned about making enough runs on a dubious pitch. In fact, Australia won the toss, made 310 for four when the pitch was at its best and had settled the match by then. We might have got away with it if we had won the toss but, in retrospect, I doubt if we were very bright to discard the accuracy of Cartwright and Underwood.'

Among the few bright points for England, as they lost by 159 runs, were six second-innings wickets by Pat Pocock and in the final stages an unbeaten 87 by Basil D'Oliveira. Down at Edgbaston, meanwhile, Warwickshire were humbling Yorkshire, thanks to Tom taking seven for 36 and three for 48. So it was no surprise when his name was in the thirteen summoned to Lord's for the second Test.

The squad was announced on the morning of Sunday 16 June, but Tom had other things on his mind that day.

It was the last summer before the introduction of the John Player Sunday League, and each week BBC2 broadcast a game between one of the counties and an International Cavaliers XI that was made up of a mix of overseas players and former greats. The matches were staged on behalf of that county's beneficiary, and the previous year Warwickshire had held Jim Stewart's Sunday benefit match against the Cavaliers at Stratford-upon-Avon.

"You could pack in about 6,000 there," Tom says, "and it was heaving. So, when they had a meeting in the winter, I said I'd like to do mine at Edgbaston, and they wouldn't have it. Eventually this guy, who came from Surrey, said, 'Look, it's Tom's benefit, why don't you let him have it where he wants?' and reluctantly they agreed."

The International Cavaliers recruited the Australians Bobby Simpson and Colin McDonald, the West Indian Clive Lloyd, the Pakistani Saeed Ahmed along with Godfrey Evans, Trevor Bailey, Fred Trueman and the returning local hero Mike Smith. Warwickshire fielded their full side, including Rohan Kanhai, Lance Gibbs and Bob Barber. Tom was a county stalwart, soon to become the only Warwickshire player ever to score 10,000 runs and take 1,000 wickets; he was just the sort of cricketer for whom the benefit system was devised.

Sunday morning for the beneficiary was an anxious time. "We got up, and there was dense cloud over Solihull, and I thought, 'Oh my god, it's grey.' But by the time we set off, you could sense the sun trying to get through. Then, when we got to Edgbaston, it had broken through further and I was staggered by all the people outside the ground. At two o'clock we took the field and, after a while, when you looked round, all you could see were people streaming down the aisles. A message came out, calling me off the field. They wanted my permission to open the wicker gates and just take the money from people without recording them. It was like a circus outside. There were people queuing all down to the Pershore Road."

Tom and David Brown survey the crowd

It was a glorious afternoon's cricket. The Cavaliers scored 232 in their 40 overs, with the crowd treated to runs by Simpson, McDonald, Lloyd and Saeed Ahmed, and Tom showed his worth by bowling nine overs for 14, taking the wickets of his former captain Mike Smith and the England selector Don Kenyon. Then after tea Bob Barber and Billy Ibadulla batted freely against the ageing Fred Trueman before Dennis Amiss hit a century and Tom weighed in again, this time securing the victory with 33 not out.

"It was a brilliant game. I remember Clive Lloyd running out Billy Ibadulla from the covers. He dived full stretch and threw the ball from prone."

The afternoon raised £3,295 for Tom, contributing to a record Warwickshire benefit of £9,592. "If I'd really pushed, I could probably have put another three or four thousand on the figure, but it's embarrassing to do it. You've got to be pretty thick-skinned. All I really hoped for was to pay off the loan on the house."

Edgbaston, Warwickshire versus International Cavaliers, June 1968

Tom was on top of the world. He was one wicket away from being the first bowler to take 50 that summer, he was in the England party and likely to play at Lord's, and his benefit fund was brimming.

But alas, when he got up the next morning, he was in no physical state to play cricket.

"I'd been waking with a stiff leg for some time. I used to slide off the bed before I could bend it. But that morning I could hardly bend it at all."

He drove to Coventry where he did not bowl in the Warwickshire second innings, and he pulled out of the Test squad. His place was taken by Barry Knight, the Essex all-rounder who also bowled seam and whose Test career had looked to be over two years earlier.

The England selectors chopped and changed. There were so many cricketers to choose from in the county game, and perhaps – with Colin Cowdrey as captain – they were more than ever inclined to engage in speculative ideas. "Colin was a thinker. He liked to work things out. But he had far too much theory. He was a wonderfully talented batsman – but, if he'd been a real thickie and just gone out and played, he'd probably have got thousands more runs."

The team at Lord's showed five changes from the one beaten at Old Trafford and, when the thirteen was reduced to eleven on the morning of the match, the two to be omitted were Basil D'Oliveira and Pat Pocock who, as Bobby Simpson pointed out, 'were the only two successes at Old Trafford.'

"It was a fumbling time," is Tom's verdict on it all.

Cowdrey wrote later that D'Oliveira was dropped because his bowling – more swing than seam – had not been effective at Old Trafford and would be even less suitable at Lord's. Hence they would have played Tom and, without him, turned to Barry Knight, who in the event had a good game in a rain-ruined draw in which England bowled out Australia for 78.

MCC were due to play in South Africa that winter, and the prospect of D'Oliveira, a Cape Coloured, being a member of the touring party was already creating much speculation and comment. So inevitably, when he was not in the team on the morning of the match, there were plenty who saw hidden meanings in the decision and some of them wrote angry letters to Cowdrey.

None of this touched Tom at all. His first task was to get help from Warwickshire's physiotherapist Bernard Thomas, and he was given a seven-pound boot. Before and after each day's play, and at every interval, he would sit for ten minutes and raise the foot from the ground to a horizontal position and back. "I did it for years. When I left Warwickshire, I had to give the boot back and Dad made me a replacement. He took a shoe and fixed on the bottom of it some lead sheeting that he'd picked up when they'd pulled down the church hall up the road."

Tom returned to the Warwickshire side and struggled on. "If you're a bowler, most of the time you've got something that hurts. You'd never get up in the morning if you gave in to pain. And usually you can run it off."

In the third week of July, he bowled 51 overs on Sunday and Monday at Taunton, then travelled to Lord's where on Thursday and Friday, seeking to winkle out Middlesex batsmen struggling for the draw, he sent down another 61.2 overs. 'Cartwright sapped the Middlesex foundations,' Alan Gibson wrote in *The Times* of his efforts on Thursday. 'He is the sort of bowler who might have been invented for a situation such as this.' Then on Friday, 'Cartwright again bore the heat and the burden of the day.'

Alas, it was too much. His shoulder was now the problem, and it froze completely. Despite the best efforts of Bernard Thomas, he was out of action for weeks. "It got so painful," Tom says. "It was impossible to go on." He even missed his main benefit match at Edgbaston against local rivals Worcestershire.

England, meanwhile, continued to shuffle their pack. When an off-spinner was needed at Edgbaston, it was Ray Illingworth, not the previously successful Pat Pocock – and at Headingley, with half the first-choice batting injured, the net was cast far and wide. The day before selection Ted Dexter made a double century in his first championship match for two years and was called up, and as late as Wednesday morning, on the eve of the Test, Phil Sharpe was about to face the first ball of a county match at Westcliff when he was called off the field and summoned to Headingley. But there was no call for Basil D'Oliveira, whose batting for Worcestershire had been woeful all summer.

After four Tests, with weather twice saving the tourists, the series still stood 1-0 in favour of Australia. The Ashes could not be regained, and it was only left for the selectors to choose a team for The Oval and to start pencilling in names for the tour of South Africa.

"I was in the treatment room at Edgbaston," Tom recalls, "and Doug Insole came in and sat down."

There followed a conversation that in a matter of weeks would plunge Tom into the centre of an international crisis.

"We're looking at the winter, Tom. Would you be available to tour South Africa?"

"But I haven't been playing for weeks."

"Well, forget that. Would you be available to go?"

"I suppose so, yes."

Tom took the field once more on Tuesday 13 August at Lord's for the Gillette Cup semi-final against Middlesex. It was a dramatic match. Fred Titmus had just resigned from the captaincy of the home team, and Peter Parfitt, his replacement, was looking to start with a sparkle. But he ran into a typical spell from Tom – 12 overs, three wickets for 26 runs – and his team made only 162 in their 60 overs. It looked for a moment as if it might just be enough, as a sudden crash of wickets left the visitors on 148 for seven. JM Solan in the *Birmingham Post* described the moment of crisis: 'In a bizarre setting compounded of black skies and sunlight on the square, it was Tom Cartwright who had the nerve-jangling job of seeing them through when they needed 10 runs off the last 10 balls.' Out came Tom's trusty sweep, and it brought a four, a two and a four, and for the third time in five years Warwickshire were in the final.

That Sunday the England selectors chose their team for the final Test at The Oval and, according to Colin Cowdrey, he left the meeting unhappy with the bowling options he had been given. He had just played at The Oval, scoring a century for Kent, and he thought the pitch unsuited to the fast bowlers they had selected. His latest theory was that England would do well to have a medium-pacer on standby, in case the pitch was of similar character, and he persuaded the selectors to agree to his sounding out the options and to inviting along a 13th man.

Tom was first choice to be added. He bowled 12 overs that Sunday, but his shoulder had reacted badly and he declared himself unavailable. Then Barry Knight was approached, but he too reported himself less than 100% fit. So, in a most unexpected turn of events, Cowdrey turned to the bowler who was fifth in the national averages, with 55 wickets at 14.87 each, the man who had hardly scored a run all summer, Basil D'Oliveira.

Then on the eve of the match the opening batsman Roger Prideaux pulled out with a virus infection, and somehow Basil – despite his lack of runs – came in as a batsman. And he scored a magnificent century that threw the selectors' thinking for the winter tour party into confusion.

"Before that last Test had been played," Tom says, "they'd have had a frame of people they wanted for the tour, and Basil wouldn't have been in it. Then he turned it all upside down with that big score. But do you change your thinking on one performance? It was a difficult decision for them."

D'Oliveira had made 158 when under the greatest pressure of his life, but he had not had a good tour the previous winter in the West Indies. There were cricketing arguments for including him and also for leaving him out. And there were non-cricketing pressures as well, among them messages from South

Africa. The selectors met on the Tuesday evening, after England – thanks to the bowling of Derek Underwood – had snatched a last-gasp victory over Australia, and they were joined by several other MCC officials and even by Mike Smith, there to offer his experience of South African conditions from the previous tour. They were up till midnight, wrestling with their decisions.

The bombshell was dropped the next evening when the names were read on the radio: Cowdrey (captain), Graveney (vice-captain), then in alphabetical order Barrington, Boycott, Brown, Cartwright, Cottam ...... Edrich. There was no D'Oliveira.

For some in the world of cricket there was real regret that no place had been found for Colin Milburn, a great entertainer, while several journalists were astonished to find Tom's name on the list, particularly as he was still out of action with a bad shoulder. But inevitably it was the omission of Basil D'Oliveira that covered the front pages of all the newspapers the next morning, and the controversy grew in intensity as the days passed.

It was a summer of turmoil in the world. The Vietnam war raged, generating a bitter presidential election in the United States, an election which saw the shooting dead of a leading candidate, Robert Kennedy. The American civil rights movement had turned to violence following the assassination of Martin Luther King, rioting French students had come close to toppling General de Gaulle, and Soviet tanks had just crushed the reforming government in Czechoslovakia. The anti-apartheid cause was growing rapidly amid a mushrooming sense of injustice, and this exclusion of Basil D'Oliveira set off a great wave of protest.

"I had a phone call from a woman at the BBC," Tom says. "She asked me very aggressively how I felt. 'Well, aren't you sorry?' And I remember saying, 'I'm sorry for a lot of people. I'm sorry for Alan Jones of Glamorgan. He's had a brilliant season, and he's very unlucky not to be picked.' Frankly at that point I hadn't given it a lot of thought."

All Tom's attention was on getting fit for the Gillette final on Saturday, and he attended hospital in Birmingham on the Friday where he was given several deep injections of cortisone into his shoulder. "The doctor told me that, if he hit the point of inflammation, I might be lucky. But he also said I wouldn't sleep in the night when the stuff that masked the pain had worn off."

The doctor was right. "Joan and I went down to the Clarendon Court Hotel in London, and I hardly slept a wink. In the morning, when I tried to bowl in the dressing room, it was impossible. I never even went to the nets."

It was Sussex versus Warwickshire, the two early giants of the one-day game, and Tom's twelve overs were bowled by Dennis Amiss and went for 63 runs. Warwickshire were left to score 215 for victory, and Jim Stewart made a good start with 59 – but wickets fell and, at 155 for six, in the words of Gordon Ross in the *Playfair Cricket Monthly*, 'it was all Lombard Street to an orange that Sussex would win the Cup.' With only Blenkiron, Brown and Gibbs to come, everything seemed to fall onto the shoulders of the young Dennis Amiss and his captain Alan Smith, the latter – as so often – opting for the high-risk approach and carrying the day. 'What a captain's innings!' wrote Ross. 'The match was won, as indeed cricket matches were designed to be won, by someone taking the bat to the ball pretty firmly.'

For the second time in three years Warwickshire were Gillette Cup winners.

"That evening," Tom says, "we went back to the Clarendon Court and, when I walked in, Gary Sobers was in the bar across the lounge. He came over straightaway and said, 'You've had a bad knee.' I said, 'How did you know that?' 'Because I had a bad shoulder and, before it, I had a bad knee. Fred Titmus pointed it out to me.' And he said how it came about from trying to bowl on the front leg when the landing knee was a problem."

On the same day Donald Carr, Assistant Secretary of MCC, appeared at Tom's side: "You're our property now," he said. "We want you to see Bill Tucker." Tucker was an orthopaedic surgeon with consulting rooms in Park Street, off Park Lane. A big man, an ex-rugby player, he had attended King George VI, worked on Denis Compton's knee and, according to Tom, "looked after a lot of the jump jockeys who'd had terrible falls." He was the best, and Tom saw him the following Wednesday.

"He used cold sprays on my shoulder to numb it. Then he manipulated and stretched it. He gave me this massage, and he put his knuckles deep into my shoulder. Excruciatingly, I may add. He'd measured my reach up the wall beforehand, and I had three extra inches after the manipulation. Also, for the first time for years, I was able to lift my arm sideways above the horizontal."

Bill Tucker sent a report to Donald Carr at Lord's:

It is possible that with treatment and graduated exercises over the next fortnight the shoulder will recover completely and he will lose his symptoms. However, as he has had a previous injury and a shoulder that has been giving trouble off and on over the last ten years, it would be difficult to guarantee that he will not get recurrences. This is made more likely because the x-rays show that he is beginning to get early signs of wear and tear in the shoulder joint itself and in his neck.

W.E. Tucker, C.V.O., F.R.C.S
Consulting Orthopaedic Surgeon

The fixture list presented Tom with one last opportunity of a game. The Saturday following the Lord's final, Warwickshire as cup holders were to play a Gillette Invitation XI at Edgbaston. "Give it a try," Bill Tucker said.

The game was ruined by rain, but there was time for Tom to bowl ten overs for 35 runs and to take the wicket of the England captain, Colin Cowdrey, who – perhaps already sensing what might happen if Tom pulled out of the tour – was very keen to see the bowler in good shape.

"Colin liked to mouth down the pitch to me when I let go of the ball – 'in', 'out' – and in the middle of one over he mouthed 'out' and shouldered arms. It was my in-swinger, and it came in and bowled him. And I've never been sure when I've looked back, whether he deliberately got it wrong to encourage me – because you get to the point where your mind is so suspicious about things. Was it a genuine deceiving on my part, or was he trying to say to me, 'You're bowling well, you're OK'? I wasn't sure. I'm still not sure."

The *Birmingham Post* was delighted. 'Tom Cartwright came triumphantly through his ten overs, adding piquancy to the trial of his much publicised shoulder by bowling Cowdrey. His bowling action looked precisely as it always has, completely relaxed and energy conserving.'

Tom was sore the next day, and on Monday he returned to London to see Bill Tucker again. A week and a half on from his original selection, the controversy was still raging, and his own perspective had altered somewhat.

"At the time I was picked, I still thought it was the right thing to go out there and to try to influence the people, to get across the message to the Africans that there were white people in the rest of the world who had different ideas. And I also had this fear that, if South Africa changed overnight and you took all the brains and money out, the situation would be even worse for the ordinary people. But I read a little news item in the *Daily Express*; it said that, when the tour party was announced, the parliament in Cape Town was in session and the whole house stood up and cheered. When I read that, I went cold. And I started to wonder whether I wanted to be part of it."

Another worry on his mind was the prospect of leaving his young family for a whole winter. They were a close-knit group, and previous absences had been traumatic. Jane had refused to eat for several days when he had toured South Africa in 1964/65, and Jeremy had been no better when he and Joan had gone with Warwickshire to Kenya and Uganda. Now they were facing a full five months without him.

While Tom was making his first visit to Bill Tucker, Joan's thoughts were published in a *Birmingham Evening Mail* feature, written by a Maureen Messent:

> For weeks they have lived in doubt. Not knowing if Christmas would be a family affair or just an all-too-brief telephone conversation spanning 6,000 miles. … Tom Cartwright wanted to take his wife and children to South Africa. Understandably his wife would love

to go but she is still too much of a school marm to allow Jane to miss four months' schooling. … "Jane wants us all to go, but Jeremy wants us all to stay at home."

The little boy interrupts. He says firmly: "Just all stay together here, play in the garden and go shopping with Daddy on Saturday. That's nice."

"Jane and Jeremy get weepy when they see his case coming out. This does churn me up a bit, I'm afraid. Especially as I know he's feeling the same as us but trying to hide his emotions. When the team names for the tour were announced, Jeremy dashed up to ask if his father was included. He suddenly got furious. Began shouting that he wouldn't let him go because we all needed him at home too much. Of course we do. But you can't change a man's way of life when you marry him, can you?"

The family at home
Tom with Jane, Joan and Jeremy

Tom travelled to London to see Bill Tucker for a second time on Monday 16 September. His shoulder was sore, his family were not happy and he had been made sick by the South African response to D'Oliveira's omission.

"Donald Carr took me across to Bill Tucker's, and Bill laid out the options. I could go to South Africa, and I might be all right; on the other hand, I might make the shoulder worse, and I'd never be able to bowl again. Or I could come back to him and have an operation under a full anaesthetic and spend the winter recuperating."

Tom was digesting the advice as he rejoined Donald Carr in the reception area outside the consulting room. "As soon as Donald opened the front door, we saw god knows how many cameras there so Donald pushed me back and shut it again. We went out the back, climbed up on some bins and jumped over a wall. As fortune would have it, there was a taxi just coming past. He hailed it, and we jumped in. I was completely confused. Donald was brilliant, he really looked after me, but I didn't want to run away from the press; I wasn't sure it was the right thing to do. As soon as we walked through the gates at Lord's, Alex Bannister of the *Daily Mail* came round a wall and almost bumped into us. 'There's nothing to say,' Donald said, and off we went."

It was decision time for Tom, and he was soon sitting with Billy Griffith and Donald Carr, secretary and assistant secretary of MCC, and with Doug Insole, the chairman of selectors. They all wanted him to tour – "and I was half tempted. I had such mixed emotions about it all. There were such an awful lot of things in the mix." The issue under discussion was his shoulder: "I had a wife and two kids, I didn't have any other profession or trade or training, I didn't think I should risk not being able to bowl again." But there were other matters on his mind: the feelings of his family, the cheering in the South African parliament and all the intrigue in which he was now caught up.

"A part of me wanted to be shot of it, to be honest. It would have been the easiest thing in the world to go to South Africa. That's what everybody wanted me to do, but I was sitting there, asking myself, 'Do you really want to be part of all these things?'

"Eventually Billy Griffith said, 'Look, this has got to stop. Tom obviously feels uneasy about all of this and unhappy about his condition. We've had the report from Bill Tucker. I think we've now got to go with what Tom's feeling.'

"As soon as he said that and it was agreed that I would pull out, I felt much better. I knew immediately I'd done the right thing, even though it created a lot of upset."

Tom left Lord's to catch the train back to Birmingham, where he picked up his car at the station. He drove home and, as he parked on the drive and got out of the car, he could hear the telephone ringing. "It's Lord's," Joan said, appearing at the front door. "I think it's Colin Cowdrey."

"I took the phone, and Colin said, 'Will you agree at least to start the tour? When you get out there, if things go wrong, there are people out there who are coaching, like Don Wilson, who we could bring in.' Basil certainly wasn't mentioned. Nobody had suggested to me that, if I dropped out, Basil would be the one who took my place. I wasn't privy to anything like that. It was Don Wilson's name I remember being mentioned. But I just said no, and Colin said, 'OK, fine.'

"I honestly don't think there was a conspiracy. It wasn't anything like as clear as that. Doug Insole got a lot of flak; people accused him of all sorts of skulduggery. But I've always felt sorry for him. There was so much confusion, so much interference, and they were trying in the middle of it all to do what was for the best. I may be naïve, but I never found Doug anything other than straight. I had no feelings that would make me suspicious of him. He just got stuck dealing with something that was horrible."

The next morning the newspaper headlines told of D'Oliveira's selection in place of Tom, and immediately the South African Prime Minister John Vorster called off the tour, calling the selected party 'the team of the anti-apartheid movement, not the team of the MCC'.

"The telephone kept ringing," Tom says. "Journalists from everywhere, including South Africa. I'd put it down, and it would ring again straightaway. In the end I stopped answering it. All sorts of suggestions were flying around. Was I really injured? Or had somebody arranged for me to pull out? There was even an accusation that I'd had money paid into my benefit fund by the anti-apartheid movement as a bribe to get me not to go."

"We had all these journalists camped out on the drive at one point," Joan says. "I wanted to go shopping, and I could hardly get down the driveway for all the pressmen."

"You're never sure what people think of you," Tom says. "For a while everybody seemed to be looking at me. I went to a cricket club dinner, at a colliery near Nuneaton, and all evening this vicar was staring at me, all through the speeches and everything. Then he came sidling up to me, almost tentatively, and he said, 'You didn't really have an injury, did you? You did it out of conscience.'"

Fortunately the Cartwrights had already booked a fortnight's holiday in Majorca and, though Tom spent much of it exhausted by the trauma of it all and suffering from a stomach bug, he was glad to be out of range of the press. "By the time I came back, I'd lost a stone and a half."

The house was quiet when they returned – "but I had a very funny feeling when I came in. You can say I'm paranoid, but it was as if there was a sort of presence there. I did feel that – especially when I went upstairs. I remember opening the drawers in the bedroom and sensing that somebody had been there."

For those like Colin Cowdrey who had hoped that they could somehow find a solution to the crisis, that there would be a way around the problem if Tom would only agree to fly out, it must have seemed very unfortunate that it was Tom that they had had to persuade: a man who found such politicking distasteful, a man who still remained loyal to his Labour background and whose natural sympathies were with those who were protesting. Tom was a minor pawn in the affair, but in his own way he takes a pride in the fact that his final decision came down on the side of what he believes to be right.

"It would have been far better if the South Africans themselves had seen the need to do things differently but, looking back now, I can see that the people there were never going to change without outside pressure. And the cancelling of that tour did set a lot of things in motion."

In later years Tom spent many a Sunday afternoon in the company of Basil D'Oliveira, changing at adjoining pegs during matches for the Old England XI. "Naomi talked a lot to Joan about it all, but Basil and I never, ever discussed it at all. During that time there were people going off on rebel tours to South Africa, and sometimes it would come up in conversation in the team. And Basil and I would just look at one other. It was like there was a magnet drawing our eyes together, and sometimes there'd be half a smile of acknowledgement. But we never said anything."

Perhaps there was nothing to say.

CHAPTER 15
"IT WAS LIKE BEING REBORN"
1969 – 1972

The shoulder injury, and the resulting controversy over the South African tour, disturbed the even rhythm of Tom's life, but there was greater disturbance in store for him the following year.

In the autumn of 1968, as advised, he returned to Bill Tucker's Park Street rooms to have his shoulder manipulated under a full anaesthetic. "Bill was a big man; he'd been a second-row rugby forward. But he said, 'What I need to do to your shoulder will take more than I can manage on my own.' And he introduced me to this huge man who'd been a wrestler and who was going to help him. I don't know exactly what they did but they put me to sleep and, when I came round, I had to rest. They left me lying in a bed all night in the building, all on my own, just with a porter who came and checked on me every now and then. I had to rest the shoulder completely for six weeks. Then I had to bowl six balls a day for a week, then twelve, then eighteen, all of which I did religiously. And for years afterwards I used to call on Bill in his garden flat in North London; we'd have a glass of beer, and he'd give me some butazolidin tablets. Closey used to have them as well. It's what they gave horses to get them to recover quickly, though I think it's banned now."

May 1969 was wet, but Tom showed the worth of Bill Tucker's work in the first rain-free championship match, taking twelve wickets for 55 runs in 39.4 overs in a dramatic five-run victory over the reigning champions Yorkshire at Bradford. 'I doubt if the season will provide a better example of the medium-paced bowler's skills, or of more insistent control, than Cartwright's performance,' wrote Peter West in *The Times*.

Three weeks later, against Sussex at Edgbaston, Tom hit a 'rumbustious' 90 that brought the county a second victory. The following week, against Somerset at Edgbaston, he tasted further glory with the only hat-trick of his career. The victims were the first three wickets to fall: Tony Clarkson, Greg Chappell and Merv Kitchen. 'A haul of big fish,' Alan Gibson called them in *The Times*. 'It was a proper hat-trick, and it adds a pleasing flourish to the brave banner of his career.'

Tom was back in the best of form. His season's tally of 108 wickets was only one fewer than Bob Cottam, the country's leading wicket-taker, and in its first summer he topped the Sunday League bowling averages with 22 wickets at an average of 11.18 at a rate of under three runs an over. 'No other county cricketer could match his performance in 1969,' wrote his captain Alan Smith.

It was not, however, a happy summer at Edgbaston. It had started with a dispute about pay in which Tom was once more cast in the role of shop steward and trouble-maker. Mike Smith had agreed to come out of retirement for the Sunday League games, Bob Barber also made himself available and, when it emerged that they were to be paid considerably more for their appearances than the full-time members of staff, a meeting was arranged with the chairman Edmund King. "He was an accountant, with a very ruddy face that he'd probably got from the drinks cabinet in the committee room," Tom says. "We sat down, and he said, 'Now I'm not going to tolerate any car workers' attitudes here tonight.' We were sitting in the opulence of the committee room, all paid for by the Supporters' Club through the pockets of the people at Longbridge, and I still regret that I didn't get up and walk out."

Their spokesman at the meeting was Jack Bannister, a leading light in the newly formed Professional Cricketers' Association. "There were threats of all sorts, but what I knew – which the others didn't – was that Jack had just been offered the position of cricket manager. So, when we came back down to the dressing room, I said to the younger players, 'Jack's going to be your manager. Look after your futures, sign your contracts and don't get involved in anything.' Already I was feeling, 'I don't like the way things are going.'"

Officially Jack Bannister was vice-captain to Alan Smith, but – with the development of Bill Blenkiron and the arrival from Lincolnshire of Norman McVicker – Jack could not get into the side. Following the brouhaha over the South African tour, Doug Insole and Peter May had retired as England selectors, and Alan Smith had been appointed to fill one of the vacancies. The Warwickshire captain also sustained a hand injury in mid-season so the county was often without an obvious captain. The young Dennis Amiss was tried for some matches, but this was not considered a success.

Meanwhile, behind the scenes, the chairman Edmund King single-handedly made major changes to the selection committee, including the removal of its three main figures: the chairman of the committee Esmond Lewis, second eleven captain Ray Hitchcock and coach Tom Dollery, Tom's inspirational first captain. Perhaps it was time for change – Tom Dollery had many other interests, including the pub he ran – but bad feeling was created, particularly by the manner in which the changes were carried out.

"It was all done behind their backs," Tom recalls. "Tom Dollery and Ray were away with the second team, and Esmond Lewis was on holiday with his family. Ray and Tom had served the club for years, but at least they were professionals. Esmond was an amateur, giving all his time to the club for nothing, and to treat him that way wasn't acceptable."

In early August, when there was a three-day gap in the programme, Tom took a phone call at home from Alan Smith. "He wanted me to go back to Birmingham that night. He said the chairman wanted the two of us to run cricket affairs at the club. And I didn't want to do it. I didn't want to be caught up in it all. I was put on the spot. I liked Alan. He was a good guy. We were from very different backgrounds, but I liked him. 'No,' I said. 'We've got people staying. I can't get away.' I'm afraid I lied."

Tom was a political animal. He had grown up among the trade unionists of the car factories, but he has never been comfortable doing deals behind closed doors. "There was a lot going on that I found unpalatable, and I really didn't want to take over the captaincy for the rest of the season. But in the end I agreed."

He had already stood in on four occasions, winning two of them, and the next match at Weston-super-Mare, scene of so much success in his career, saw him prominent on all three days. On the first he led the batting out of crisis with a top-scoring 75, on the second he took six wickets and on the third, when Somerset needed 211 for victory, he helped to reduce them to 81 for seven.

Alan Gibson, himself a West Country man, was reporting the game for *The Times*, and his imagination was caught by one member of the crowd:

A jolly, red-faced, tubby chap, he was all I suppose Somerset supporters ought to be. In the morning he had repeatedly declaimed, in reference to the early Somerset batting: "What a click!" Yet the stand which followed, between Robinson and Langford, prospered so well that we began to think, incredulously, that Somerset might win. And now his cry was: "We got un, boays!"

At 147 for seven, 64 needed, with more than an hour to go, it was possible for a Somerset realist to be optimistic. Then Cartwright bowled Robinson, and soon afterwards it was all over.

It would be Cartwright. It was Cartwright who had got Denning and Rose out. It was Cartwright who had twice saved the Warwickshire batting, and bowled Somerset out in the first innings. Yes, it *would be* Cartwright. "What a player the bloke is," said my Somerset supporter; at least that was his meaning, if not exactly his phraseology.

Rain ruined the next two matches, but the championship programme ended with two more victories and fourth place in the table. Of the county's seven championship wins that summer, five had come from the games when Tom had been captain.

Yet Tom was unsettled. He was 34 years old, he had been threatened by a career-ending injury, and he decided that it was time to start planning for a life after cricket. Inspired by Tiger Smith, he thought that he should look for a coaching appointment, ideally one that would allow him to continue playing for a while. The Warwickshire post, filled for so long by Tom Dollery, was vacant, but he received mixed messages about whether they wanted a member of the current team to apply for it.

He wrote a letter to the county, stating that he wanted to look at options further afield and would not be signing his contract for 1970. He was going on holiday to Corfu, and he asked that no statement was issued till he returned. "There was a chap in the hotel in Corfu, a journalist from Leamington Spa, and he came up to me. 'Have you seen the papers? I didn't realise you'd retired.' And that made me angry."

When Tom returned to his home, he received a visit in person from Edmund King. "He came into my lounge. 'Sit down,' I said, and he said, 'No, it's all right, I'd rather stand.' And he was wandering around the room, looking over the sofa and at the back of the chair. It was like a farce. I told him, 'There's no tape recorder anywhere, you know.' We talked about his trying to find me a local school. Then soon afterwards I got a phone call from John Solan from the *Birmingham Post*. The county position had been advertised and he said, 'I've been talking to the chairman and, if you apply, they'll view you favourably.' I said, 'John, if he wanted to say that to me, why didn't he tell me himself? Why's he doing it through you? Thanks for telling me, but I'm not going to apply.' It was embarrassing. I didn't want to put the club in a position where they felt under pressure from me. If I had applied, I think I would have got it, but it wouldn't have been the right way to set off in the job."

Tom had offers from several counties, including Gloucestershire, Sussex and Northants. Leicestershire came up with the most attractive financial package, including free private education for his two children, but he had set his heart on working in a school. "By that stage I wanted to go and find a future somewhere new. I wanted to work with kids, and I wanted to spend more time with my family."

Brighton College were keen to recruit him, though there was no immediate vacancy, and the same was true at Millfield School, where Colin Atkinson, the former Somerset captain, was deputy headmaster and where there were plans to build a new sports hall.

"It meandered on for a long time, and we were living on money which I'd saved. In the end I had to sign on, and that was a dreadful experience, queuing with these young men who looked so unprepared for life. They were downcast; they didn't look you in the eye. There were no job centres in those days, nobody to help. It affected me so much that I couldn't eat when I got home."

Eventually Colin Atkinson put together an offer to play for Somerset in the summer and to work for Millfield School for the rest of the year. It was for £700 a year less than Leicestershire had offered, £600 less than

Warwickshire, but Tom was taken with Millfield School, the brainchild of the eccentric Jack Meyer, Somerset captain back in the 1940s. There was a great emphasis on sport, and the fees were based on the ability to pay, with the wealthy subsidising the less well-off. "It was like Robin Hood, robbing the rich to pay the poor."

He and Joan took a while to make their decision. "It was a colossal wrench. The kids had to change school. But it gave me the opportunity to see another side of life. And after I'd been there a while, I knew it was going to be good."

There remained the matter of his registration to play county cricket. Even though he was out of contract, he could not make an immediate move without the permission of Warwickshire. Tom Graveney had had to spend a year out of first-class cricket when he moved from Gloucestershire to Worcestershire, as had Peter Richardson, moving from Worcestershire to Kent, and Barry Knight, from Essex to Leicestershire. In the circumstances of the falling out, Warwickshire insisted that Tom did the same.

"I was angry," he says. "I was married with kids, and all I was looking to do was to pursue my profession, to build a future. I had no freedom of movement. It was an appalling situation. I thought it was quite unacceptable for them to try to block me like that."

He appealed to the Registration Committee of the MCC, going down to Lord's where Jack Bannister, on behalf of the Professional Cricketers' Association, represented him and Bunty Longrigg, Somerset's President and a lawyer himself, spoke on behalf of his new county. "While they addressed the committee, I had to sit in Donald Carr's office. There were two phones on the desk, one red, one black. He said, 'If this one rings, don't touch it. But if that other one rings, you're to go downstairs.'"

In time the telephone rang, and he was escorted towards the double doors behind which the committee had been deliberating his fate. Remembering his national service days, and the arrangements when you were on a charge, he turned to his escort. "Are you my marching relief?" he asked, and he could hear the chuckles from behind the double doors.

"The chairman of Surrey, Maurice Allom, announced their ruling. 'Tom,' he said. 'I want you to sit down there. Don't say a word; just listen.' And he told me that I would be free to play for Somerset immediately and that Jack Bannister had spoken very well on my behalf. I said, 'Thank you very much.' And that was the end of it."

Tom had become the first professional cricketer to move without the approval of his county and not to serve a period of residential qualification. "It was thoroughly unpleasant," he says now. "I had a non-contributory pension, and Warwickshire refused to transfer it; I think I'm the only player ever they've

159

withheld it from. I could have taken them to court over it, but I didn't want to do that – because in the end the game suffers. However insignificant it might be, it becomes another blot on the game, another chip off it."

Tom was making a fresh start, but one shadow from his past returned before he had bowled a ball for his new county. The South Africans were scheduled to tour England that summer, and there was much political debate whether, in the light of their refusal to accept Basil D'Oliveira two years earlier and their subsequent refusal to grant admission to the American tennis player Arthur Ashe, the tour should be allowed to proceed. The Professional Cricketers' Association conducted a ballot of its members and, Tom believes, he was one of only seven to vote against playing the tourists.

The South Africans were due to visit Taunton in late August, and immediately Tom was required to make his position clear. "I told Jimmy James the secretary that I was strongly against playing against South Africa, and he brought the chairman Colonel Grey out onto the middle to meet me. It was my first meeting with him, and his first words after shaking hands were, 'I understand you have a reluctance to play against South Africa.' 'I have a very strong reluctance, sir,' I said, 'but I've made a verbal contract with you that, if you say I've got to play, I will. But my contribution to the game will be very minimal.' He was a very nice man and he said, 'If you feel that way, we'll not ask you to play.'"

In the end the matter did not arise. The protests grew stronger, the police warned that they could not guarantee security at the grounds and, after pressure from the Home Secretary, the Cricket Council withdrew its invitation to the South Africans.

It would be hard at that time to make a cricketing move with more contrast than the one Tom was making: from the West Midlands heartland of industrial England to the slow-moving market town of Taunton, from the county with the healthiest bank balance to the one closest to bankruptcy. "We bought a house in Wells, and I went three months before I got my first pay."

At Edgbaston the facilities were the best in the country. "All the players had got big lockers and their own spaces in a big airing cupboard. But at Taunton the walls used to stream with water; you couldn't hang your clothes up in the dressing room and leave them overnight. And the ladies' toilets were in a terrible mess. Joan used to put toilet rolls round them on Saturday mornings.

"Roy Virgin said to me, 'How could you leave Edgbaston to come here?' But I didn't mind that everything was run down. In a way I liked the nostalgia of it all, and the smells. As Warwickshire had become more affluent, it had changed its identity a bit. When I started at Edgbaston, the members would park in the forecourt behind the pavilion, and you'd mingle with them. There was a little coffee room next to Leslie Deakins' office, with a waitress, where members would come in the morning, even when there wasn't a game on. You talked to them, and they talked to you. And you had a drink with them at the end of the day in the same bar. But as the ground changed in structure, there grew up a separation from the members. You didn't see them, and you became almost disconnected from them. It had all lost its family feeling and become more like a business.

"But at Somerset it was exactly the same as it had always been. There was still a real connection between the spectators and the players. Somerset people are fairly down to earth. They're not over-impressed by flannel. Families would go and watch; ladies would go with their husbands. They were country people; they all had glowing, ruddy faces. Their faces stood out at away matches in early season, when most people had a pallor.

"I wanted to play somewhere that was fun to play, in nice surrounds. Driving from Wells to Taunton each day, through the country roads of Somerset, it was like having an extra salary. And I loved playing at Weston. We had so much fun, driving across the Mendips, family days out in school holidays with pubs to eat at en route home. Those things beat all the dressing rooms and the facilities. For me, moving to Somerset was like being reborn."

Somerset as a cricket team were at rock bottom. In 1969, even with the young Greg Chappell playing for them, they finished bottom of the championship table with just one two-run victory at the start of the summer; they were bottom-but-one in the Sunday League, and they were knocked out in the first round of the Gillette Cup.

Their captain that summer was the off-spinner Brian Langford. "Fred Rumsey had just left," Brian says. "They'd got rid of Bill Alley, and Peter Wight and Graham Atkinson had gone. I was called to a meeting at Glastonbury and told by Len Creed the vice-chairman that I was the captain. I was trying to work out afterwards if it was an honour or not. He said to me, 'We don't expect you to win a game. We're going to be rock bottom. Just go and try your best.' It was a battle. You don't mind getting runs scored off you if your own batsmen are scoring runs. But we weren't getting any runs that season."

"We were in the lifeboats," slow left-armer Peter Robinson says. "We had no opening bowlers. Brian and I would be bowling by twelve o'clock. I fielded that year at bat-pad, and it's safer now in Iraq. Teams without bowling do struggle a bit. If we had even half a good morning, the wheels would come off between lunch and tea."

The batsmen did not score runs. The bowlers could not exercise control. Even the wicket-keeper Charlie Carter, an Old Radleian who was a protégé of Bill Andrews the coach, was not – in the opinion of Peter Robinson – up to county standard: "He couldn't keep pigeons," he says. "We'd have been better off with a coat. At least it would have had four pockets."

The summer of 1970 saw some improvement, with four recruits from other counties: the fast bowler Allan Jones ('Jonah') from Sussex, the unpredictable batsman Maurice Hill from Notts via Derbyshire, the wicket-keeper Derek Taylor from Surrey and, most significantly of all, Tom.

"Jonah had pace," Peter Robinson says. "He might knock over a few with the new ball. Then we could turn to Tom, and suddenly, with Langy still a good off-spinner, we had some control. Roy Virgin had a great season with the bat. We had Merv Kitchen and Graham Burgess. And Derek Taylor was a very good wicket-keeper. We became a much tighter unit."

'Cartwright was the natural linchpin of the whole effort,' *Wisden* reported, 'and bowled much more than anyone else.'

"Tom and I were in the same mould," Brian Langford says. "We had the same feel for the game. It's very easy to bowl when it's turning and bouncing, but on a good wicket, if you're bowling well, that's when you come into your own."

"The best bloke I ever bowled with was Fred Titmus," Tom says. "He bowled with the same philosophy as me, building pressure. And bowling with Brian Langford was a joy, too. He had the same mindset. We used to bowl overs 9 to 24 together on Sundays. It was a crucial time, and it was brilliant to have him at the other end."

The Sunday League programme began with five victories in the first six games, there was a run to the semi-final of the Gillette Cup, and a late flurry of wins lifted the county four places to 13th in the championship table. But, as so often, Tom's most colourful memories are of matches at Weston-super-Mare.

The festival, which attracted substantial holiday-making crowds, began with a Bank Holiday victory over neighbours Gloucestershire, in which Tom – with six for 29 – caused the main damage on the final day. Then came Worcestershire, captained by Tom Graveney. There was intermittent rain on the first two days and the visitors, replying to Somerset's 183, had only reached 35 for no wicket when the last day began. A hot sun was beaming down, the pitch was awkward as it dried out, and Tom and Graham Burgess soon had them all out for 132. The crowd, brought alive by the fall of wickets, expected quick Somerset runs and a declaration, but neither happened and soon after tea their mood turned sour.

"Len Creed started it off. He got up out of his deck chair, moved to the trellis and started the slow handclapping. Some chaps began to walk back and forth across the sight screen. Then another man came right out to the middle of the pitch. He looked just like Norman Wisdom, and he pulled this big, juicy pear out of his pocket and smashed it down right on a length. He had another one in his other pocket, but he couldn't get it out."

According to *The Times*, he was Mr Michael O'Reilly, a holiday-maker from Birmingham, and he explained his protest: 'The target was stiff enough if Somerset had declared at tea. I couldn't believe it when they went on afterwards.'

"I recognised him from Edgbaston," Tom says. "'I'm sorry, Tom,' he said. 'I'm sorry. I had to do something.'"

The declaration never came and, when stumps were drawn, an angry group of some 200 spectators assembled outside the pavilion. One of them dropped the Somerset flag to half mast, and for a long time Brian Langford did not dare to emerge from the dressing room. "We found his youngest boy Scotty in the marquee. We told Brian to drive off, and we passed Scotty through the car window as he went. Then I got on a box and addressed the crowd. I told them they were like soccer hooligans. And they all started to drop their heads and slunk out of the ground."

The next day, Saturday, saw a third match at Clarence Park, Weston, against Kent. The committee, however, had a policy of taking the Sunday matches around and about the county, and at close of play they dismantled the stands and drove them down to Devonshire Road, the Weston club ground a quarter of a mile away. There Tom played the match that, above all others, he wishes he could forget.

Tom is one who thinks that one-day cricket has had a negative impact on the skills of the game. "Before it was introduced, the bowler's job was to take wickets. The bowler asked questions, and the batsman had to answer them. But one-day cricket changed that totally. The bowler's job was to react to the batsman, to try to stop him scoring; you could win without taking wickets. It's all had a very negative effect on the skills of bowling. When I bowled on Sundays, I used to reduce my lateral movement – because the edges often went into gaps. Most of the time my idea was to get the ball to go to the field I'd set, and to do that you needed to hit the middle of the bat."

Tom was a master of the form. In the first six Sunday matches that summer he had bowled 48 overs, taken ten wickets and conceded only 84 runs. But his afternoon at Devonshire Road, Weston, was to put a major dent into those figures. Fielding at slip he dropped the Kent opener Brian Luckhurst early on. Then, when he came on to bowl, Luckhurst opted for an adventurous approach, hitting him repeatedly across the line.

"There was a huge gale blowing," Tom remembers. "Brian was a bottom-handed player. He just put his foot down the wicket and hit it. I had Tony

Clarkson fielding on the deep square leg boundary; he'd run in for the catch and the wind would carry the ball over his head. It was like a nightmare. I kept thinking, 'It can't go on.' All the time I had this feeling that I was going to get him out. And he just went on and on."

"It was more exposed than at Clarence Park," Peter Robinson says. "It was an amazing afternoon, like seeing Joel Garner being whacked. It's the only time I saw it happen."

Tom – 'Mister Credit Squeeze himself,' Alan Gibson called him in *The Times* – bowled his eight overs for 74 runs, only five short of the league record at that time. His friend Mike Brearley was at Lord's the next morning: "We were looking at the scores in the paper," he says, "and I do remember reading out Tom's figures. Eight overs, nought for 74. We all enjoyed that."

By Thursday life was back to normal. On an unpredictable pitch at Leyton, Tom bowled 44 overs in the day, taking twelve wickets for 86 runs. Somerset's fortunes were looking up.

Tom spent the winter at Millfield School. The new sports hall was not built, and his duties included the running of the under-13 football team – "I scored a lot of goals that winter" – and working with Kenny Palmer on the grounds. "I wanted to learn about ground management," he says, "and it kept me fit."

Jack Meyer
They say he could always find what he wanted!

Power had effectively shifted from the founder headmaster Jack 'Boss' Meyer to his deputy Colin Atkinson, and Tom's memories of Meyer suggest a man whose visionary qualities had slipped almost completely into eccentricity. "He lived in the tennis hut during the day. You could hardly move for papers and things when you went in there. He'd walk around the grounds with his golf club. 'Bowl me one,' he'd say, and he'd turn the club up the other way. When children came for interview, he'd get me to put a couple of coats down for goalposts. 'See if you can score,' he'd tell them."

Tom was no nearer to realising his ambition to coach young cricketers, but his second summer at Somerset saw further progress with the arrival of three exciting recruits: fast bowler Hallam Moseley from Barbados, leg-spinner Kerry O'Keeffe from Australia and, above all, the former England captain Brian Close, sensationally sacked by Yorkshire the previous November.

Tom, turning 36 during the summer, took 100 wickets once more, and in the Sunday League he was the only bowler in the country to go for under three runs an over. 'He bowled superlatively well,' *Wisden* recorded, 'and, accepting missed catches and very long spells as all part of the day's play, he made a wonderful professional example.'

Once more his best days were at Weston, where in Northants' only innings he took seven for 72 and in the next match, when Gary Sobers hit a hundred, he took seven for 74. The latter match is remembered among Somerset players for a moment of pure Brian Close. "Sobers was coming out," Brian Langford recalls, "and Closey gestured to us to gather round him. We thought we were going to hear some mind-boggling idea he had, and all he said was, 'This lad's left-handed.' He was bloody serious, too."

The 40-year-old Brian Close, freed of the cares of the Yorkshire captaincy, averaged more than 40 for the first time in his long career. He was also fearless as ever at short leg, where his 34 catches put him third in the national list.

"At Somerset he batted at three," Tom says. "He could just go in and play; he could present what was Brian Close in a natural way every day without having to consider other issues and other people. He looked a very good player, and he had a very good summer."

"When we played against him in his later years at Yorkshire," Peter Robinson recalls, "we felt he was just a slogger. But when he came down to us, we realised what a good player he was."

"Closey's personal figures suffered at Yorkshire," Tom says. "Had he been a number three all his life, I think you'd have seen a lot more runs behind his name and a lot more outstanding innings. Because, whatever little gems of 50, 60, 70 he will have played, people don't talk about them like they do about a well-cobbled 150, even if the 150 didn't have as great a bearing on the match."

First day back, April 1971

Standing: *(left to right)* Derek Taylor, Roy Virgin, Hallam Moseley, Allan Jones,
Maurice Hill, Tom Cartwright
Front: Merv Kitchen, Brian Langford, Brian Close and Thumper

Brian Close had hit only two centuries in his last four summers at Yorkshire, yet in 1971 he hit five for Somerset. One was on debut at Leicester, one against the touring Indians and one – almost inevitably –against his old county at Taunton. But the one that is most remembered came against Surrey, also at Taunton.

"We were playing on the Sunday at Torquay, and he top-edged a ball into his mouth," Brian Langford tells. "He lost a few teeth and went off. He went back to the Crown and Sceptre that evening, got some scotch down him and in the morning I picked him up and took him to the dentist. 'There's no way you can play today,' the dentist said, but he wouldn't hear of it. He was next in to bat, and he was sitting in the dressing room, with his mouth swollen and his nerve ends hanging out.

"Maurice Hill came in. He was twelfth man, and he hadn't been playing on the Sunday at Torquay. 'I don't think I can play today,' he said. 'I've got toothache.' The dressing room erupted."

166

A wicket fell immediately. Brian Close stepped out to bat and, still in a painful daze, he found himself on the receiving end of a Robin Jackman bouncer that somehow he top-edged for six. "That really brought me to my senses," he says. "After that I got my head down." 'He was not especially in form,' Alan Gibson reckoned, 'and his runs did not come smoothly. But his hundred was the innings of a man determined to make runs.'

Somerset finished that summer in seventh position in the championship table, and at the beginning of August they were top in the Sunday League.

For Tom, though, the highlight of the summer was an innings victory over his old county at Glastonbury. Warwickshire were top of the championship table, looking to repeat their triumph of twenty years earlier, and on the Monday, resuming at 52 for none in reply to Somerset's 258, they lost 20 wickets for a further 112 runs, with Brian Close taking five catches and Tom finishing with match figures of 42 overs, eight wickets for 37 runs. According to Alan Gibson, 'Close collected the catches at short leg as a man ticks off the items on an account' while 'Cartwright, unchanged and unchangeable, was bowling with what in a more flamboyant character we might have suspected to be a knowing grin.'

"It was one of those days," Tom says. "The odd cloud drifted over from Bridgwater and, once the sun went behind them, the pitch cooled and started to seam more. I always used to tell Billy Ibadulla that I could smell the rain clouds coming. And he came out to bat. 'Is it going to rain?' he asked me. 'Can you smell it?' 'No,' I said, 'but watch that cloud over Bridgwater.' We'd bowled them out a second time before tea, and they were booked to go round Morlands the next morning. I wasn't very popular."

Tom Cartwright and Brian Close. The two men at the heart of Somerset's renaissance were very different characters: Tom the meticulous professional and Brian the unpredictable adventurer. Inevitably the stories about their newly-arrived Yorkshireman piled up, and no one can tell them better than Peter Robinson:

> Brian would bowl these little seamers, and he'd say, 'I used to be as quick as Fred, you know.' Ted Dexter made a comeback that year, playing in the Sunday League, and the first ball Brian bowled at him at Bath was an absolute long hop that Ted nailed straight to mid-wicket. 'I always do Ted, lad,' he said.
>
> He was an amazing cricketer. He was the best bowler of a full toss and the best batter of one. If he bowled it, he got a wicket; if he batted it, he got a four.
>
> He had more excuses than anybody. He dropped a skier in the deep once. 'It just came down quickly at the last minute,' he said. When

he got out, we used to sit and wait for what excuse he was going to come back with. 'Do you know why I got out today?' 'Why's that?' 'I never had my chewing gum in.' Another time he played an awful shot just before lunch and got out – and, when I came in, he looked at me: "Your running between the wickets is diabolical. And another thing, why didn't you tell me it was one o'clock lunch?"

There wasn't a braver, more stupid fielder in the world than Brian. I was pleased when he came. Up till then I was doing bat-pad. 'I'm going in there, lad,' he said and I thought, 'Thank God for that.' I'd been trying to ditch the job for years.

He used to get hit in the shins, and all he'd say was 'Keep them up, lad.' His legs sounded better than some bats. He got a nasty one at Kent. The lad Nicholls hit him in the collar bone. He just went off for a bit, had a fag and came back. He was unbelievable.

I saw him walk down the wicket once to Andy Roberts, and he let the ball hit him on his chest. I said, 'What are you doing?' 'I just wanted to see how quick he was.' I remember him saying about the Ali-Frazier fights, when Ali let Frazier hit him. 'Well, I'd fight like that. How would they knock me down?' And he'd believe it.

I could write a book on him.

"He'd always have a reason for everything," Tom says. "Every time he came back after getting out, I'd light a cigarette for him and put it straight in his mouth. If you could stop him speaking for five minutes, you'd be all right."

But, if Brian Close the cricketer occasioned plenty of stories, Brian Close the driver generated even more.

"I remember driving into Taunton one Saturday morning," Tom says, "and, when I got to the bend at Borough Bridge, there was this car perched on top of the hedge, with about twenty or thirty yards of hedgerow before it all flattened. I thought, 'That looks like Closey's car.' I got to the ground, and there he was, with his pot of tea, his *Sporting Life* and a fag. 'Have I just seen your car?' I said. 'Is it still there, lad?' Apparently, going round the bend, he'd been leaning across to grab his portable radio. And he'd come off the road and ploughed along the top of the hedge.

"Another time we were playing a Sunday League match at Worcester, and I was driving home with Joan and the kids on the M5. It was dark, and the car in front wasn't lit up. 'Look at that idiot,' I said to Joan. I kept flashing it, and nothing happened. Then I saw the top of Peter Robinson's head on the passenger side, and I realised it was Closey. He was in the middle lane so

I went out into the outside lane, got alongside him and looked across. And he'd got the Sunday paper spread across the steering wheel. I could see Robbo slumped back – probably praying. It took me ages to get Closey's attention.

"The Yorkshire lads told me there was a time when they were going down the Edgware Road in London, and the inside lane was all dug up and cordoned off. And when they went past, there was a car down in the hole, with its top level with the road. "I bet it's Closey,' they said. And it was. He'd probably been reading the paper and driven straight through the barrier into the hole."

For the summer of 1972 the Somerset committee decided that they wanted Brian Close to take over the captaincy. He did not especially want it; he had enjoyed his year without responsibility. But he agreed.

"I'm not sure it was a good decision," Tom says. "Langy was a good captain by that time. He knew the game, and he was popular with the players and the members. And Closey was batting like he hadn't for years."

Tom spent a second winter at Millfield, but Colin Atkinson had bad news for him. The plan to build a sports hall was being postponed. The cost of transporting the children to and from the houses at lunch time was too great, and they had decided to prioritise the building of a refectory on the site of the orchard. It was a disappointment to Tom but, when he returned to Taunton in April, an offer soon arrived via Harold Gimblett, the former Somerset batsman who was running the shop at Millfield. "I was lying in one of those slipper baths in the old pavilion, and he poked his head round the door. 'Colin's sent me down to see you,' he said. 'You can buy the school shop if you like.' I said, 'That's generous but, to be honest, Harold, I'm too tired to think about it.' I'd been bowling all day. I turned it down, probably one of the worst decisions I've made. I'd have had a captive audience with money to spend."

Then came the phone call that launched Tom into the next stage of his life. The secretary Jimmy James asked to talk to him, and they met at the Star Hotel in Wells. "He pumped me for quite a while about what I thought was wrong with the club, and he finished up offering me the post of player-coach. I was free to play all summer, then in the winter I was to set things up."

Tom was to replace Bill Andrews, who had been with the county – player and coach – since 1930 and who, as he liked to tell everybody, was being 'sacked' for the fourth time: "I've got the scars on my heart." He also liked to tell everybody that he had bowled Bradman in 1938, when the Don had reached 202 and was looking to get out. "Shake the hand that bowled Bradman," he would say to one and all. Such boyish enthusiasm was not to everybody's liking, however, and Tom recalls being accosted by a member in

Torquay, an unusual character in a pin-stripe suit who strode right out to the middle at the end of a game. "He grabbed me by the hand and said, 'I just wanted to shake the hand that's bowled every other bugger but Bradman.'"

Peter Roebuck was a promising, young cricketer at this time, a boy at Millfield where his parents were both teachers. "My parents didn't quite know what to make of Bill. The first time we encountered him was at a trial game at Street when at the tea interval he went out onto the pitch, lay down and fell asleep. He was a big-hearted man, full of enthusiasm, but he was chaotic. The under-19s would have no matches for three weeks, then somehow there'd be three in one day."

"If he got up a team," Peter Robinson says, "he'd have either nine or thirteen. I don't know how good a judge of young cricketers he was. He told Kenny Palmer he wasn't tall enough to be a bowler. And he was always finding another Peter May or Fred Trueman, usually from Weston. But he loved the game. He was probably more suited to coaching the kids."

"He came to a Sunday game at the Imperial ground at Bristol one time," Tom recalls. "I think he spent the afternoon in the marquee. Then he came into the pavilion. He flopped out in this big armchair, stretched his legs out in front of him and went fast asleep. We all showered and changed and left him there."

"We were playing Wiltshire at Taunton in the Minor Counties," Peter Robinson remembers, "and we were getting a bit of a smacking. A few minutes after the start Bill would nip out the back and go into the Ring O' Bells. He came back just before lunch, saw the score and started having a go. John Martin was the captain. 'John, you bowled like a pr-pr-proper idiot.' He used to stutter. 'But I haven't had a bowl yet, Bill.' 'Don't you argue with me.' We saw him a bit later, and he'd nodded off."

"Tom was completely different," Peter Roebuck says. "He was quiet, efficient, thoughtful."

"I loved my years at Somerset," Tom says. "There were so many characters, so much atmosphere. After what had gone on at the end of my time at Edgbaston, it was quite a release for me."

Somerset cricket was entering a new era. They had never had a captain like Brian Close, nor had they had a coach like Tom. During the next five years the two of them would oversee the flowering of a new generation of cricketers, a generation that would include Viv Richards and Ian Botham. They would be the most fulfilling years of Tom's life.

CHAPTER 16

TOM'S BOYS

1972 – 1975

The summers of 1972 and 1973 were successful ones for Tom and for his veteran captain Brian Close.

In first-class cricket Tom's 98 wickets in 1972 made him the joint leading wicket-taker in England, and in 1973 he topped the national averages with another 89 wickets. In *Wisden* Eric Hill paid tribute to him:

> Once again Cartwright was superb: the indispensable player. In his 38th year, he bowled almost as much as any two other Somerset bowlers and, even when not taking wickets, could always be relied upon to control any situation. His wonderful skill and energy through dozens of long spells – several during tropical August weather – were monuments of true professional application. At second slip he was one of the few safe catchers in the side.

His contribution in the Sunday League was no less impressive. In 1972 he conceded his runs at 3.03 an over, second only to John Snow's 2.87 in *Wisden's* list of economical bowlers, and in 1973 he was in first place with 2.38, and the second-placed bowler was far behind at 2.94.

Immediately after Christmas 1973 Tom made a third trip to East Africa, this time at the invitation of Mike Brearley, who was raising a party on behalf of the MCC. Tom had decided never to leave his family for another overseas tour, but it was only for three weeks, Mike Brearley was keen to have him and Joan told him to go.

"Things were changing in East Africa," he says. "There were still some Asians playing, though a lot of them had left. And, when we went to Dar-es-Salaam, the Tanzanians had a lot of Chinese troops there and people from the Eastern block countries. Bob Barber and I stayed with a bloke from the Consulate. 'Don't worry,' he said. 'You were all vetted very closely before you came here. We know all about you and your families.'"

It was another successful trip, with Tom the outstanding bowler, and it ended with victory in a three-day match at the Gymkhana ground, Nairobi against an East African representative eleven. Mike Brearley remembers debating a declaration in the MCC second innings and Tom arguing adamantly that they should go on: "Get a decent score, keep the fielders in position and I can bowl properly for you." Then, when the quick bowler John Hutton was given the end with the wind behind him, Tom expressed his views a second time: "If you want me to float up a few half-volleys,

Michael, I'll bowl at this end. But if you want me to bowl properly, I need the other end." In due course he was switched, and inevitably he finished off the match with five cheap wickets.

NAIROBI, 18-20 JANUARY 1974.

CARTWRIGHT, 30 OVERS, FIVE FOR 53. 18 OVERS, FIVE FOR 30.

At home, however, Tom's absence created disruption. A teacher from Jeremy's school called to see Joan – "Has something happened at home? He seems very low in spirits" – and it was a while after Tom's return before the family settled down again. "It was a marvellous tour," Tom says, "but I've always regretted going."

While Tom was at Somerset, he sometimes drove up to Bristol for treatment at the home of Les Bardsley, the physiotherapist for Gloucestershire and Bristol City. "I can remember Les saying to me, 'You can't be a good pro without abusing your family.' I think that probably goes for people in quite a few walks of life."

Tom might be in his late 30s, but he was still as successful a bowler as any in English cricket – and Brian Close, four years older, was among the most successful batsmen. In 1972, for the first time in his long career, he averaged over 50 with the bat and, at the end of the summer, his distinctive style of captaincy was recognised by the selectors who appointed him to lead England in the first ever series of one-day matches, against Australia. It was an ironic appointment as, only two years earlier, Yorkshire had cited his lack of belief in the burgeoning one-day game as their reason for dispensing with his services and, in truth, not everybody at Somerset thought that his captaincy was at its best in the shorter game.

"He was great in the three-day game," Peter Robinson says. "He'd set the declaration to give time to take ten wickets, no matter whether they'd got Kanhai or Sobers playing or what, and he'd find ways of getting people out."

"I remember one of his first games when I was still captain," Brian Langford says. "I was bowling to Basil D'Oliveira. 'He plays with his pad a lot,' Closey said. 'I'll go and stand in front.' He stood right up close, and the third ball went straight into his hands.

"When he was captain, he was moving the field all the time. I was fielding mid-off in one game, and he moved me six times in one over. Barrie Meyer was umpiring. We went off for lunch and Barrie said, 'I'm the only bloke he hasn't moved.' Robbo said, 'It's your own fault. Don't look at him. If you look at him, he'll move you.'"

"But he wasn't a good captain in the one-day game," Peter Robinson says. "He was still thinking he'd got to bowl them out. He wouldn't appreciate it at all if nothing appeared to be happening, if you were strangling it."

"One-day cricket," Tom says, "is mostly about being clever in defence, and that just wasn't in his nature. He never defended in his life."

Brian Langford agrees. "He was a great captain when we were attacking but, when we were trying to defend, he'd get bored. Tom and I would build a bit of pressure. Then Closey would come on and bowl five or six overs of rubbish, and he'd take all the pressure off. I tell you, Tom used to do his nut."

Some remember the occasion when he summoned up the burly non-bowler Richard Cooper who proceeded to bowl high full-tosses to the big-hitting Mike Procter, but Peter Robinson's memory goes straight to the Gillette Cup match against Leicestershire in 1973.

That summer the 41-year-old Jim Parks had come down from Sussex. Mostly Jim played as a specialist batsman, leaving the gloves on the capable hands of Derek Taylor, but sometimes in the one-day matches he wore them – as he did that day at Taunton.

Somerset made 212, a good score in those days, and some time after tea, Leicestershire had slumped to 127 for seven. Tom and Brian Langford had bowled out their overs and, though Chris Balderstone was still at the wicket, it seemed to be just a matter of how long it would take Allan Jones, Hallam Moseley and Graham 'Budgie' Burgess to mop up the tail.

"Jim Parks took a blow on the thumb," Peter Robinson remembers, "and he said he couldn't go on with the keeping. Brian Rose had done it a few times, but Closey said, 'I'll do it. I kept in a Test match once.'"

"Before you could turn round, Closey was strapping the pads on," Tom says. "He couldn't wait for his chance; he never even tried to talk Jim round."

"He caught a little skier off Budgie," Peter Robinson goes on. "'There you are, lad.' But when Jonah came back on, Closey suddenly said, 'These bloody gloves are too small' and took them off. And that was red rag to a bull to Jonah, who started bowling faster and faster."

"The only thing that would have incited Jonah more," Tom says, "was if Closey had stood up to him. Jonah was bowling from the river end. Closey was trying to catch the ball as it went past him, and it was going straight through him, hitting the wall and coming all the way back to the middle. I said to him, 'Just line the ball up with your head and take it in front of you.' And he said, 'Don't tell me how to keep, lad. I've done it in Test matches.'"

Fourteen byes were conceded, the last four bringing the visitors victory with an over to spare. 'By the bye Leicestershire are through,' was the *Times* headline. "It was like knocking somebody down for 14 rounds," Peter Robinson says, "and losing in the 15th."

"It was a big match," Tom says, "and in lots of ways it was farcical."

Allan Jones and his captain were both strong-willed characters, but they were never kindred spirits and it did not help Brian Close's mood that Balderstone, who made 119 not out, had been dropped twice by the fast bowler, once when he had only scored 16. "Chris got a top edge, down towards the Stragglers," Peter Robinson remembers. "Jonah trotted round, dropped it and kicked it into the Ridley Stand."

Allan Jones was not a good fielder, and he left Somerset two years later, moving to Middlesex where his fast bowling helped to bring the championship title to Lord's for the first time for nearly thirty years. That summer, when Middlesex came down to Bath to play Somerset in the Sunday League, he was fielding in the deep on the leg side when Brian Close was batting. When the ball flew hard and wide of him, it was somehow inevitable what would happen. "He had to run backwards," Peter Robinson says. "He ran round the boundary, and he finished up catching it over his right shoulder." The irony was not lost on Alan Gibson in *The Times*: 'Jones has not been hitherto distinguished by brilliant running catches on the boundary.'

At the end of all the laughter, however, Tom has immense respect for Brian Close as a captain. "Maybe he didn't have the ability to think about defending, but he was a very positive cricketer and he had a genuine feel for how the game should be played."

Tom finds a parallel in the West Indies–England Test in Port-of-Spain in March 1968, when the series was locked in stalemate and Gary Sobers sought to bring it to life with a declaration that resulted in England regaining the Wisden Trophy. "I've had so many arguments with West Indians about that game. It was a brilliant declaration; it made for a great game of cricket. Close and Sobers, those people are worth ten of the others."

*

In the autumn of 1972 Tom began his work as Somerset coach.

"Len Creed asked me to go to his area meeting in Bath. There were about thirty or so people in the pavilion there, and he wanted me to tell them what I was going to do. I sat in front of them, and I said, 'First of all, can I say what I'm not going to do? I'm not going to confuse activity with achievement. I'm not going to get 500 kids on a register and say at the end of the winter, 'This is what I've coached.' I'm going to get about 50 kids of real quality together and, if I don't produce a team within five years, then sack me.'"

The invitations went out to clubs throughout the county, to send along their promising young players.

"My first session was on a Tuesday evening, at Peter Wight's indoor school in Bath. And the only people who turned up were Jimmy James the secretary, a photographer, a journalist and me. Then we had a session on Thursday at

Taunton, and this time Keith Jennings came as well. I said to him, 'What do you do?' 'I bat and bowl,' he said. 'Same as me,' I said. 'I'll bowl at you, and you can bowl at me.' It was the start of my coaching at Somerset."

It was all very well to have great ambitions, but a new culture had to be created. Bill Andrews had exuded good cheer, but his sessions were more likely to end up with his selling the youngsters kit from the back of his car than with his imparting to them any cricketing skills. "Dear old Bill," Peter Robinson laughs. "He's the only person I've known who could sell a pair of wicket-keeping gloves to an off-spin bowler."

"Nothing had been done for years," Tom says. "There wasn't any confidence that it was worth coming."

Another approach was made to the local clubs, and slowly a momentum developed. One of the first to come along to Bath was Colin Dredge, an 18-year-old apprentice toolmaker from Frome who, within five years, would be opening the bowling for Somerset, his ungainly action – all elbows and legs – drawing gasps of horror from the purists. "He wouldn't have a chance in the game today," Tom says. "He didn't fit any of the biomechanical templates. I remember when he first came to Bath. He used to terrorise the batters; his head almost hit the floor when he bowled. It was one of the great achievements of my coaching that I managed to get it up a bit."

Some young talent was already emerging from the independent schools. Peter Roebuck and Phil Slocombe had been in that summer's first eleven at Millfield, Vic Marks and Jeremy Lloyds at Blundell's. But Tom's eye was wandering further afield, as it had one evening the previous year when he and Brian Langford had looked into one of Bill Andrews' sessions in the Barracuda at Millfield School, a marquee designed for indoor tennis that was kept up by hot air.

"In the middle was a portable net with a tubular frame, and in it Peter Roebuck was bowling leg-breaks to Phil Slocombe. And around the outside of the hall were all these little groups, and one of them in the far corner was with Brian Lobb. They were practising the drive by hitting tennis balls."

Slocombe was a neat, stylish batsman, who was already attracting attention with large scores in schools cricket. For Bill Andrews there was the added excitement that he came from Weston, and he eagerly drew Tom and Brian Langford towards the young batsman.

"My eye kept going back to the lad playing the drive in Brian Lobb's group," Tom remembers. "His arms were working so well together when he hit the ball."

"Who's that boy in the corner over there?' Tom asked.

"Don't worry about him, my old beauty. I want to show you my boy over here."

"But who is he?"

"Oh, he's from the sticks," came the exasperated reply. "He's a kid called Bottom. Now come and look at my boy."

Ian Botham was only fifteen at the time, but he was sent for a trial at Lord's and offered a place on the ground staff there for the summer of 1972. His father Les was sceptical about the idea, and Tom remembers being called into a discussion in which Roy Kerslake, a local solicitor who was Somerset's chairman of cricket, was trying to persuade Les to let his son go.

"Les was insisting that Ian had to go into an apprenticeship. So I joined in and said that he possibly had a brilliant future. I often wonder, had Roy not been so insistent, if Ian would have finished up as a plumber or an electrician."

During Tom's first winter as coach, Somerset received the news that their Australian leg-spinner Kerry O'Keeffe was not going to return for a third summer. At that time counties were only able to sign an overseas player without residential qualification once every three years. It was impossible to replace him for 1973.

Some at the club wanted to secure the services of the Australian all-rounder Graeme Watson for the summer of 1974, but Tom was more interested in finding a developing talent, a young unknown who would grow to maturity alongside the young players he was starting to identify.

Tom attended a Professional Cricketers' Association meeting in Birmingham and got talking with Mike Brearley, who had been out in the Caribbean, guesting for the touring Kent team. "I asked him if he'd seen any good young players, and he came up with the name Richards. 'Ask Bob Woolmer if you want confirmation. He smacked us all over the ground.' I spoke to Rohan Kanhai, and I asked him the same question. 'There's a boy called Richards,' he said. 'I haven't seen him, but people are saying he can play.'"

Fate was at work. By the time Tom got back to Taunton, bearing the name of Richards, Len Creed the vice-chairman had flown back to Heathrow from a Mendip Acorns tour of the West Indies and he had with him the very same Vivian Richards, held in immigration while they sorted out a work permit.

"When he arrived that night, Len said to me, 'I've got this player.' And I said, 'I know all about him, Len.' He said, 'We've got to persuade the committee. Will you have a look at him?' And he brought him down to a first-team practice. Viv batted for half an hour. He didn't hit the ball off the square, but he looked magnificent. You could have put a pint of beer on his head, and he wouldn't

Hallam Moseley

"I remember sitting up in the box by the winning post at Derby with Denis Smith, the Derbyshire coach. He was a big man, carved out of granite, a bit like Tiger; he used to sit there with his cap on, smoking his pipe. 'I see you've signed that lad Moseley,' he said. 'We had a look at him. He lets the ball go in front of his head.' I looked at Hallam in the nets, and he did. He was collapsing on his front leg. We worked on getting him up, and he fractured his patella, his knee cap.

"Years later, I was at Lilleshall with Micky Stewart, before the England team went out to the World Cup. I was watching Geoff Arnold with Syd Lawrence, and he was trying to get him to get up on that front leg. I wanted to say something, and I thought, 'It's not my place." I always wish I had – because he fractured his patella that winter. He hardly played after that."

Viv Richards was the first of the six youngsters to make his mark. "I remember sitting down with Pete Roebuck, waiting to go out to bat in a little pre-season practice," Vic Marks says. "Bob Clapp ran in to bowl, and Viv played this rasping square cut. We just looked at each other and thought, 'We ain't going to get in in front of him.'"

Somewhat older than the others, at 22, Viv was in the team from the start of that summer of 1974. His debut came at Swansea in a Benson and Hedges match in which he hit an unbeaten 81 and won the Gold 'Man of the Match' Award.

"That was a great innings," Tom says, "but the real test for him was in the next Bensons game against Gloucestershire, facing Mike Procter. We all knew what was going to happen."

Saturday 4 May 1974. Somerset versus Gloucestershire at Taunton. The young Viv Richards up against the menacingly fast South African Mike Procter. "There's not been too many times in my life when I've been on a ground with an atmosphere like there was that day when Viv came out to bat."

Tony Brown was the Gloucestershire captain, and Viv did not appear till the Somerset score had reached 81 for two and the change bowlers were on.

"As soon as Viv walked out, Browny brought Procter back, and the first few balls he bowled to Viv were incredible. I think there was a drive off the front foot, a drive off the back foot, then came the inevitable bouncer."

The moment they had all anticipated. The moment of moments, and it was all over in the whizz of a ball and the flash of a blade.

"The ball finished up in the organ works. You could hear it rattling round the machinery in there, never to be seen again.'

WISDEN, 4 MAY 1974. 'THE NEWCOMER RICHARDS STRUCK HIS FIRST OVER FROM PROCTER FOR 15 RUNS.'

"It was a magical few minutes, it really was. And that six, it was one of the most electrifying moments in cricket that I've ever witnessed."

Before the year was out Viv was playing Test cricket, hitting an unbeaten 192 against India at Delhi.

"Viv was probably the best destroyer of bowling ever," Brian Langford reckons. "I remember Sam Cook umpiring a game, and he said to me, 'I bowled at Bradman, but this Richards is something else. With Bradman I still had two slips and a gully. But Richards, there's nobody close enough for him to talk to, they're all spread out and he's still smashing the ball everywhere."

"He was such a good player," Tom says. "I'm not sure how much I helped him. I hope I was an influence."

Viv's autobiography provides the answer: 'Tom had played with and against some of the best cricketers in the world, and he had plenty to pass on. He was definitely an influence on my development; he would tell me to be myself and work on my strengths. When things did not go well he was fine, but he was even better when things *were* going well because he could spot things that maybe you got away with and he made sure you did not do them again.'

"People said Viv was arrogant," Tom says. "When he walked onto the field to bat, everybody was aware of him. Everybody stopped and watched him, even when he was young. He walked out with an air that was different from other people. But it wasn't arrogance. He was seeking to impose his will on the people out on the field. That's what cricket's about. If you're going to get to the top, you have to have that ability to impose yourself on the person at the other end. It's got nothing to do with arrogance. Viv was the least arrogant person I think I've ever worked with. He was a smashing kid."

Another who quickly learned how to impose himself was Ian Botham, and his first day in the headlines came a month after Viv, in a Benson and Hedges quarter-final match against Hampshire at Taunton.

Early in the day he had a brief moment of glory when he bowled to Barry Richards and the dangerous South African, attempting to cut a long hop, edged the ball onto his wicket. But Somerset looked to have lost the tie when, needing 183 for victory, he went out to bat at 113 for seven. At the other end Tom was immediately caught at mid-on, and it was 113 for eight – with only the bowlers Hallam Moseley and Bob Clapp left to bat.

Eric Hill was in the press box, and he recalls how one of his fellow journalists sent in an early report of a Hampshire victory, leaving his editor to fill in the final details. However, the 18-year-old Botham and his partner Hallam Moseley had other ideas. Astonishingly they took the score past 150, and Botham was soon back on his feet after a bouncer from Andy Roberts had loosened a tooth and had him spitting blood onto the grass. 'The sheer heroism of it was stirring,' Eric Hill wrote. 'He ruefully rubbed the growing bruises around his eye and, from the boundary edge, seemed to turn down with some vehemence suggestions that he might go off.'

"He took them on," Tom says. "I couldn't watch it. I remember disappearing from the dressing room and wandering out into the streets outside the ground. It was very eerie; there was nobody in the vicinity as if they were all inside, watching the game. And I could hear the cheers. It wasn't just the winning of the game that stirred me; it was that it was one of my boys and that I could see this vision of the future. All my good days were when these lads started to do well. In a way I got too involved. I'd go home at night and worry whether they were playing well or not."

Ian Botham, after being hit, with Hampshire's Peter Sainsbury

Two more of Tom's six youngsters, Peter Roebuck and Vic Marks, were on duty that day. "We were putting up the score in that old brown scorebox," Vic says, "and we got so excited that we kept cocking it up. We all knew Both was a bit special, though we never dreamt he'd become what he became, and we always wanted to watch him – not just because he was Both but because he was the same age as us. If he could make an impact, perhaps we could as well. And that day was very exciting. We had an old phone that went through to the scorers by the press box, and we were getting all this abuse from the crowd: 'It's all wrong. The score, the overs.'"

181

Their fellow 18-year-old hit Roberts for six over fine leg, then a six off Herman sailed over the Priory Bridge entrance. As the runs required dropped into single figures, there was a tense hush as each ball was bowled, and Andy Roberts finally trapped Hallam Moseley lbw. Struggling to keep the strike, Ian Botham reduced the target to three. Then he hit a flowing cover drive to the boundary and was promptly mobbed by a delirious crowd. 'The greatest cricket match I've ever seen,' Eric Hill called it. Another of Tom's youngsters had established himself.

Tom's contribution to the development of Botham the batsman was limited: "I think I was good for him because I allowed him to develop the way he naturally batted." His contribution to the development of Botham the slip fielder was also limited, though it is acknowledged by Ian himself: "I always felt that one of the most frustrating things as a bowler was when you got the outside edge and it dropped short of the slips. So I came a little closer, and I took a couple of catches. I remember Tom and I discussing it. With Tom you could always sit down and talk something over. If he didn't agree with you but you explained why you did it, he'd listen. And he said, 'If that's the way you feel, field closer. Go out and prove people wrong.' I took some stick over the years, but I'm sure I took a few sharp chances that wouldn't have reached me if I'd stayed put."

Botham's natural talent with the bat and in the slips would have flowered without Tom's presence – but would Botham the bowler have happened? "The year he was at Lord's," Tom says, "they thought he was a joke bowler; they didn't let him bowl."

Tom remembers their conversation back at Taunton.
"How much bowling are you getting?"
"They think I'm a joke."
"Do you want to bowl?"
"Well, yes, of course I want to bowl."
"Well, if you want to bowl, I'll work with you because I think you could bowl."

"There were times when I got a bit down," Ian recalls. "But Tom kept pegging away at me. 'You're an all-rounder, you can be a very good one – so get on with it.' He had a lot of time, a lot of patience and he gave me a great deal of encouragement. As a youngster, if you've got somebody like that pushing away at you, it's a real buzz. I owe him a lot.

"We talked about what length to bowl and how to bowl at the different batsmen but, more than anything, he worked on my thinking, my mental strength. He and Closey, they were magnificent. Those two guys gave me my direction. They encouraged me, and they kept my feet on the ground."

In 1972 he was a joke bowler at Lord's. In August 1986, at The Oval, he was nipping the ball back into the pads of New Zealand's Jeff Crowe and celebrating as the umpire's raised finger took him past Dennis Lillee to become the greatest wicket-taker in the history of Test cricket. To this day, he remains England's greatest.

"I can honestly say that he was one of the most receptive people I've ever worked with," Tom says. "He learned to swing the ball both ways in a very short time, literally in weeks, and to have control in doing it. He had so much ability to grasp what was going on around him and to work. He was a classic example of somebody interpreting what he learned within his own physical and mental capabilities.

"Closey said, 'He's going to be a fast bowler, lad.' And I'd say, 'No, he isn't. He hasn't got an action to bowl quick, quick, quick. He's got an action to bowl at the top end of fast medium.' There were times when we'd walk onto the field arguing.

"Tiger said to me, 'Lots of people will offer you help. In the end it's down to you to think through what you've been offered. It'll be down to your judgement in the end.' It really is down to the individual: the learning, the ability to teach yourself.

"You have to do so much for yourself – and Ian did. People may think that life came easy to him as a cricketer, but he worked damn hard. He really did. I have as much admiration for him in the way he buckled down as for anybody I've ever been with."

Peter Roebuck's debut came in August that year, against Warwickshire at Weston. "I'd wanted him to play for some weeks, but Closey wouldn't. He wasn't that keen to have young players; what he wanted was good ones. You could be 40, and he'd pick you if you were good enough. In the end I said, 'If you don't pick him this time, I'm going to resign as coach.'

The 18-year-old from Millfield opened the batting with keeper Derek Taylor, and he scored 46 out of an opening partnership of 104.

"Warwickshire had a curious attack," Peter remembers. "David Brown led the way with his height and pumping elbows, and AC Smith the former wicket-keeper bowled in-swingers in a cravat. When I got out, Brian Close – without quite remembering my name; he had a habit of calling everybody 'doo-dah' – told me that I'd had a hundred there for the taking."

"Peter should have played for England," Tom says. "He was good front foot and back foot, and he had such a good brain. Not just an academic brain. I used to pick him up in Street and take him to games so we travelled together in the car a lot. That was when he was young and growing. And I just felt he had an incredibly shrewd cricket brain. It was the one real disappointment for me in my coaching career that he didn't play for England. It was injustice. I thought, on ability, he was a certainty."

In time Peter Roebuck would take on the captaincy of Somerset, his period of office forever enveloped in the storm that led to the departure of his two colleagues from those early days, Viv Richards and Ian Botham.

Tom, however, prefers to point to his later captaincy of Devon when, in four successive summers, he led them to the Minor Counties title. "He was a brilliant captain. They were all Devonians apart from him. It was an enormous feat. You're coping with all kinds of things as captain of a minor county – and to win four times, he really doesn't get the recognition he deserves. I feel the world hasn't treated him as well as it should have done."

Philip Slocombe was the fourth of Tom's six to join the first team, playing from the start of the next summer, 1975, when he hit a century in his third championship match and completed 1,000 runs.

"He had talent," Tom says, "and there was a single-mindedness about his batting that meant he would get hundreds. But I always felt he was a coached player, very schooled, very chiselled. There were days when that bore fruit, but he didn't have the natural look of the others. And if you rely on the stereotype, there will be periods of play in matches that will take you into places that you're not equipped to deal with.

"I never really had the coaching agreement with him that I had with the others. Once he got into the first team and started scoring runs, he didn't want to know."

At the start of his second summer Slocombe was chosen by MCC to play at Lord's in the season's curtain-raiser against Leicestershire, the county champions. He made an unbeaten 34, and John Woodcock in *The Times*, liking his patient, neat, correct style, thought that 'he could just be ready for a tour of India when the MCC side comes to be chosen in August.'

He did not progress as hoped, and he did not hold his place in the Somerset team throughout the season. "I remember him coming to me at Yeovil," Tom says. "'What's wrong with me, Tom?' I'd tried to tell him before the season that the pick-up of his bat wasn't on as true a path as before so I'm afraid I was a bit hard on him. 'It's a little late for that now, Philip,' I said. 'I tried to talk to you weeks ago.' As a boy he'd been heavily pushed by Bill Andrews, and I never felt that he discovered himself in the way the others did."

Vic Marks also made his Somerset debut in 1975, by which time his batting was making an impression at Oxford University. "I always thought Vic was at his best going in at six or seven, having the freedom to play his strokes, because he was a good player when he was hitting the ball. I was a bit surprised when he became an England strike bowler because, when they were young, Jeremy Lloyds spun it a lot more. But Vic acquired good change of trajectory and flight, and he's intelligent, you see. I'm a great believer in having cricketers with a brain – because, if you haven't got one, you struggle. And Vic taught himself so much. I just hope somewhere along the line that the things I was saying to him helped to point him in the right directions."

Vic Marks played six Tests, scoring fifties in each of his last three innings for England. He captained Somerset, then he retired from the game to become cricket correspondent of *The Observer*, a newspaper Tom and Joan read each Sunday. "He's a lovely boy," Tom says with real fondness, though Vic's gently uncontroversial articles do not always meet with the full approval of Tom's fighting spirit. "If you're speaking to Vic," he says with a chuckle, "tell him to get down off the fence."

Of the original six that Somerset recruited for the summer of 1974, only John Hook did not progress to a substantial career in the first-class game.

"It was a wonderful time in my life," Tom says. "Peter and Vic used to call at our house in Wells. They really were like an extended family."

Peter Denning and Brian Rose were only a little older so suddenly the Somerset team, instead of being held together by old campaigners recruited from far and wide, was filling up with youngsters from within the county.

"They came from all over the county, too," Tom says. "Ian from Yeovil, Vic from Chinnock, Colin Dredge from Frome, Keith Jennings from Milverton. Little Martin Olive from Wells, which hadn't had a Somerset cricketer for years. There was Dasher Denning from Chewton Mendip and Rosey from Weston. And, among the older players, Budgie from Glastonbury. There was hardly anywhere not represented. I remember the committee used to talk about the difficulties they had filling the marquees, and I said one day to Roy Stevens the secretary, 'If you get all these youngsters playing, coming from all over the county, you'll have people falling over themselves to hire those marquees at Bath and Weston.' And it turned out exactly like that.

People were out there, just waiting for something to catch on."

The golden years of Somerset cricket were fast approaching. "It would be conceited of me to say that it all happened because I was there – Roy Kerslake was a huge figure in it all, Colin Atkinson the Chairman at that time and Peter Robinson, who was my assistant, they were all important – but, had I not been there, I honestly don't think it would have happened like it did. The boys had to be nurtured. I think the committee thought it all happened naturally, that it was inevitable. It was only when it was all gone that they realised."

The arrival of the youngsters in the summer of 1974 had a rapid impact on the older players at Somerset, but the youngsters, arriving in a group, also had to adapt to the strange world of professional county cricket.

"I turned up on the first morning," Vic Marks recalls. "I was excited. It was my first day as a professional cricketer. And we were in the old dressing room, with a gas heater in the middle. And the first hour or two is spent huddling round this gas fire with Merv in particular going through all the details of our expenses. 'This meal allowance is an absolute disgrace. The petrol money, that can't be right.' For two hours we were listening to this outrage about the allowances. Merv got the same driving in from Yate as Keith Jennings got cycling in from Milverton. It went on and on and on."

"That was Merv," Peter Robinson confirms. "His first words, when he met you in April, wouldn't be, 'Hello, lads, how are we all doing?' It would be, 'Well, how much is the meal money and the travelling this year?' Our big pre-season treat was to go over to Weston for a brine bath and a football match. Merv would have his dog Thumper with him, and he used to bring the ball. And one year he didn't think the sides were fair. 'Come on, Thumper, we're off,' he said, and off he went with the ball."

"He walked off once at Taunton," Tom remembers, "and, when we got back to the dressing room, we found he'd washed Thumper in the slipper bath and used all the towels to dry him. They were all covered in dog hair."

For the youngsters, there was also Brian Close to adapt to, with early stints as twelfth man seeming to be less about extra sweaters than trips to the bookmakers. "The main thing was to know the numbers for Joe Coral and Taunton Turf," Peter Robinson recalls. "And you'd have to ring up some stable lad. 'What have you got for Brian today?'"

"For one dog race he told me to put five pounds on number three," Peter Roebuck remembers, "and I put three pounds on number five. Even though it won, he still seemed disgruntled."

"Tom and he were a beautiful contrast," Vic Marks says. "One paying attention to detail and wanting to create all the good habits, the other a wild card, a maverick you thought was mad but whom you had to respect.

I remember turning up 45 minutes late to a game once, I'd had a bit of a prang on the way, and Closey hadn't noticed."

"He'd struggle to know people's names," Peter Robinson says. "Keith Jennings made his debut in a Sunday League match. I thought, 'I hope he gets Keith on early.' Next thing you see is Rosey bowling. He probably didn't realise Keith was in the side to bowl till somebody told him."

"Tom was so good at bridging the generation gap," Vic Marks says. "I think he loved it that he had some young players who listened wide-eyed. He was a terrific enthusiast; he had a clear idea how the basics worked, and he could articulate that."

Close and Cartwright. Peter Roebuck, recalling Britain's successful wartime coalition, calls them 'the Churchill and Attlee of cricket'. "The two best pieces of advice I got in cricket were one from Tom, about the use of the left shoulder and dropping the bat down through the ball, and the other from Brian Close who said, 'Players with lazy minds can't make it.' Thirty years later, I find those two things are the core of the coaching I've done. I was very lucky to have those two influences – Close the great fighter, Cartwright the great technician.

"Botham was lucky to have them, too. He used to combine Close's gambling and bravado with Tom's thorough professional sense that cricket was a craft, a battle of skills. Between them, because they were so different, Close and Cartwright brought out those characteristics in Ian. They may have come out anyway, for all I know. But Botham was lucky to have the two of them there."

"We still think of ourselves a bit even now, thirty years on, as Tom's boys," Vic Marks says.

How sad that it would all end in acrimony in 1986. Peter Roebuck as captain would be a party to the decision to release Viv Richards, and Ian Botham would walk out in solidarity with Viv. Tom had been gone for ten years by that time, his brand of kindly discipline no longer keeping events in check, but he remembers hearing the news on his car radio.

"They were interviewing Brian Langford, who was Chairman of Cricket, and I felt sad, really sad, because it was like my family being torn apart. In a way I still felt possessive of them, that they were my boys. I just wish I'd been there. I'm certain I could have stopped it happening."

CHAPTER 17

TEN MINUTES IN A SMELLY WESTON TOILET
1976

In the summers of 1974 and 1975, as his youngsters began to break into the Somerset side, Tom's own cricket suffered setbacks, with injuries significantly reducing his appearances.

The summer of 1976, however, offered the hope of a return to full fitness. Tom worked hard in the pre-season nets and, in the first Benson and Hedges match against Gloucestershire at Bristol, he won the Gold award.

"Tom was such a great bowler," Brian Close says, "and it's amazing what difference a great bowler can make to a side. He can shoulder responsibility and help the other bowlers along. They have less responsibility and fewer overs to bowl so they can concentrate more – and, as a result, their confidence develops and they become better bowlers. We'd missed Tom for much of the previous two summers and I really thought that night, with him back in the team and winning the award, we were going to have a good season."

The next day, Sunday 2 May, Tom dashed all the hopes. Diving into the crease to complete a quick single in a televised Sunday League match against Sussex at Taunton, he collided so heavily with the fielder John Spencer that he was thrown into the air and landed on his head and shoulder. "There was a huge crack," he recalls, "and my right shoulder blade was split down the middle. It swelled up, and I was like the Hunchback of Notre Dame. I remember Derek Taylor driving me home, and he had to stop several times for me to be sick."

"In all my years in sport," Brian Close says, "I've never seen such a crestfallen team as we were that evening."

Weeks of intensive manipulation and physiotherapy followed for Tom. However, during that time, his 45-year-old captain's career took another remarkable twist. The West Indians were touring England, and at Lord's in late May a strong MCC batting line-up looked apprehensive against the pace of Holding, Roberts and Holder and capitulated feebly. So, when the West Indians came to Taunton for their next match and Brian Close hit a typically battling 88, Alan Gibson in *The Times* was quick to champion him as the answer to England's problems, even suggesting that he, not Tony Greig, should be captaining the side:

> It was sad when he failed to get his hundred. He was out just after tea, from a bad stroke to a bad ball. I suppose this, too, is part of his character. When the West Indians went in again, they scored runs

without difficulty. Bang-bang went Greenidge's sixes to long leg and fours to square leg. The Old Bald Blighter stood steadfastly at short leg, for as long as it was useful. Then, as evening clouds drew round the Taunton ground, he dropped back a little, ruminating like a Wharfedale bull who is trying to remember spring. He nevertheless made one marvellous, sudden, stooping stop.

Oh bring back yesterday, bid time return! What the very dickens and devil of a cricketer Close ought to have been for England. The historians, in the future, will be puzzled about it all. Was it his own fault? Very possible, though others might also be to blame. Even now, from the shadows, if we really want to beat the West Indians next week, this dour, difficult and daring man might be recalled to the sunshine.

Two days after these words appeared in print, the selectors announced the Test team. There was a first call-up for Tom's friend Mike Brearley, eleven years – including several of university lecturing – after their tour to South Africa. And, to the amazement of many, there was a comeback for the Somerset captain, 27 years on from his debut. Peter Robinson was in the car with him, driving to a Sunday League match at Portsmouth when he heard the news. "Do you know, lad," he said, "it's the first year I haven't put the dates in me diary."

Against a fearsome West Indian attack Brian Close did as well as anybody in the first two Tests, top-scoring at Lord's, but before the Old Trafford match he was summoned by Tony Greig to the captain's room and given a new role.

"He said to me, 'Brian, the selectors and I have been talking. We want you to open the innings.' 'You must be joking," I said. 'I haven't opened in a first-class match for years. Anyway, what's Bob Woolmer in the Test side for?' 'Oh,' he said, 'we think he's got a lot of Test cricket left in him. We don't want him killed off.'"

England were bowled out for 71 in the first innings, and by Saturday evening Brian and the 39-year-old John Edrich were going out to bat for a second time, needing 552 for victory. "It was a very hot summer, and I've never seen a wicket as bad to play Test cricket on. The faster you bowled, the more it went through the top and flew."

There followed a period of eighty minutes, in which the two batsmen scored 21 runs and survived numerous blows to the body. "Bill Alley was one of the umpires, and at one stage he warned Holding that he was bowling too many bouncers. I said to him, 'What the hell have you done that for, Bill? The bouncers are going over our heads. It's the ones that are more pitched up that are hitting us.'"

"If you watch the film of him that evening," Tom says, "you'll see that, when he got hit, he visibly shook, almost an involuntary reaction, and I'd never seen that before. It was very harsh to put him in that position at his age."

On Monday the two survived another hour before Brian Close was bowled by Roberts for 20. England subsided from 54 for no wicket to 126 all out, and the selectors replaced the pair of them for the next Test.

Tom made his comeback on Monday 9 August, captaining the second eleven against Shropshire at the club ground in Bath. It was another pitch suffering from the heatwave, and Tom returned figures of six for 24 in Shropshire's first innings of 99. "It was a minefield," Peter Roebuck remembers. "The batsmen were trying to counter him by going down the wicket so the keeper was standing up. Tom wasn't just bouncing the ball, he was cutting it, and the ball was going all over the place. I was at slip, and I had to take it several times."

Somerset managed 138 in reply. Tom was unable to bowl a second time but, with Bob Clapp taking five wickets, the game was completed that evening. Together with the game at The Oval in 1953, Tom reckons he may be the only cricketer to have played in both two-day and three-day matches that have finished inside one day.

The first team was playing at Weston-super-Mare and, with his shoulder still feeling the painful after-effects of bowling, Tom drove there the next day. Somerset were among the front runners in the Sunday League, raising hopes of a first trophy in the club's history, and news of Tom's success against Shropshire led the chairman Herbie Hoskins, a farmer from Yeovil, to tell Tom that he had to play in the first team the next Sunday.

What followed was the saddest episode in Tom's life. He and his family were settled in Wells, he took great pride in the achievements of his young players and, in his own words, "I was happy with Somerset and, to be honest, I saw the rest of my life there."

He had already received a letter from the committee, telling him that his contract expired at the end of the summer – "There was some new legislation about severance pay, and they'd got in a panic over a technicality" – but he did not really think that his position with the club was insecure when Herbie Hoskins confronted him in the Weston toilet.

"I told him I wasn't fit. I couldn't even bowl in the second innings at Bath," and he said, 'We've got a chance of winning the league. You must play.'"

The discussion became heated, and Tom only remembers parts of it. "He said, 'The doctor says you're fit.' The club doctor was a paediatrician, and I was certain he'd said no such thing. 'Are you going to take the word of a paediatrician over me?' I said. 'I know when I'm fit to bowl.' … 'Anyway,' I

190

said. 'You've sacked me. I've got the letter to prove it.' 'We had to write that to cover ourselves,' he said. … Keith Jennings was sitting outside, and I said, 'He's your future. Play him.' … It was the interval, and Peter Robinson was out marking the pitch. Herby said, 'Look, there's a man who'll do anything for Somerset.' And I said, 'Herby, that's Peter Robinson. This is Tom Cartwright. And I won't do things that I know are not right.' … The argument lasted about ten minutes, all in that toilet in Weston. I can smell it to this day."

Rumours of the row reached the press, but Tom still did not expect what followed. The chairman convened a meeting and some days later, at the end of a day when Tom had been watching the second eleven at the county ground in Taunton, he received a message that the secretary Roy Stevens wanted to see him in his office. Tom was giving Peter Roebuck and Martin Olive a lift home, and he left them in the car.

"Roy was as white as a sheet when I got there, and he looked a real mess. 'I want you to sign to say you've received this envelope,' he said. He'd been a Royal Marine. I played against him for the Army against the Navy. I had no inkling of what was coming, and I remember I joked with him. 'I was taught in the army never to sign for anything,' I said. 'But I'll sign for you anytime, Roy.' And as soon as I'd taken the envelope, he hurried out of the office, locked the door, rushed off to his car and drove off. I walked back to my car and, when I opened the envelope, it had a cheque in it and a letter saying that I was to clear my locker and never come back to the ground. I didn't say anything to Peter and Martin. I drove home, and I talked to Joan. It was horrible, really horrible. They put around the word that I'd refused to play, and I hated it that people thought I'd deserted the youngsters. The day we packed up and drove out of Wells was one of the worst days of my life."

Tom's professional pride and refusal to kowtow to committees had locked him in a dispute with an obstinate chairman, and it had all gathered momentum, leading to a conclusion that nobody wanted: not Tom, not the young players, not even the committee members who had decided his fate.

"A decision taken at the end of a hot day through the thick bottoms of whisky glasses at Weston," Tom calls it now. "Just about every one of the people on that committee has sidled up to me over the years and said, 'I wasn't part of it.' Even Herbie. 'You know, Tom,' he said. 'I hated writing that letter. They made me do it.' And he was the chairman."

In the end the Sunday League title was lost on the last day. Several thousand Somerset supporters made their way to Cardiff, flooding into the ground long before the arrival of the gatemen, and Glamorgan secretary Wilf Wooller sent out stewards with buckets in a forlorn effort to recoup the lost admission charges. 'With not a Welsh accent within hearing,' Alan

Gibson wrote, 'Sophia Gardens might have been Bridgwater Carnival.'

Glamorgan made 190. Then, late in Somerset's reply, the total was mysteriously increased to 191. Many of the crowd were unaware of the alteration and, with the other results that day meaning that Somerset only needed to tie to win the title, their final score of 190 led to initial cheering. In fact, with Colin Dredge run out inches from the crease, they had lost by one run. Brian Close, dropping a crucial catch and making only one run before being caught on the boundary, was left reflecting that 'the game's been like my ruddy life, a cock-up.' 'It was enough to make a Somerset man weep,' wrote Alan Gibson, 'though mostly, as they departed from the ground, they just swore instead.'

It would be another three years before Somerset, under the captaincy of Brian Rose, would lift the county's first ever trophy. Tom had persuaded them to take on six youngsters for the summer of 1974, and four of them – Botham, Richards, Roebuck and Marks – would be prominent in the one-day side that would go on to win five trophies in five years, with Slocombe also playing in some of the games. It was success on a scale that the county had never experienced before; it has never been repeated since.

Tom's position as coach was passed to his assistant, Peter Robinson.

"I learnt so much about coaching from Tom," Peter says. "He had a knowledge of the game and a passion for it. And he's never lost it. He's still got it now."

"Peter doesn't get the credit he deserves," Tom responds. "He was a good cricketer and a good coach, and he's done so much for Somerset over the years."

In time Peter would be coach, groundsman, scorer, even – in his last post before retirement – the club's health and safety officer, a posting his wife called "a square peg in a round hole, if ever there was one."

"He was willing to do anything," Tom says, "which kept him on the staff. But he was always going to be shunted from place to place because, if you're that kind of person, you do get shunted. I remember coming back with the Glamorgan team some years later, when he was still coach and they had this Aussie physio. There was a net up in the morning, and Robbo was standing there with a bag of balls while the Somerset team were running round the outfield. 'You might as well use the net,' he said to me. 'I keep coming out, hoping somebody will want a practice.'"

"In some ways," Peter says sadly, "the game has been hijacked by fitness people, and the skills have to take care of themselves. I think the balance has got slightly wrong."

Tom has a more robust response. "If I'd still been coach, I'd have stopped all that but Robbo didn't have the clout."

The year after his dismissal Tom returned to Somerset to attend a funeral. "We went back to 'Dasher' Denning's uncle's pub, and Herbie sat next to me. He was a lovely old boy, really. 'Tom,' he said. 'What we need is a good coach.' And I said, 'I thought you had a decent one, Herbie.' I'm sure, if I'd offered to come back, he'd have snapped my hand off."

"At the time," Vic Marks says, "we didn't take in the consequences. 'Tom's going.' We all respected him, and we were disappointed. But we were young, naïve and quite full of ourselves. 'We'll cope,' we thought. But, looking back now, his contribution seems even greater than we realised at the time."

"Any county could do it, you know," Tom says. "You only have to have somebody in charge who knows what he's doing."

A young Tom absorbs Len Hutton's 'Just My Story'

'Unfortunately, with the ever-increasing tempo of modern life – call it jet-age jitters, if you like – the demand for speed appears to be uppermost in the minds of most young people. They are constantly searching for something quicker and better. Often, in the end, they find that what they get is slower and inferior!

'Cricket doesn't lend itself to this hurly-burly, and never will. The youngster of today who is enthusiastic about the game and enters it in the right spirit will obtain as much exercise as he needs on any one day and he will find it as exciting as any other form of amusement. Cricket doesn't always sprint along but when the last ball is about to be bowled, it's four to win and the last man in, I think everyone on the ground is gripped by a feeling that doesn't come over the spectator of any other sport.'

CHAPTER 18

A SIX-BALL OVER

1

"Excellence is always determined by the quality of the interaction between bat and ball at any given time. If you accept that, then you must not take that away. It has to fall away naturally, when the bowler gets tired or the batsman gets out – and the battle is won. You must not take people out in an artificial way. If you introduce anything that's artificial, then you detract from excellence.

"If you take the one-day game, and the best player on one side is the opening bat and on the other the opening bowler, when the game starts the potential for excellence is at its very highest level. Then, after a few overs, that is diminished when the bowler is taken out of the attack because of the constraints of the match.

"It's as if the bowlers are sharing around a chore; they don't learn to take responsibility, and it carries across into the four-day game. There are very few counties who can win a game by bowling a side out for 180 or 200 in the fourth innings by using three bowlers.

"The by-product of the restriction on the bowler is that the batsman's potential for improvement is impaired as well – because the challenge becomes less.

"So your excellence level immediately falls. If you multiply that by all the games that are played at all the age group levels and then look at the restrictions on bowling for kids and all the other things, then the detraction from potential excellence is monumental. I can't understand why people can't see that.

"I do feel sorry for the bowlers in one-day cricket. Batsmen used to wonder what bowlers were going to do. Now it's reversed. Bowlers are trying to second-guess the batsmen. You can't learn the skills of bowling, of taking wickets, within that framework."

2

"The Australian game is based on pace and wrist spin, as it ever was. If you look at our game, the finger spin and swing and seam have been greatly reduced – with too much limited overs cricket and with covered pitches. It's had a devastating effect on the quality which we produce in depth. The depth was greater in county cricket in the 1960s. If there was still that depth now, then the quality of the players coming out of it would be greater – because of the interaction that they would daily face.

"It's a dumbing down. It's a horrible American phrase, I know, but it's true.

"The pressures on the bowler were far, far greater when you were playing on uncovered pitches. Much of the time you'd be bowling on good batting wickets. But if you were bowling on a pitch that was damp and green and seaming and you were going to get seven wickets, you'd got to get them for 35 or 40. If you got them for 70, you'd lose. When runs were at a premium, you couldn't make up the difference with the bat.

"If you look at the number of bowlers who got their 100 wickets at under 20 apiece, that tells you something about their control.

"If the pitches are always in the batsmen's favour, the bowlers don't learn anything. They then become percentage cricketers, looking to come out of their spell of bowling at 4 an over, 3½ an over. A negative approach. It's an inevitability."

3

"Cricket, like other sports, needed sponsorship. But I can never understand why it capitulated to that sponsorship in making so many changes when other sports have hardly changed a jot. In so many ways we changed how we delivered a day's cricket whereas 200 metres is still 200 metres. Nobody brought it down to 170 to make it more exciting.

"Cricket, above all sports, singularly perhaps, is the one that has changed its format, its method of playing, almost totally. It's so dramatic the change. I much prefer to see people play natural cricket. Then you get a multi-faceted game. When you take away some of the facets, which we have done, it shrinks in its artistic form, certainly in the disciplines required, and therefore the overall product is diminished.

"It's like so many things that you buy. All the emphasis is on presentation and packaging. Nearly always the thing itself is inferior in hand-crafted quality.

"The game in my day wasn't macho. I can remember at Edgbaston, when I started there, Tiger saying the best ball-player was Jimmy Ord – and he was a little, short man from Durham. He had this lovely touch, lovely balance on his feet. I was only 16 at the time, and I'd sit and watch him. He was a beautiful ball player.

"Probably Ian Bell is closest to him, and Michael Vaughan, a beautiful stroker through the covers. And several of the Indians, of course. They're that type of person, with touch and with a lovely balance that goes with it.

"We had so many players like that. Tom Graveney: he was so elegant, I could watch him all day. Arthur Milton: Arthur Cloth-bat they called him because there was no sound on the bat. George Emmett, Joe Hardstaff, Dennis Brookes, Gilbert Parkhouse. There was a craft, a caress about the way they played. There was something gentle and pure, right through from the way they looked so well turned out.

"Now it's all more butch. It's all big hits. It's the same with the bowling, the obsession with pace. The bowler no longer caresses the ball when it comes out. That finesse, that artistic thing, it's something quite different from bludgeoning the ball or hurling it.

"I do honestly believe that our level of technical skills – batting, bowling, wicket-keeping – has diminished. That's no slight on the current player. It's the environment he's playing in. It's the environment that will always shape your ability."

4

"Sledging is infantile playground behaviour, isn't it? I can't believe it goes on. The wicket-keepers are expected to orchestrate all this noise, and the players are telling you all the time who they're going to target. It's pathetic. It's a huge tragedy that it's been allowed to happen like this. Not enough people speak out against it.

"We do it because the Aussies do it, but why do we have to copy what they do? Step outside cricket and think. Is that the sort of ethic we want to encourage in the world, the way we want adults to deal with each other? They say it's a test of mental strength, but it's got nothing to do with that. It's a complete abuse of what sport is about, and we just accept it. I can't watch the television with the sound on.

"I say to my kids, 'The umpires are responsible for the laws of the game; the players are responsible for its spirit.' Unless people understand that, the real feel for the goodness of the game will go.

"I had a boy keeping wicket in my final trials a couple of years ago, and he went up for a catch down the leg-side when he knew the batter hadn't hit it. I said, 'That's cheating.' 'No, it isn't, Tom.' I said, 'It is. You knew he hadn't hit it. I don't ever want to see that again on the field.' He came to me afterwards and apologised.

"I can remember going to a Test and County Cricket Board meeting at Lord's in the early 1980s. Gubby Allen proposed that only the keeper, bowler and first slip should be allowed to appeal for lbw – because appealing from other positions is cheating, isn't it? You're guessing – or trying it on. Tony Brown and I strongly supported him. They went off to lunch, chewed it over

197

and came back and said, 'Let's leave it. There's a lot to discuss this afternoon. We'll look at it again another year.' It's always bothered me that it didn't happen. If they'd have acted then, they'd have stopped it in its tracks. Now they're trying to claw it back. The kids do it; they're all shouting.

"I remember one year my under-16s were playing against the West of Scotland, and they were making all these comments aimed at the batsmen. I just walked onto the field. 'Do you mind if I talk to my players?' And I said, 'I don't want to hear anymore. The next one that says anything doesn't ever play again.' I wish umpires would do it, but they won't.

"Religion brought a semblance of order to the community, and it's gone. And sport did a similar thing. There was a discipline and an order. These things fashioned people's lives.

"What was precious in our game is being destroyed, thrown away."

5

"If Test cricket is not going well, they go straight to the grassroots. They ignore the bit in the middle – county cricket: the development of quality. Not only have they ignored it, they've destroyed it.

"When I played county cricket, we had the opportunity to play every day, and we had to prove ourselves. It was like a market force. Playing is important. You've got to play a lot of cricket, and it's got to be the right sort of cricket. Any national team in any sport reflects the domestic game.

"Now the England team is like an elite club within a country. It's become almost completely disconnected from the rest of the game – and the journalists that cover it are an elite group, too, all within this bubble.

"Not only has the Test team become disconnected from the county game, the county game has become disconnected from the recreational game. There used to be associations in each county that looked after recreational cricket, and they were made up of people who were elected from the grass roots. Now in most counties they've been replaced by bodies where the members are appointed by the counties. It's all become top-down, and it's disillusioned and demoralised so many of the people who did so much voluntary work in the game. If you want the best at the top, there has to be a connection right the way down to communities.

"It was the people's game when I played. Then it started to shift from that to becoming financially driven. Now marketing and sponsorship have totally taken over. The game was run by people in sports jackets, and now it's become suits, hasn't it? It may sound glib, but it tells a huge story.

"The more people become organised, the more it detracts from why they are there. I remember Peter Cranmer, one of my first second-team captains at Edgbaston, saying, 'You can be over-organised if you're not careful.' You lose the free natural progression; you've strangled it at an earlier point.

"Most of the people in these jobs – because of their lack of ability, or confidence in their ability – try to have cushions. They have people between whatever they're dealing with and themselves. The responsibility is deflected; they bring in people to absorb the pressure, whereas people before stood on their ability.

"They create work to keep themselves going, to pay their salaries and their pensions. They're not interested in passing on their knowledge and skills – because their interest is not there in the first place. They could be organising transport, couldn't they?

"So much of their innovation is born of job justification.

"The people who used to be in charge of cricket were ex-cricketers. The other people were brought in and used for what they were good at. Now they've stayed and they've multiplied, and the ex-players, with a conscience about how the game should be, have gone.

"I'm staggered by my own thoughts now. I'd rather see the thing go back to being controlled by the MCC of yesteryear, that type of person, rather than the hard-bitten professional who's come out of the City. I look at John Barclay at Arundel, an Old Etonian, and he's trying to spread joy. His bounce is telling you that. It's joy. And I find myself wishing that people like him were running the game."

6

"I feel very strongly about every kid having the opportunity to attain and achieve what the great players before them achieved, to wear the crown and three lions of England. Now you have officials at the ECB, wearing the coronet and three lions to give them a bogus credibility, and it devalues the achievement of playing for England. It all becomes disconnected from the past – and meaningless.

"It's not a snob thing. It's like the green baggy cap. You won't find the Australians giving that away to anybody of dubious credibility. They value the history of their game; they pound their players with it. The magic comes from the past and from the folklore of it all.

"Every development has to be comfortable with the past. Otherwise the whole thing's lost.

"The person I look up to more than any other in sport is Brian Clough. I had tremendous admiration for him. He had a unique way of producing high quality teams, and it almost flew in the face of FA policy. That's why he was never manager of England. All that bragging was just a game. He was shrewd. He got his players to do very well the things which they did naturally; individuals shone in his teams.

"He held on to the discipline of the game, and he had an unswerving attitude to the freeloaders, the people who battened on to the game; he never backed down from that. There was a fearlessness about the way he took on the pretenders who latch on to sport and ruin it. I know he had his faults at a personal level, but to me he stands out like a beacon in the world of sport.

"I just hope that long after I've gone there will still be enough people around who love cricket more than they love money. If there are, it will be OK. But the way we're going, we're almost knocking the love of cricket out of people."

The grandchildren learn cricket
Thomas, aged 10, is bowling on the left
Matthew, aged 8, is being shown how to bowl by Grandpa

CHAPTER 19

INTO WALES

1977 –

It was John Arlott who came to the rescue when, for a second time in his cricket career, Tom found himself out of work. Arlott often reported on Somerset matches, staying at the Rose and Crown in East Lyng where at night he would invite chosen players for dinner with him in the parlour of the pub – and Tom was one who received more invitations than most. So he wrote on Tom's behalf to Ossie Wheatley, the new chairman of Glamorgan. As a result Tom and Joan moved to Neath, back among Joan's folk, and Tom played one last summer of first-class cricket.

"In some ways I knew what to expect when I moved to Wales, but it was around the time that they were starting to put all the road signs in Welsh as well as in English so it was also a bit of a shock. It wasn't another county; it was a nation – and a very proud nation. People use the word 'nation' a lot in Wales."

Glamorgan were going through hard times. The previous summer, the last of Majid Khan's four-year reign as captain, had seen them finish at the bottom of the championship table, bottom-but-one in the Sunday League and eliminated at the earliest stage from both knock-out cups. The club had lost the winning ways that had brought it the championship in 1969 or – as its former captain and long-serving secretary Wilf Wooller put it in *The Cricketer Spring Annual* – 'Glamorgan has been going through a period of transition.'

"That was always Wilf's stock reply to criticism," recalls Peter Walker, a key member of the 1969 championship side. "I don't think the playing staff ever had any idea where we were in transit from or to."

Wilf Wooller, a sledger before his time and an outspoken champion of right-wing political causes, was not a man to whom Tom warmed. "He was appalling. When I was only about 19 or 20, I was batting against Glamorgan at Edgbaston. He was fielding at mid-wicket, and he stopped Jim Pressdee halfway through an over. 'Hang on, Jim,' he said. 'This little bugger couldn't hit it off the square.' He came right in at forward short leg. I played this full-blooded sweep, and the ball cracked very hard onto his shin. That was a very satisfying moment in my life.

"I always wanted to take Wilf on, because he was a bully. We had a big slanging match one year at Swansea. He was at the back of the members' seating, and he started to shout out all these criticisms. He accused me of bringing all these English people into the club. And I started to shout back.

I think he would rather have somebody shouting back than crumbling. I said, 'I suggest you have a recount. I think you'll find there were more Englishmen in your sides.' It was like *High Noon*.

"Another year there was a Balconiers do at Swansea, and he made a reference to all the languages in the team, with people like Javed and 'Smoky' Featherstone. It's the one time in my life that I've regretted that I couldn't speak Welsh. I really wanted to get up and answer him in Welsh – because I'm not sure he'd have been able to reply.

"Wilf once told me that, when he was captain, he wanted his players to be more afraid of him than of the opposition." Tom smiles. "He probably achieved that. I know Bernard Hedges used to say that, if he was walking towards him on the pavement during the winter, Wilf would totally ignore him."

However, it seems that not everybody was intimidated by Wooller. "When I was at Somerset, we played a Sunday League match in Pontypridd and we couldn't find Jeremy at the end of the game. He was only about eight, and we were in and out of all the marquees. Then we ran into Wilf; he was carrying some crates and bottles, and behind him was Jeremy with some more bottles. There was this monster of a man and this tiny little boy. I said, 'What do you think you're doing, Jeremy?' He said, 'I'm helping Wilfred.'"

Tom was 42 years old in July 1977, and his contributions on the field that summer were limited. Nevertheless, with Alan Jones as captain and Tom himself taking on the role of first-team coach, the results improved a little, and there was an end-of-season fillip when they won through to the Gillette Cup final. Never before had the county reached even the semi-final of one of the Cups, and a great army of Welsh supporters travelled in good voice to Lord's. At one point it looked as if their opponents might be Somerset – "I really didn't want to play against them," Tom says. "They were all my kids" – but in the event Tom's last appearance at Lord's was against Mike Brearley's powerful Middlesex side. He bowled his 12 overs for 32 runs, took the wicket of Michael Smith, and, though the match was lost, Welsh spirits were still high at the awards ceremony when the strains of *Land of my Fathers* and *Ar hyd y Nos* rang out in the damp September air.

"It was a very emotional day," Tom remembers. "I'd been to Lord's finals three times with Warwickshire, but this was very different. There was a lot of feeling, lots of singing and a great party afterwards. But at the end of the season I went to the cricket committee and I said to them, 'Don't be fooled. We've only papered over the cracks.'"

Tom was offered the newly created post of cricket manager. "They also wanted me to carry on playing, but I said, 'It's pointless. Get the young players in; find out if they're good enough.' Sometimes it can be a brutal process, but you need to give young players the opportunity, even if you're only proving that they're not quite good enough."

During the summer of 1978 Tom travelled about the country with the first team, but the job was not that well suited to his abilities and coincided with a period in which Glamorgan's fortunes did not improve. "It was a non-position," Tom says. "When Ossie asked me to do it, he said, 'We really want you to be a fireman' – whatever he meant by that. It frustrated me. You can't muck around with people during the summer while they're playing at that level. The real work is outside the first team, preparing the young players and rehabilitating the ones who have been dropped."

Alan Jones, Tom and Ossie Wheatley

Alan Jones captained again in 1978. "Alan was a great batsman, one of the best technically that I've played against, and he's a very nice bloke. But I'm not sure he especially wanted to be captain. I went to a cricket committee meeting at Tony Lewis's house, and Tony said, 'We need somebody fresh. Is there anybody finishing with another county, somebody with lots of experience who could give us a lift?' I could only think of Hobbsy in Essex, and Tony said, 'Great, go and see him.'"

So began a disastrous chapter in the career of Robin Hobbs. He was working for Barclays Bank, taking wickets aplenty for Suffolk in the Minor Counties, and Tom met him twice at Paddington Station, where over several cups of coffee he persuaded him – against the wishes of his wife – to give the Glamorgan captaincy a go.

"I was selling Barclaycard, and it was getting a bit boring," Robin says. "Tom said, 'We're not doing that well; we need you to put a bit of life in the team.' I'd always enjoyed playing against Glamorgan, and I agreed to do it. That first year I stayed in the Angel Hotel, Cardiff and the Dragon, Swansea, and I drove back to Essex whenever I could. It was hard work, especially when we went the whole season without winning a game."

With Malcolm Nash injured, the batting rarely making a decent total and the only overseas player the little-known Rhodesian Peter Swart, Glamorgan were at rock bottom in the summer of 1979. Robin's chirpy East London manner somehow failed to lift dressing-room spirits, where he was less prepared than Tom for the Welshness of it all. "A lot of them spoke Welsh among themselves in the dressing room," he remembers.

"We nearly won a game," Robin says to console himself. "We had Gloucestershire nine wickets down at Cardiff, and we had over an hour to bowl out the last pair, David Graveney and John Childs. You know how you get a gut feeling in a game. I said to Swart and Ontong, 'Bowl some bouncers at them.' But we never looked like getting the wicket. Mike Procter was captaining Gloucestershire. I was talking to him about it a few years later, remembering how tough it had been, and he said, 'Hobbsy, if we'd known it was that desperate, we'd have let you have the wicket.'

"We were a pretty poor side, and nothing seemed to go right for us. If you look through *Wisden* – and I don't, I keep that one sealed – you'll see that we always seemed to be on the wrong end of the weather and the uncovered wickets."

Robin was on a three-year contract which, despite cartilage problems, he saw out. But after one year he passed on the captaincy to Malcolm Nash, who was fit again and who led the team to four victories. "Nashy was a bloody good new ball bowler," Robin says, "and we had Javed Miandad and Ezra Moseley. You're always going to win a couple of games with guys like that in your side."

Tom remained Glamorgan's cricket manager till 1983, by which time the captaincy had passed from Malcolm Nash to Javed Miandad and Barry Lloyd, then to Mike Selvey. At one stage Tom even tried to tempt Vic Marks across the Bristol Channel. They were not successful years, and Tom was happy when he relinquished his position.

For most of this time Tom had also been Director of Coaching to the Welsh Cricket Association. The post had been created by Ossie Wheatley in his role as Chairman of the Welsh Sports Council, in an attempt to get recreational and county cricket moving in the same direction. "He asked me to build a structure of development throughout Wales," Tom says, "to produce a Welsh nucleus to take things forward. It was a two-fold task; I had to produce excellence, and I had to sustain the depth of club cricket in Wales."

Tom worked closely with Bill Edwards, Chairman of the Association: "He was marvellous. He's done so much for cricket in Wales, and he always gave me unflinching support, never interfered." The first task was to divide Wales into eleven regions, from Anglesey to Gwent, and to find a structure of coaching for each of those regions. Tom was set a target of recruiting and training 100 coaches in his first year, and by the end of it – after long hours of driving the minor roads of Wales – he had 120 qualified coaches in action. These were days before the growth of central grants, and much of the work had to be self-financing. "We were lent rooms in the universities and colleges in Bangor, Aberystwyth and Swansea; there was so much goodwill."

The link between Glamorgan and the whole of Wales was reinforced – 'Develop as a nation, play as a county' was the approach – and from the summer of 1980 Tom took over the Welsh under-16 team. His first captain was Hugh Morris, and they reached the finals of the inter-county Texaco competition held at Uppingham School. In Tom's first twelve years in charge his under-16 sides reached the finals six times, more than any other county except Yorkshire.

"My great regret was that I deliberately kept Jeremy out of that first side. He was good enough to play, but it was all a bit messy at that time and I thought it would be easier if I didn't pick him."

For 27 years now, from 1980 to 2006, Tom has run the under-16s, and he is starting his winter's work again with a new group for 2007. Always keen to have his young cricketers in action on the field, he accompanies them through the summer holidays as they play three fixtures each week, including an annual tournament in Jersey.

The youngsters feel a pride in playing for the nation of Wales, but Tom does see a downside to this. "They do have a little bit of an inferiority complex. They need to play against people a few times before they realise they're better than them. When I organised the fixtures myself, I used to make sure they played mostly away games, in England, to get them over this."

Of all counties in recent years Glamorgan has come closest to fielding home-grown sides. Many of the boys who have passed through his teams have gone on to play for the county, among them Robert Croft and Simon Jones.

Robert turned up as a mad-keen nine-year-old, good enough to hold his own in Tom's under-11 sessions – while Tom had known Simon from a baby, from playing Old England cricket with his father Jeff. "When he was 16, Simon was yards quicker than anybody else we played against – but I was always worried whether he would stand up physically to being a fast bowler. He had the shape of an athlete, and that doesn't give you the durability you need."

When Glamorgan won the championship in 1997 most of the side had come through Tom's under-16 teams, as have most of the players who three times in recent years have won the first-class umpires' award for fair play.

"He's been superb," Robert Croft says. "He's got a fantastic technical knowledge of the game and a very good eye for talent. No matter what your age is, he's never been scared to put you in the deep end if he thinks you can handle it. For all of us guys who've come through into the Glamorgan team, he's been a real influence; he's added an extra edge of discipline and professionalism."

"The best coaches should work with the youngsters," Tom says. "That's the point at which you can have most influence."

For 23 years, from 1977 to 2000, Tom was Director of Coaching in Wales, with his family supporting his unstinting efforts and his home the centre of a cottage industry. Joan took all the telephone calls, Jane provided secretarial support and Jeremy's cricket progressed so successfully that he in turn has made a career in coaching, first at Edgbaston and now as Cricket Development Officer in south-west Wales.

"It's been a wonderful adventure," Tom says. "Wales is such a beautiful country. I've never grown tired of seeing it in all the different seasons. I used to drive through the Brecon Beacons as the sun was coming up. The road was deserted, and the mountains on one side were all white; on the other they were a deep burgundy, from the reflection of the sunshine. It felt like the beginning of the world.

"I never took any holiday. Apart from a few days when I had a hernia operation, I had two weeks off in 23 years. The first was in 1987, when I went to Trinidad to run a coaching course. That was a bit daunting. The West Indies had conquered the world, and everything was different. The second was when I went back 18 months later and did the advanced course with them. In terms of quality, it was the best course I've ever done. There was so much talent there. Deryck Murray's father Lance was the leading light. He asked me to write up some sort of structure for them, and I remember writing at the end of it, 'Whatever you do, I hope you pursue a structure within a West Indian way of playing cricket.' If you were to stifle their natural inclination, you'd lose something precious."

On his second visit Tom was struck by one of the 18-year-olds. "He was bowling leg-spinners. Then I saw him bat, and he was very special." Tom had been at Taunton when Viv Richards had first arrived in England, and it had been one of the great joys of his life to see him develop. Perhaps it could happen a second time. "I went up to him afterwards, as the bus was revving up to take them back. 'Would you like to play in England?' I asked him, and he said, 'Yes, sir, I'd love to.' I didn't have any paper so I bent down to pick up a cigarette pack that somebody had discarded, and I got him to write down his address and telephone number."

Alas, it is a story without a happy ending for Tom. His car, containing his briefcase and diary, was stolen from outside the national sports centre in Cardiff, and the name on the cigarette packet – Brian Lara – was lost for ever to Glamorgan cricket.

Tom's work has not been glamorous or high-profile, and inevitably he has had his arguments. "He's very strong-minded," Robert Croft says. "He won't just say things to please. If he believes in the opposite, he'll say it."

On one occasion, a group of young cricketers from Wales, potential county players, were sent to the Lilleshall National Sports Centre for a week-long course. One of them, who had just started on the Lord's ground staff, was a little overweight. In time he would play for Glamorgan but, when he arrived for the week, "They did the Pinch test, to check his bodyweight index, then the Bleep test, timing him as he ran between cones, and they failed him. He hadn't even opened his cricket bag, and they sent him home.

"His mother rang me to tell me he'd had to leave. During the phone call his father walked in the door. He'd driven him up to Lilleshall from Pontypridd, and he had to go straight out to collect him from the railway station. You can imagine how the lad must have felt going back to Lord's, having to tell them they'd thrown him out. I was furious."

Tom wrote to his former protégé Hugh Morris, now the ECB's Technical Coaching Director: "'I thought this was supposed to be a class act, not a crass act.' I don't think the letter went down very well. You think of some of the great cricketers of the past – people like Colin Milburn – they wouldn't even get close now."

Tom retired from full-time work at the age of 65. He has not let go, however. He runs the under-16s, he remains in demand as a coach, and he gets angry at the changes that have been made since his retirement.

His post was sacrificed in a shake-up that saw the creation of a Cricket Academy, as prescribed by the ECB. For Tom the operation has become more top-down from Lord's, less rooted in the regional coaching associations that he created. He is also hostile to what he sees as the excessive elitism of the academy system, pulling youngsters too early into too rarefied an environment.

"They haven't played enough so it all becomes based on people's opinions rather than on performances. You're saying to kids of 13, 14, 15, 'You're a county player', to others, 'You're not.' You're setting them apart with sweaters, shirts and track suits all with the logo on. And that's destructive. You can't pick county players at that age. Somebody at Lord's, who's handing out the money, wants to see a certain number on the books, and you don't get the same number each year. And they don't stay in the system long enough. It's almost an abuse of young people, the way they're running things.

"Counties should not be under the direction of the ECB. Nothing from the centre ever succeeds. It all becomes about number crunching and ticking boxes. Most of the phone calls now seem to be about computers.

"It's got to be much more flexible. If you had a nation of artists, they wouldn't all be taught to develop in the same way.

"You can't impose a system that's the same in Yorkshire as it is in Essex or in Wales. Each county should develop as a county. Every area has a different history and different social and economic conditions. When I played, swing and seam bowlers in Sussex and Essex weren't the same as in Glamorgan, where you got a lot more rain and the local soil was different. The batting was different in the north. The top hand was much further round the bat, and somewhere like Lancashire there was a different mindset about how to establish your innings to get a working total. It's like dialects. It's what makes things interesting."

Tom's brief as Director of Coaching was not only to create excellence but to support and strengthen recreational cricket at every level, and he takes as much pride in the thousands of people who attended his courses on coaching as in the few who progressed to the county game. "Some came to improve their own game, some because their kids were playing, and some went back to their clubs to coach."

At every level Tom sought to spread his passion and his knowledge.

"It's nice to get to the top, but the real joy is playing. If you can achieve your full potential in a club 3rd XI, you'll experience the same joys as the people achieving their potential in county cricket. Coaches have a responsibility to realise that."

In 1999 Tom became the first cricket coach to be inducted into the National Coaching Federation's Hall of Fame, receiving his award from Princess Anne on the same day as Alex Ferguson and Walter Winterbottom. Then in the Honours List of New Year 2000 he was awarded an MBE for services to cricket coaching in Wales.

"I never think of these awards as just for me," he says. "They're a recognition of all the work of all the coaches in Wales, so much of it voluntary and unpaid. People like Stuart Owen, a town-and-country planner in Carmarthenshire; for twenty years he and his wife Jan provided the administrative support for my under-16s. He organised festivals of cricket for different age groups, he coached and ran junior cricket in Swansea and every summer he'd umpire 70 or 80 games. Bob Miles, who umpires the under-16s; he and his wife Margaret travel to all the games with us. And Richard Kemp, a zoologist at Aberystwyth University who's been chairman of the development committees for so many years. He was a good cricketer as a boy, but he caught polio at 17 and he's in callipers. He's a great inspiration.

"Self-help is so important. It's how you build up communities. People will only do it if they're appreciated, if they're listened to. If you start imposing on them from above, you'll lose them. In the end everything comes down to having good people."

Kevin Lyons, Glamorgan's second team captain from 1978 to 1983, was assistant to Tom in his role as county coach, and he saw at first hand how Tom approached the task.

"Coaching is about people coming to terms with themselves, with the coach pointing them in the right direction. Tom would explain things and make you think. He had this huge knowledge of the mechanics of the game, at a time when other coaches didn't – I'm not sure they've got it now – and he made it seem simple.

"It wasn't stuff he'd learnt on courses. It was knowledge built up over years of playing the game, of absorbing ideas, of thinking things through. He made it all seem so basic, so much so that I don't think people always realised just how good he was. Coaching now is all about the coach imposing himself on the players, and Tom never did that."

"Playing is the secret of development," Tom says. "Coaching is only a small part of it. We've got to the point where we're not playing enough; we're not going out and doing the things enough. It's then that you learn about yourself, then that you learn how to do it. A moment in cricket – one good drive, a stop in the field – can stay with you for a week. Nothing in a net will replicate that.

"Coaching is sometimes in danger of selling itself too strongly. The art of coaching is to prepare people so that they can teach themselves. If you impose on people, they don't make decisions for themselves.

"If you're a coach who tells a player how to do something and he repeats it, then I don't think that's ever going to benefit the guy more than for that moment. The long-term benefit comes from getting him to understand how it's working for him, getting him to understand his body.

"I remember having three hours with Hugh Morris in the nets at Neath. He was having a bad run, and we worked on picking up the bat. The next day he caught up with the boys at Taunton and got 140. That doesn't make me clever. It makes him clever. All I was trying to do was to get him to understand how his body works best for him.

"I want my players to think and react *like players*, not like coaches. Too many people are being pushed into thinking like coaches, in all sports, and you lose the individual flair. You look at Kevin Pietersen; he stepped right outside any coaching, he did what was innate in him.

"You teach everybody the same way, but they will all interpret your teaching within their own physical and mental capabilities. You teach 24 people, and you get 24 different interpretations – because everybody is unique. If you forget that as a coach, if you try to over-ride it, you end up going down a blind alley. Coaches are there to prepare people to think and to learn about themselves, not to clone people."

The tributes are many.

Robert Croft: "He's a fantastic point of reference. He's seen me grow up, and I still go back to him when I need help. He's always made me feel the door is open, and I get the feeling that he gets enjoyment out of trying to help. Whether you're 9 or 39, he's got an understanding."

Steve Watkin, an early member of Tom's under-16s and now director of the academy that Tom so dislikes: "If I've got a bowler I'm not sure about, Tom's always my first port of call."

Kevin Lyons, now Head Coach at Cardiff's University Centre of Cricketing Excellence, a better set-up in Tom's view because the students there are older and have three years in the system: "I thought Tom was on a different level to everybody else. I think he still is. When he comes in to help, I say to my guys, 'He won't say that much, but hang on to his every word.' I've learnt more from Tom than from all the other people put together. For a man of his calibre not to have been involved in the higher echelons of the game is criminal."

Robin Hobbs, still working with Essex under-12s and always happy to speak his mind: "It's the biggest tragedy in English cricket that he was never appointed England's bowling coach. The guys they've had, they're not fit to lace his boots. He's the best bowling coach this country has ever had."

"I've only really felt confident about two things in my life," Tom says. "One was playing cricket, and the other was getting other people to play. Because I know how it works. I do feel I know how it works. If I could work with money in the same way, I think I could be quite rich. Some people know how to work with money, don't they? I don't know that, but I know how it works with cricket."

CHAPTER 20

THE FLAME STILL BURNS

Sixty years have passed since that summer's day in 1947 when Eddie Branson took Tom to the Coventry Schoolboys' trial and Tom, having heard his name read out at the end of the afternoon, ran home full of excitement to his mother. A flame was lit by the devoted schoolmaster, and it has burned all through Tom's life, a life devoted to cricket.

An honest man, a man who has stayed true to the values of his upbringing, Tom played for 26 years as a county cricketer, and he has spent longer still passing on to younger generations what he has learned through the years – and what Tiger Smith before him had learned in a career that went back to the start of the twentieth century. And who knows from how far back the wisdom of Tiger Smith came? Who knows from what previous generations he received the flame?

We live in an age when, in the thinking of many, new theories are of greater value than such passed-down wisdom, and at times Tom's voice has come to seem a discordant one, one that does not fit readily into a world in which experts in sports science are heard with greater attention than people with a lifetime of experience in the game.

"It's staggering," Tom will say. "You've got people bowling for England who have served no apprenticeship in the game at all, and they're being guided by coaches who have never even been successful in county cricket. They're nice lads, good coaches in the right setting, but they're like the St John's Ambulance. You're pleased to have them at the village fete, but they aren't expected to perform heart by-pass operations, are they?"

Tom has become an outsider, refusing to pay lip service to these developments. He is not a loudmouth, not an ogre, but his unyielding honesty has made people in the higher reaches of the game wary of him. One day at Lord's Micky Stewart, at the time England's cricket manager, stopped him. "Why's everybody frightened of you?" he asked. "I'm not."

"I think maybe Micky would have liked me to have more of a role, but he knew that I wouldn't go along with things like everybody else did. You do pay that price if you challenge people."

The changes in English cricket have frustrated Tom, but he has never lost his commitment to his work in Wales. "To be honest," he says, "I'd rather be with the kids.

"When a player in a Test match produces a beautiful drive or bowls a magic ball or takes a blinding catch, and everybody celebrates, it should be seen as a celebration not just of that moment but of how that person started, all the long hours they spent when they were young with schoolmasters and coaches."

Tom is still a port of call for cricketers wanting advice, and Joan provides a cheerful, if not always reliable, telephone answering service.

"Is that Mrs Cartwright?" she remembers one caller asking. "It's Matt Windows here."

"No, thank you very much," came the reply. "We don't need any double glazing." Down went the receiver.

Tom sees less of his 'Somerset boys' now that life has spread them far and wide about the world. "The last time I saw Ian was at the launch of his book *Botham's Century*. I went up to the Café Royal in London and, when I got there, I was one of only two people in the room not in a dark suit. Vic Marks saw me straightaway and came over. 'Now then, Tom,' he said. 'Is this a political statement?'"

Through the years, till he was 67, he continued to enjoy a few games of cricket every summer, playing for the Old England XI that the brewer Sam Whitbread sponsored. Jim Parks has been their manager, each year arranging six or eight Sunday matches against club sides who hoped to use the visit of the old cricketers to raise money for themselves or for charity.

"They were wonderful days. We used to leave here in Neath on Sunday morning, drive maybe 250 miles, play a game of cricket, then drive back. About 12.30 or one o'clock in the night, if you called in at the Leigh Delamere service station on the M4, you'd always find Joan and me, David Allen and Joyce and sometimes Jeff Jones having a cup of coffee. 'DA' and I were still playing together thirty-odd years after we'd toured South Africa."

The memories flood back: John Edrich's superb century at Shepperton, the cluster of spectators that gathered whenever Derek Randall fielded on the boundary, the devotion with which Raye Luckhurst, Brian's wife, recorded the direction of his every scoring shot, the sight of Basil D'Oliveira fielding deeper and deeper in the slips as the years went by, the rainy day at Eaton Hall when Brian Close fell from grace by tipping his cigarette ash into the Duke of Westminster's precious ornaments ... and that wonderful innings of Arthur Milton at Bromyard.

"Arthur was such a gifted sportsman. They say he wouldn't play golf for months and he'd go round in one over par. I remember in my benefit year we were playing Gloucestershire at Coventry, and the Midlands Snooker Champion was there. He wanted to know if anybody wanted to play him. Nobody in our dressing room would do it so we went into the Gloucestershire dressing room and they all said, 'Get Arthur.' And Arthur beat him.

Old England XI

Standing *(left to right)*: Robin Hobbs, John Snow, Jim Watts, Tom Cartwright,
Dougie Slade, Peter Sainsbury, John Edrich
Sitting: Roy Booth, Alan Oakman, Jim Parks, Sam Whitbread,
David Allen, Mike Harris

"He was such a bright bloke, and he could play any game if he wanted to. That day at Bromyard he was in his sixties, and he came at the last minute, got his bat out of the attic. He played in his pumps. It was a wet ground, and he never fell over. He had an incredible balance. He got a hundred that day. People like that, days like that, they're very special in your life."

Finally Tom retired, but three years later at the age of 70 he found himself back on the field of play for one last time – at Broadhalfpenny Down, the ground in Hambledon where English cricket started to take shape in the 1770s, where Silver Billy Beldham scored his runs, where John Small the elder's batting triumphed over the bowling of the broad-shouldered Lumpy Stevens.

It was Saturday 17 September 2005, a great gathering of the cricketers of Tom's time, all there at the invitation of his Warwickshire and England team-mate Bob Barber who had flown over from his home in Switzerland to celebrate his 70th birthday. There were so many guests there who had meant so much in Tom's life, among them Jim Stewart, with whom he'd travelled on the train each morning from Coventry to Birmingham, Peter Richardson, with whom he'd opened the batting for the Combined Services, Mike Smith, who had been his captain for so many years at Edgbaston, Alan Smith, his ever-enthusiastic wicket-keeper, Fred Rumsey, fellow-toiler when they made their Test debuts together at Old Trafford, Ossie Wheatley, the visionary who established Tom's coaching role in Wales, Ted Dexter, John Jameson, Doug Insole, David Brown and Peter Walker.

Then there was Mike Brearley, kindred spirit in South Africa, Alec Bedser, his bowling hero, and, all the way from Miami, Lance Gibbs. What did he say? 'Dis tent, man, will be biscuits and cheese to dem elephants.'

The match had complicated rules, with batsmen often going out in pairs, and Tom was put in charge of organising the batting order for Bob Barber's team. He and Lance were the last two names on the list, unrequired as it worked out. "If I do have to bat," he explained, "I'm going out with Lance."

The sky was blue, there was a gentle air of autumn about the rolling hills, and in the late afternoon, when Tom's turn to bowl came round, there was a leap in the delivery and his arm was high. Donald Carr looked on with admiration: "He wouldn't know how to bowl a bad ball," he said.

"It was a magical day," Tom says. "A living evidence of what is really good about playing cricket. When you looked at the different backgrounds of all the people there and the way they'd come together in cricket and played on equal terms, it really brought home what cricket can be in people's lives."

Back in 1950 Eddie Branson had presented Tom with a book called *The Young Cricketer*, and it carried the story of Hambledon told by John Arlott:

> On the Down it is a great match day, and there are some thousands patiently and anxiously watching every turn of fate of the game, the old farmers leaning forward upon their tall old staves and the whole multitude perfectly still. But whenever a Hambledon man made a good hit, worth four or five runs, you would hear the deep mouths of the whole multitude baying away in pure Hampshire: "Go hard – go hard! – tich and turn! Tich and turn!"

For Tom the magic of cricket has always been that it carries a tradition, and that day at Broadhalfpenny Down he was glowing. "I've never played here," he told me, "but I did visit here once. I went out on my own into the middle, and I listened to all the ancient voices. And I knew which end I would have bowled. Uphill, into the wind, like Lumpy Stevens used to do."

214

Where others played in track suits, Tom was immaculate as ever in his whites – and uphill into the wind he bowled for one last time.

In the marquee in the evening Dennis Silk, former Warden of Radley College and a past President of MCC, was the main speaker. He paid tribute to the day's organisers and to Bob Barber, he welcomed the guests from distant parts and he told some amusing stories. Then suddenly, before a multitude of the great and good of cricket, he singled out Tom for special mention, for all that he had done for English and Welsh cricket over the years, and the applause that followed was long and loud.

"I've always had this thing about Tom," he says. "He's tremendously respected by his fellow cricketers. He's kept up such high personal standards without making a meal of it. And he's put so much back into the game, patiently and generously. He's one of the great unsung heroes of English cricket."

"Cricket has given me such enormous pleasure," Tom says. "I suppose that's why I've done what I have with my life, why I still do it. Cricket has been such a wonderful life for me, and I try to provide for other people something that might come close to what I've enjoyed. Headmasters should insist on its being played in their schools. Parents should take their kids along to play.

"Cricket is not like any other sport," he says. "It has a purity, and that purity is being taken away. It's so important that people who love cricket stand up and fight for it."

A BRIEF STATISTICAL DIGEST
T.W. Cartwright, M.B.E.
Born: 22 July 1935

BATTING IN ALL FIRST-CLASS CRICKET

Year	Matches	Innings	Not Outs	Runs	Highest	Average
1952	1	2	1	104	82*	104.00
1953	9	16	1	260	83	17.83
1955	7	14	1	221	58	17.00
1956	18	29	4	411	50	16.44
1957	18	32	2	606	84	20.20
1958	23	36	3	902	128	27.33
1959	31	54	6	1282	101*	26.70
1960	16	28	2	543	77	20.88
1961	34	65	11	1668	119*	30.88
1962	28	42	7	1176	210	33.60
1963	26	41	1	687	85	17.17
1963/4 East Africa	1	1	0	2	2	2.00
1964	28	45	3	624	54	14.85
1964/5 South Africa	8	10	4	293	111*	48.83
1965	23	34	8	392	112*	15.07
1966	25	35	7	504	65*	18.00
1967	30	40	10	550	47*	18.33
1968	18	14	1	176	61	13.53
1969	26	42	3	779	90	19.97
1970	24	44	9	766	63*	21.88
1971	25	32	2	632	127	21.06
1972	21	31	3	497	93	17.75
1973	20	25	1	338	57	14.08
1973/4 East Africa	1	2	1	32	23*	32.00
1974	7	8	0	185	68	23.12
1975	2	3	0	0	0	0.00
1976	2	1	1	4	4*	-
1977	7	11	2	76	22*	8.44
TOTAL	**479**	**737**	**94**	**13710**	**210**	**21.32**

BATTING IN ONE-DAY CRICKET

Matches	Innings	Not Outs	Runs	Highest	Average
144	105	18	1254	61	14.41

CATCHES

Test cricket 2   All first-class cricket 331   One-day cricket 52

TEST CRICKET

BATTING	Matches	Innings	Not Outs	Runs	Highest	Average
	5	7	2	26	9	5.20

BOWLING	Overs	Maidens	Runs	Wickets	Average
	268.3	97	544	15	36.26

BOWLING IN ALL FIRST-CLASS CRICKET

Year	Overs	Maidens	Runs	Wickets	Average
1955	2	0	15	0	–
1956	11	2	32	1	32.00
1957	58	8	180	2	90.00
1958	236	88	495	18	27.50
1959	843.3	300	2033	80	25.41
1960	442	157	1168	25	46.72
1961	846.1	302	1969	77	25.57
1962	923.2	338	2126	106	20.05
1963	888.1	359	1786	100	17.86
1963/4 East Africa	36	14	81	6	13.50
1964	1146.2	501	2141	134	15.97
1964/5 South Africa	366.3	141	817	25	32.68
1965	735.1	306	1505	108	13.93
1966	842.5	307	1795	100	17.95
1967	1194	495	2282	147	15.52
1968	608.4	258	1145	71	16.12
1969	878.5	373	1748	108	16.18
1970	851.4	317	1891	86	21.98
1971	976.4	407	1852	104	17.80
1972	863	373	1827	98	18.64
1973	810.4	349	1410	89	15.84
1973/4 East Africa	48	20	83	10	8.30
1974	273	130	493	22	22.40
1975	49.3	24	87	5	17.40
1976	77	32	138	4	34.50
1977	131.3	52	258	10	25.80
TOTAL	**14139.3**	**5653**	**29357**	**1536**	**19.11**

BOWLING IN ONE-DAY CRICKET

Overs	Maidens	Runs	Wickets	Average
1248.3	286	3481	172	20.23

BOWLING ON DIFFERENT GROUNDS

First-class cricket *Qualification: 250 overs*

Ground	Overs	Maidens	Runs	Wickets	Average
Weston-super-Mare	428.4	195	751	77	9.75
Coventry	501.4	188	1057	74	14.28
Swansea	324.5	122	673	47	14.31
Derby	333.5	150	632	40	15.80
Leicester	275.3	101	585	33	17.72
The Oval	325	131	701	37	18.94
Edgbaston	4139.2	1675	8643	445	19.42
Bath	488.2	205	970	49	19.79
Taunton	1233.3	499	2453	117	20.96
Trent Bridge	555.3	214	1170	55	21.27
Lord's	403.1	149	851	40	21.27
Worcester	296.5	119	585	26	22.50
Old Trafford	337.2	149	643	18	35.72

ECONOMICAL BOWLERS IN ALL ONE-DAY CRICKET

Qualification: 500 overs at under 3 runs per over

		Overs	Runs	Runs per over
1	F.E. Rumsey	800.2	2185	2.73
2	V.A.P. van der Bijl	872.5	2385	2.73
3	T.W. Cartwright	1248.3	3481	2.78
4	J. Garner	2226.3	6598	2.96

BOWLING IN THE TWELVE ENGLISH SUMMERS 1962-73

MOST FIRST-CLASS WICKETS

1	T.W. Cartwright	1251	6	R. Illingworth	969
2	F.J. Titmus	1187	7	N. Gifford	955
3	D.L. Underwood	1119	8	D. Shackleton	951
4	D.J. Shepherd	1012	9	D. Wilson	918
5	J.B. Mortimore	979	10	R.M.H. Cottam	832

BEST AVERAGE   *Qualification: 250 wickets*

		Wkts	Ave				Wkts	Ave
1	J.B. Statham	725	16.81	6	D. Shackleton	951	17.99
2	T.W. Cartwright	1251	17.19	7	H.J. Rhodes	651	18.06
3	J.A. Flavell	624	17.39	8	F.S. Trueman	763	18.07
4	D.A.D. Sydenham	373	17.66	9	O.S. Wheatley	615	18.28
5	M.J. Procter	397	17.94	10	R. Illingworth	969	18.39

OVERS BOWLED IN AN ENGLISH SUMMER

These figures include all cricket: first-class, limited over and Twenty20

	Most	Average 2003-6
J.M. Anderson	690.5	358
S.J. Harmison	609.5	396
M.J. Hoggard	659.1	396
S.P. Jones	338.2	168
S.I. Mahmood	379.2	291
L.E. Plunkett	558.4	322
		Average 1962-73
T.W. Cartwright	1206	969

YOUNG BATSMEN IN COUNTY CHAMPIONSHIP CRICKET

SCORES OF 80+ UNDER AGE OF 18

17 yrs	39 days	T.W. Cartwright	82	Warwks v Notts	1952
17 yrs	227 days	N. Peng	98	Durham v Surrey	2000
17 yrs	247 days	G.J. Bryan	124	Kent v Notts	1920
17 yrs	270 days	D.N. Patel	107	Worcs v Surrey	1976
17 yrs	276 days	G.S.F. Griffin	88*	Middx v Sussex	1900
17 yrs	296 days	T.W. Cartwright	83	Warwks v Notts	1953
17 yrs	344 days	J.A. Hopkins	88	Glam v Glos	1971
17 yrs	365 days	C.J. Barnett	80	Glos v Glam	1928

ACKNOWLEDGEMENTS

Much of this book has been written from conversations with Tom Cartwright, and I would like to thank him for all the time he has given me. We began in October 2003, and it has taken me three years to clear the decks and get down to the writing. So I would especially like to thank Tom for his patience during this time. Usually we met in *Y Mochyn Du*, the pub beside Glamorgan's ground at Sophia Gardens, Cardiff, but on several occasions I have been to Tom's home in Neath and I would like to thank Joan for her hospitality on those occasions.

I would like to thank the following for giving up their time to talk to me: David Allen, Jack Bannister, Bob Barber, David Belchamber, Bill Blenkiron, Lily Bosworth, Ian Botham, Mike Brearley, Brian Close, Robert Croft, Eric Hill, Joan Hill, Robin Hobbs, Martin Horton, Brian Langford, Kevin Lyons, Vic Marks, Lorna Marles, Liz Price, Peter Robinson, Peter Roebuck, Dennis Silk, Graham Sewell, Alan Smith, Mike Smith, Jim Stewart, Brian Timms, Alan Townsend, Sheila and John Walker and Steve Watkin.

I would like to thank David Smith of Corsham for his careful reading of the manuscript. His observations on content and literary style, coupled with his keen eye for factual errors, make him a vital person in the writing of the book.

I would like to thank Phil Britt, the librarian at Warwickshire County Cricket Club, and Tony Stedall, of the Somerset County Cricket Club museum, for their assistance, also Norman Rogers in Coventry and Graham Sewell at the Coventry and North Warwickshire Cricket Club.

The statistics in this book have been provided by Peter Griffiths and his superb CricketArchive website. Tom himself has been amazed by some of these statistics, saying to me several times, "I wish I'd known this at the time. I'd have put in for a pay rise."

A number of the photographs in this book are reproduced by kind permission of their copyright owners, and I would like to thank the following:
the late Bill Smith F.R.P.S. for the Courtaulds ground on page 24 and Tom bowling on pages 6 and 124 and on the jacket,
Mrs Ken Kelly for the portrait of Tiger Smith on page 58, the balcony scene on page 143, the panorama of Edgbaston on pages 144 and 145 and Tom with Ossie Wheatley and Alan Jones on page 203,
EMPICS for Tom with the Lord's cat on page 133,
the Millfield Society for Jack Meyer on page 164, and
Eddie Lawrence for the Somerset squad on page 178.
Other photographs are from Tom's own collection but, if any photographic source believes that any of the remaining photographs are theirs, they should contact me to rectify the matter.

I have made regular use of the following reference books:
Wisden Cricketers' Almanack
Playfair Cricket Annual
Bailey, Thorn & Wynne-Thomas, *Who's Who of Cricketers* (Newnes, 1984)
Swanton, Plumptre & Woodcock, *Barclays World of Cricket* (Collins, 1986)

I have also read and occasionally quoted from the following books:
John Arlott, *John Arlott's Book of Cricketers* (Lutterworth Press, 1979)
Jack Bannister, *The History of Warwickshire CCC* (Christopher Helm, 1990)
Ian Botham, *Botham's Century* (Collins Willow, 2001)
Brian Close, *I Don't Bruise Easily* (Macdonald & Jane, 1978)
Colin Cowdrey, *M.C.C. The Autobiography of a Cricketer*
(Hodder & Stoughton, 1976)
Tom Dollery, *Professional Captain* (Stanley Paul, 1952)
Leslie Duckworth, *The Story of Warwickshire Cricket* (Stanley Paul, 1974)
Eric Hollies, *I'll Spin You A Tale* (Museum Press, 1955)
Len Hutton, *Just My Story* (Hutchinson, 1956)
David Matthews, *Derek Shackleton – On The Spot* (Blackberry Downs, 1998)
Peter May, *A Game Enjoyed* (Stanley Paul, 1985)
Patrick Murphy, *'Tiger' Smith* (Lutterworth Press, 1981)
Peter Oborne, *Basil D'Oliveira* (Little, Brown, 2004)
Graeme Pollock, *Down The Wicket* (Pelham Books, 1968)
Viv Richards, *Sir Vivian* (Michael Joseph, 2000)
Peter Roebuck, *From Sammy to Jimmy* (Partridge Press, 1991)
Peter Roebuck, *Sometimes I Forgot To Laugh* (Allen & Unwin, 1984)
Norman Rogers, *Eric Hollies – The Peter Pan of Cricket*
(Warwickshire Cricket Publishing, 2002)
Norman Rogers, *H.E. 'Tom' Dollery* (ACS Publications, 2004)
Bobby Simpson, *The Australians in England 1968* (Stanley Paul, 1968)
John St John (editor), *The Young Cricketer* (Naldrett Press, 1950)
Ian Wooldridge, *Cricket, Lovely Cricket* (Robert Hale, 1963)

also from the following newspapers:
The Times, The Guardian, News Chronicle, Daily Express, Daily Herald, Daily Mail, Daily Mirror, The Sketch, Birmingham Post, Birmingham Evening Mail, Coventry Evening Telegraph and Nottingham Guardian

from the following cricket magazines:
The Cricketer, Playfair Cricket Monthly and Wisden Cricket Monthly

and from the yearbooks of Warwickshire County Cricket Club.

Stephen Chalke
Bath, January 2007

INDEX

Tom Cartwright and his family are not included

222

223

FAIRFIELD BOOKS

The following is a full list of published titles.
Those with an asterisk are out of print – but it may be possible to track down copies.

Runs in the Memory
County Cricket in the 1950s
by Stephen Chalke

* Caught in the Memory
County Cricket in the 1960s
by Stephen Chalke

One More Run
by Stephen Chalke
talking with Bryan 'Bomber' Wells

Fragments of Idolatry
From 'Crusoe' to Kid Berg
by David Foot

* At the Heart of English Cricket
The Life and Memories of Geoffrey Howard
by Stephen Chalke

* The Appeal of the Championship
Sussex in the Summer of 1981
by John Barclay

Harold Gimblett
Tormented Genius of Cricket
by David Foot

Guess My Story
The Life and Opinions of Keith Andrew
by Stephen Chalke

* No Coward Soul
The Remarkable Story of Bob Appleyard
by Stephen Chalke and Derek Hodgson

Born To Bowl
The Life and Times of Don Shepherd
by Douglas Miller

Charles Palmer
More Than Just a Gentleman
by Douglas Miller

Ken Taylor – Drawn to Sport
by Stephen Chalke

Sixty Summers
Somerset Cricket since the War
by David Foot and Ivan Ponting

It's Not Just Cricket
by Peter Walker

* A Summer of Plenty
George Herbert Hirst in 1906
by Stephen Chalke

Tom Cartwright
The Flame Still Burns
by Stephen Chalke

For full details of prices and availability,
or to join the mailing list for news of future titles, please contact
Fairfield Books, 17 George's Road, Bath BA1 6EY
telephone 01225-335813